MS Access

An Active-Learning Approach

Sue Coles & Jenny Rowley

Department of Business and Management Studies,
Crewe and Alsager Faculty, Manchester Metropolitan University

DP Publications Ltd
Aldine Place
London W21 8AW

1994

acknowledgments

This book would not have been completed or even conceived without the support that the authors have received during its production from many of their colleagues and family.

First and foremost we are grateful to the Microsoft Corporation for permission to reproduce various screen dumps and for the creation of a database package that is both powerful and fun to work with.

Secondly, teaching databases to our students on the HND in Business Studies and Finance has given us a true insight into the problems that students encounter when learning about databases for the first time. No two people approach a software package with the same knowledge and experience and expectations. We hope that, working with our many students, we have gained an insight into the use of database packages that has informed our approach in this book.

Thirdly, we are ever grateful for the competent and cheerful technical support that has been lent to us by member of the staff of the Computer Services Department in the Crewe and Alsager Faculty. We would like to make special mention of Kate McDonald, Mike Eddleston and Martin Shenton, without whose technical support we would not have been able to find the time or inclination to be able to complete this endeavour.

Lastly, but not least, we are especially grateful for the support of our husbands Martyn and Peter, and our children Helen, Lynsey, Shula and Zeta, during the final phases of the completion of this text, when they had to make do with even less of our time than usual.

A CIP record for this book is available from the British Library.

ISBN 1 85805 096 0

Typeset by Kai Typesetting, Nottingham

Printed in Great Britain by The Guernsey Press Co Ltd, Vale, Guernsey CI

contents

preface

aims

This book is intended for students on a wide variety of business studies and other courses who need to learn about databases and their application through the use of Microsoft Access, one of the industry standard database packages. The book assumes no prior experience of other database packages.

Although this book is specifically designed for business studies students the orientation will be equally applicable to students in further and higher education on many courses where students need to learn about databases.

This book is designed for business studies students on a wide range of courses, including BTEC National, BTEC Higher and undergraduate courses in business studies, accountancy, computing and information systems.

approach

This book introduces students to the basics of databases and database design through a series of applications oriented exercises. These exercises are based on the operations of one organisation, Chelmer Leisure and Recreation Centre. A series of self contained but interrelated sessions takes the student through the design of a database for Chelmer Leisure and Recreation Centre. Each session comprises a series of exercises. As each new function is introduced, the book explains both why the function is useful and how to use it.

The approach does not assume any previous knowledge of databases or the Windows environment. However, students who are familiar with the Windows environment, and, in particular other Microsoft products, such as Word for Windows and Excel will find their road into Access to be much more intuitive than students who are not familiar with these related products. Equally, students who have some familiarity with other database products may find the database concepts that are introduced in this book easier to grasp.

The approach is designed not only to introduce students to Access but also to offer them a conceptual framework for the use and design of databases that will encourage the development of skills transferable to other applications.

The learning material requires little, if any, input by lecturers, and can therefore be used in programmes based on independent learning. Students learn by practising the commands and techniques.

The text is selective and does not deal with all of features in detail, but does take students step-by-step to a level at which they can happily use the help system or software manual to master further features.

Access

Access is a powerful and exciting database management system for Windows. It provides standard data management features for data storage and retrieval but uses graphical tools made possible by the Windows environment to make tasks easier to perform.

scope of the book

This book has been specifically designed for students who will benefit from a straightforward introduction to databases in the context of a specific database package. The aim is not to be comprehensive, but rather selective. Once students have been introduced to an appropriate range of basic concepts they may use other more comprehensive or advanced sources to further extend their knowledge and skills.

The book will give students the confidence to perform and understand the central tasks concerned with database design, creation and maintenance:

❒ designing and defining a database

❒ designing and using queries

❒ designing and using screen forms

❒ designing and using printed reports

❒ using multiple tables

❒ importing and exporting data

❒ creating and using macros.

The book has been structured in such a way that those students who are embarking on a more basic course may restrict their reading and activities to the first four sessions. More advanced topics are dealt with in later sessions.

The book is written so that it can be used in conjunction with either Access 1 or Access 2. Often there are small differences, for example, the Layout menu in Access 1 becomes the Format menu in Access 2 and these are identified where appropriate. Where there is greater difference, for example in setting indexes, then each version is differentiated by an icon in the margin.

how to use this book

Students who have not used a Windows program before should first read through Appendix 1 Basic Windows Operations, which summarises the key features of the Windows environment, and then turn to an Overview of Access before tackling Session 1. Students who are familiar with the Windows environment can move straight to An Overview of Access before beginning Session 1. Appendix 3 or Appendix 4: Toolbar buttons provides a reminder of the meaning of the buttons.

Each session commences with a summary of the objectives to be achieved and skills to be gained . Each session is divided into a number of activities. Within each activity there is an explanation of concepts relating to the activity, instructions on how to perform operations, and Exercises which ask you to perform the operations. Sessions conclude with Integrative Exercises which offer you the opportunity to practice your newly acquired skills further. These exercises have minimal instructions.

This book may be used as a basis for independent study or for class activities. In either instance it is important to:

☐ work methodically through the exercises in the order in which they are presented. Data entered in earlier exercises may be re-used in later exercises.

☐ take time for rest and reflection and break learning into manageable sessions

☐ think about what you are doing

☐ expect to make mistakes. Think about the consequences of any mistakes and learn from your mistakes.

☐ use the integrative exercises at the end of each session as a means of testing whether you have understood the earlier concepts and exercises.

The following conventions have been adopted to distinguish between the various objects on the screen:

- ❏ Commands are shown in bold and italic e.g. *Format–Page Setup*, which means choose the *Format* menu and then select the option *Page Setup* from that menu.

- ❏ Buttons and icons are shown in bold e.g. **Cancel**.

- ❏ Dialog box names are shown in bold e.g. **New Report**.

- ❏ Keys are shown in bold and caps e.g. **CTRL**.

- ❏ Filenames are shown in bold e.g. **Membership**.

an overview of Access

All students, except those who have some experience of Access, should read this section before tackling Session 1. Appendix 1 (page 213) reviews the basic features of Windows for the benefit of inexperienced users or as a ready reference for those who may have forgotten some of the basic features. Appendix 1 also introduces mouse techniques and acts as a summary of the terminology used elsewhere in this book.

a tour of the Access window and the database window

It is worthwhile to study the two basic windows in Access: the Access window and the Database window for a few moments before trying to make use of Access. This section can be used as a ready reference and returned to later as necessary.

The Access window

When you first start Access, the Access Window shown in Figure 0.1 is displayed. This window is used to open a database or to perform other tasks that are not possible once a database is open. The window has the following components:

Title bar – shows that you are in Microsoft Access.

Access control menu – in the very top left hand corner. If you click on this box a menu with commands for sizing and moving the Access window, switching to other applications and closing Access is displayed.

Access main menu – shows the two pull down menus File and Help.

Toolbar – shows the help icon which can be used to call Help quickly.

Status bar – at the bottom of the screen. Shows the status of the system, and whether switches such as NUM for Number Lock are on or off. (Note: The status bar is not shown in Figure 0.1).

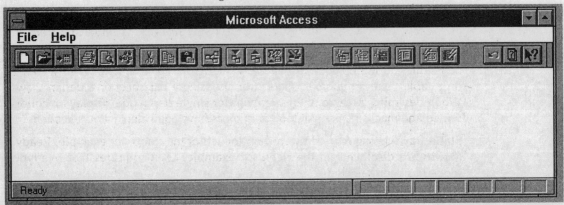

Figure 0.1 The Access window

The Database window

Once you have opened a database, the screen appears as shown in Figure 0.2 The Database window allows you to access any object in the database by clicking on one of the object buttons. Initially the Table button is selected and a window displays all tables in the database.

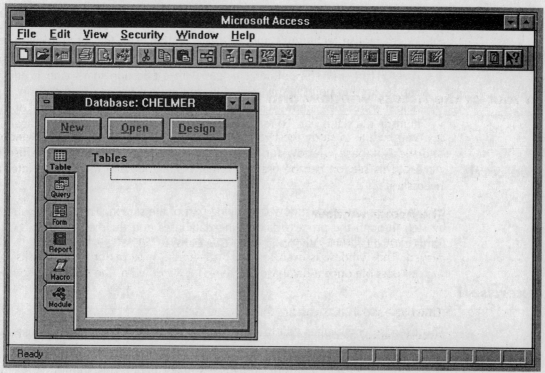

Figure 0.2 The Access window with Database Window displayed

When the Database Window is open, the Access Window has the following components:

Title bar

Access control menu

Database window main menu which shows a few more pull-down menus than the Access window, specifically, *File, Edit, View, Security, Window and Help*.

Toolbar which shows the icons for the creation of new objects. The icons vary depending on the object that you are working on. For example, when working on a table there are toolbar options for choosing a datasheet or a design view. When designing a macro, there are icons for single step mode, displaying conditioned and macro names. All toolbar choices have equivalent menu selections.

Status bar. Messages are displayed on the left of the status, for example, Ready. Modes are displayed on the right, for example, OVR indicates that overtype mode has been selected.

help

Both help and tutorials are available for Access. There are four main methods of getting into the help system:

1. Pull down the *Help* menu and select a command from it.

2. At any time you can press **F1** to get help on whatever you are doing at that moment.

3. In many dialog boxes there is a **Help** button.

4. Press **SHIFT+F1.** The pointer changes with a question mark after it and it can be used to point to anything. Clicking on that object will then bring up help. For instance, in this way you may get help on the meaning of all of the items in the status bar. To remove the question mark press **SHIFT+F1** again.

cue cards

Cue cards appear in a window occupying part of the screen. They take you step by step through the process of creating databases and their components. Cue Cards can be called by choosing *Help-Cue Cards.*

exercise 1

This exercise encourages you to explore the help system and to start to use the Access window.

❑ Click on the *Help* menu on the *Access* main menu. This should cause the pull-down menu to be displayed.

❑ Click on *Help Index* to open the *Help Index* window. View the contents of this window.

When you have finished close this window by clicking on the **Control** menu in the upper left hand corner of the window (if you are not sure where this is consult Appendix 1), and click on the *Close* option to close the window.

If you would like to examine the tutorials, click on *Help* on the *Word* main menu again, and choose *Learning Access.*

what is an Access database?

Access is a database management system and provides a means of storing and managing data or information. Microsoft refers to Access as a relational database product since it allows you to relate data from several different sets or tables. The purist would recognise that Access does not meet all of the criteria of a true relational database, but it is a sufficiently close approximation to be considered as a relational database product for the purposes of this book.

An Access database comprises all of the tables of data and all associated objects, such as screen forms and report forms, macros and program modules and queries.

Note: The use of the term database in connection with Access is broader than that encountered in earlier database products, such as dBase IV, where only the data itself is considered to be part of the database. For example, you may have an employee database, a client database and a supplier database. Each database is a separate file and there will also be additional files for reports and screen forms.

Tables

Access stores data in tables that are organised by rows and columns. The basic requirement of having a database is that you have at least one table.

Columns represent fields of information, or one particular piece of information that can be stored for each entity in the table.

Rows contain records. A record contains one of each field in the database.

Generally each major set of information in a database is represented by a table. There might, for instance, be a Supplier table. Client table and an Employee table.

We will return later to the issue of how data might be organised in tables, and how relationships can be defined between tables so that tables can be used together, in such a way, for instance, that data from more than one table can be shown in a report.

Queries

Queries are used to select records from a database. Access has three different types: select, action and parameter.

Select queries are the standard type of query. They are questions that you may wish to ask about entries in fields. They choose records from a table and store them in a table called a dynaset. Queries are specified by completing entries in the Query-by-Example window. It is possible to specify complex combinations of criteria in order to select a specific set of records.

Action queries update values in a database table. They can be used to change an entire group of records, as in, for example, the removal of all records for former employees.

Parameter queries allow you to change the criteria for a query each time that you use it. Access prompts for criteria entries with the QBE grid. They are a useful way of creating an environment for end users where users complete dialog boxes instead of a QBE grid.

Reports

Reports are used to print information from a number of records. Reports can show the data from either a table or a query. In addition to records, they may show summary information relating to the records displayed. Graphs created using Microsoft Graph may be added to reports.

Screen forms

Screen forms can be used to view the records in tables or queries, or to add new records. Unlike the basic datasheets, forms present just one record on the screen at a time. Subforms allow you to display related records from another table at the same time.

Controls are placed on a form to display fields or text. Text on the form acts as labels to controls and headings. The appearance of text on a form can be changed by changing the font or adding bold or italic. Text can also be shown as raised or sunken or displayed in a specific colour, and lines and rectangles can be added. Controls, attached labels, form sections and the form itself all have properties that can be changed.

Macros

Macros are a series of steps or keystrokes that you record and then use by pressing just one or two keys. Examples of uses of macros are:

❑ to add a button to a form so that it will open a second form.

❑ to create custom menus and pop-up forms for data collection.

Modules

Modules are programs or sets of instructions designed to perform a specific task or series of tasks. Modules are written in Access Visual BASIC code, the programming language provided with the package. Modules are a little more complex than macros and you should only attempt to develop these once you have mastered most of the basic features.

exercise 2

Answer the following questions:

1. What is the difference between a report and a screen form?

2. What types of queries may be used in Access

3. What is a table? What is the relationship between a table and a database?

4. Give an example of when you might use a macro.

designing an Access database

objectives

This session focuses on activities associated with the creation of a database table. At the end of the session you should

❏ appreciate the reasons for analysing data before creating a database

❏ understand that within a database data is kept in tables and that there is usually more than one table in a database

❏ understand that the tables in a database can be related or linked together

❏ know the component parts of a table and to be able to create a table

❏ to be able to define field properties

❏ to be able to create table indexes

Before a database can be created careful thought needs to be given to deciding upon the data that should be held and in planning the way in which the data is to be organised. This is known as data analysis and you will be introduced the basic concepts of this in the first part of this session.

The rest of the session will concentrate on the production of the tables required by a small leisure centre. The setting up and entering data into tables requires a lot of hard work and it is important that this is done correctly. By setting up the tables as described in this session the forms, queries and reports described in later sessions can be created.

The examples and exercises throughout this book use the data that you will be asked to put into the tables, so in order to execute these examples it is necessary to enter all the example data.

activity 1 data analysis

A database is used for storing data which can be used by a system. A system is not easily defined, though they abound in society and nature. Your body has many systems of which the nervous system and digestive system are examples. In society there are legal systems, political systems, educational systems, tax systems, etc. Organisations may have order systems, management-information systems, product-information systems, personnel-data systems, sales-marketing systems, etc. Libraries have cataloguing systems and information retrieval systems. In general terms, systems can be viewed as being concerned with taking inputs or resources, executing some form of regulated change and achieving results or outputs. Systems often need access to data to act upon their inputs, if this data information is easily accessible, i.e. via a well designed database then the system will perform well.

Data or systems analysts are highly trained individuals who design information systems of which databases usually form a major part. They use their skills to determine how to organise the data in the tables in the system's databases. It is not the intention of this book to impart analysis skills but to give you a practical insight into the building of a database.

We shall be considering the database needs of a small leisure centre. Data is recorded about various things, such as membership details, court and course bookings, financial information, etc. The information about these different things, or entities, may be kept in tables in the database. If data from more than one table is required to be retrieved then the tables can be linked or related together, as will be explained in a later session.

A table generally holds data about one 'thing' or entity. There are usually several or many instances of this particular 'thing', for example, the members of the leisure centre. A members table would hold details about each member.

Records and fields

For each member there is a separate record in the table. Each record is composed of data about the member, such as, name, address and so on. Each piece of data within the record is known as a field. In this Session we will see how each field in a record needs to be defined before data can be entered into the record. Fields are given names to describe the kind of data they will eventually hold. It is important to distinguish between the name of a field and the data that that field contains. For example, the field named Surname will hold people's surnames such as Harris. The field names can be considered to be the column headings in the table and each row in the table is a separate record. Therefore each record in the table will have fields with the same name but containing different data. We shall also see that fields need their size and the type of data that they will contain to be defined so that Access can store the data in the table correctly.

activity 2 defining a new database

A new database is used to store all the tables, queries, forms and reports that belong to the system. To begin with a database will hold the tables of data needed for the system.

To define a new database

1. Choose *File-New Database*

2. In the **New Database** dialog box select the drive and directory in which you wish to store your database.

3. In the **File Name** box type in a name for your database, obeying the normal filename rules. This is the only time you need to use a normal filename as .

Access stores all tables, forms, queries, reports etc. in this one file. Names used for tables etc. are not bound by the file name rules.

4.   Click on **OK**.

exercise 1 *defining the Chelmer database*

Follow the steps outlined above. If you do not change directory then your database is likely to be stored in the Access directory. Give the database the filename Chelmer. Access will give it the extension of .mdb. This file differs from traditional PC databases in that it can contain all of the tables, forms, reports, queries, macros etc. that belong to a database. The one you have just created awaits the inclusion of these as you learn to create them.

activity 3 understanding relationships between tables

Having created the database, the next step is to create the tables that go into it. How do you decide what constitutes a table and the sort of data it should contain? First consider the nature of the Chelmer Leisure and Recreation Centre.

A leisure centre basically needs a building, staff and people that use it. Often it is cheaper to become a member of a leisure centre and some centres require that you become a member before you can use the facilities. When a person joins the centre details about that person are obtained. Details about the staff that work at the centre will be needed so that they can be paid correctly. Details about the bookings of various rooms, halls and courts in the centre will be required so that the building is used efficiently. If the centre has a bar or cafe then details about food and drink kept in stock would need to be kept as well as, for example, sales records.

Let's look at the membership data in more detail. What sort of information will the centre be asking for in the membership form? Apart from name and address, date of birth is useful for targeting advertising to specific groups e.g. senior citizens. Also knowing something about the sporting interests of the member is useful. The information that Chelmer Leisure and Recreation Centre require about each new member is shown in the table below:

Surname	Occupation
Forenames	Date of Birth
Title	Date of Joining
Street	Date of Last Renewal
Town	Sporting Interests
County	Smoker
Post Code	Sex
Telephone No.	

The names in the table are the names of each piece or field of information. Before issuing a membership card the centre will allocate a membership number, which is different from any other member's number, and will charge a membership fee. The centre offers different categories of membership for which different fees are charged. Therefore it is necessary to have two additional fields, membership number and membership category.

The centre will need to hold data about the current fees charged for each category of membership, this forms another table in our system, the membership category table:

Category No
Category Type
Membership Fee

To discover the fee that a member has paid by matching their membership category with category number in the membership category table, the information in the two tables can be linked. This is known as relating the tables and by creating links between them, they appear to be one table.

One advantage of using more than one table is that less storage space is required. Consider the situation where there wasn't a membership category table and the information about category type and membership fee was stored in the table containing the member's information. Say there are 500 members, so 500 membership category descriptions and 500 membership fee details will need to be stored. If there are two tables then there will be 500 category identification numbers, which need only be one digit and if there are 6 categories, 6 category identification numbers, 6 descriptions and 6 fee details. Another advantage is that the fees can be amended and the new data is available throughout the database simultaneously so that when a new member joins or membership is renewed the correct fee details are used.

Two other tables that form part of the Chelmer Leisure and Recreation Centre system we will be building, are concerned with bookings of the room/hall/courts and the classes that are held. The centre will need to keep track of bookings of rooms to prevent double booking and to schedule classes. Rooms can be booked either by members or by a class so that there is a link between a member and a room booking and there is a link between a class and a room booking. The bookings table and the classes table are shown below:

Booking No
Room/Hall/Court
Member/Class
Member No
Class No
Date
Time

Class No
Class Day
Class Time
Class Tutor
Class Activity
Male/Female/Mixed

Figure 1.1 shows the relational database used by our system for Chelmer Leisure and Recreation Centre. It shows how the four tables, the membership table, the categories of membership table, the classes table and the bookings table are

linked together. Each table is composed of records and the fields in each table are listed in the boxes. The fields that are written in bold italics are known as primary key fields, to which you will be introduced later in this session.

Note: This is just one database structure that could be used for part of the system at Chelmer Leisure and Recreation Centre. The total system would be more complex and a number of alternative database structures are also possible. The best database structure for a given application depends upon the way in which the database is to be used.

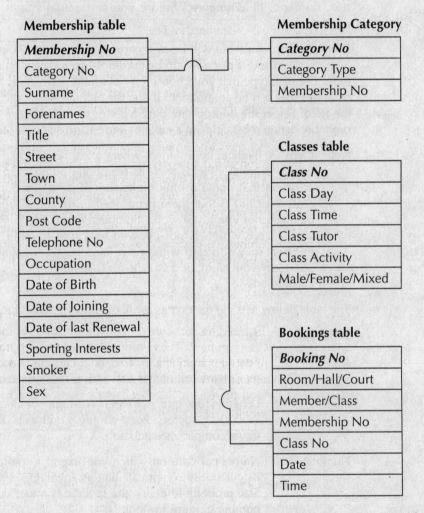

Membership table

Membership No
Category No
Surname
Forenames
Title
Street
Town
County
Post Code
Telephone No
Occupation
Date of Birth
Date of Joining
Date of last Renewal
Sporting Interests
Smoker
Sex

Membership Category

Category No
Category Type
Membership No

Classes table

Class No
Class Day
Class Time
Class Tutor
Class Activity
Male/Female/Mixed

Bookings table

Booking No
Room/Hall/Court
Member/Class
Membership No
Class No
Date
Time

Figure 1.1 Chelmer Leisure and Recreation Centre Database

exercise 2 *creating and linking tables*

The centre will need to have details of the class tutors that it employs. Design a tutors table on paper by considering the fields that will comprise the records in this table. How could this table be linked in with the tables in Figure 1.1?

activity 4 choosing data types

The first stage in building the database is to define the tables, that is, to name them and to define the names of the fields that will be contained in each table's records. The next stage is to define type of data to be stored in each of the fields. No data has yet been entered but before it can be, Access needs to know what sort of data to expect. Take the member's surname, first you need to tell Access the field name, i.e. Surname and you also need to tell Access whether the data is text, numeric, date/time etc. before you can actually start entering people's names!

Every field in your table will be of a particular data type, for example a name is alphanumeric text, a price would be currency and a date would have a date data type. The data type that you choose for your field determines the kind and range of values that can be entered into it and the amount of storage space available in the field. Select the appropriate data type for each field. For example, you will probably define most fields in a table of names and addresses as Text fields.

Note: there are likely to be instances where a text field should be used when the data is numbers. Fields such as telephone numbers, or employee works numbers that contain only digits should be defined as Text fields. The reason for this is that there is no need to do calculations with telephone numbers nor employee works numbers. Often telephone area codes start with a zero which is not allowed in a true number. Employee works numbers may also start with one or more zeros (known as leading zeros). So, reserve the Number data type for fields on which you want to perform calculations.

The table below lists the data types available in Access and their uses.

Data type	Use for
Text	Text and numbers. A Text field can contain up to 255 characters. Examples, names and addresses, class activity.
Memo	Lengthy text and numbers. A Memo field can contain up to 32,000 characters. For example, comments about a hotel, in a travel company's database.
Number	Numerical data on which you intend to perform mathematical calculations, except calculations involving money. Set the Field-Size property to define the specific Number data type. Example, number of items in stock.
Date/Time	Dates and times. A variety of display formats are available, or you can create your own. Example, date of joining.
Currency	Money. Don't use the Number data type for currency values because numbers to the right of the decimal may be rounded during calculations. The Currency data type maintains a fixed number of digits to the right of the decimal. Example, membership fee.

Counter   Sequential numbers automatically inserted by Microsoft Access. Numbering begins with one. Makes a good primary key field. The Counter data type is compatible with the Number data type with the FieldSize property set to Long Integer. Example, membership number.

Yes/No   Yes/No, True/False, On/Off. Example, smoker/non-smoker.

exercise 3 choosing data types

Think about the following questions:

1. What would be the effect of rounding on currency (money) data?

2. What data type do you think you would choose for the following fields?

   ❑ Category No

   ❑ Surname

   ❑ Street

   ❑ Telephone No

   ❑ Date of Birth

   ❑ Sporting Interests

3. Later we suggest that you use a Yes/No field for Sex. Explain this!

4. Why would you use a text field for a post code?

activity 5 defining a new table

This activity takes the form of an exercise in which the membership table will be defined. In the exercise the fields will be set up so that they correspond to the type of data that will be stored in those fields.

exercise 4 creating a new table

The database window should be active (indicated by a blue title bar if you are using the standard Windows colours).

Figure 1.2 Database Window

❑ The **Table** button should be selected as shown in the illustration above, depending upon the version of Access you are using, if it is not then click on it.

❑ Click on the **New** button in the table window to

Access 1

display the **Table** design window as shown in Figure 1.3.

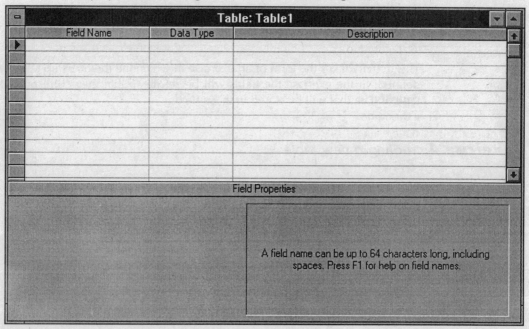

Figure 1.3 Table Window

Access 2

display the **New Table** dialog box.

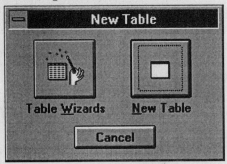

click on the **New Table** button to display the **Table** design window (Figure 1.3).

The **Table Design** window allows you to define the structure of your table. By filling in the Field Name, Data Type and Description cells and by setting Field Properties the structure of the table is defined. This is described in the following exercise.

exercise 5 *defining the fields in a table*

In this exercise the fields for the membership table will be defined, the name, data type and description will be entered into the table design window. You should be able to complete this exercise by following the immediate instructions, but additional notes are also given over the next two pages, which you may wish to consult. The membership table is defined as follows:

Field Name	Data Type	Description
Membership No	Counter	Automatic membership numbering
Category No	Number	Categories are 1-Senior, 2-Senior Club, 3-Junior, 4-Junior Club, 5-Concessionary, 6-Youth Club
Surname	Text	
Forenames	Text	
Title	Text	
Street	Text	
Town	Text	
County	Text	
Post Code	Text	
Telephone No.	Text	
Occupation	Text	
Date of Birth	Date	
Date of Joining	Date	
Date of Last Renewal	Date	
Sporting Interests	Memo	
Smoker	Yes/No	
Sex	Yes/No	

❐ To display the table design window, from the database window with the table button depressed, click on the **New** button.

❐ Enter Membership No for the first field name. Do not type a full stop after No as these are not allowed in field names. For more information on field names refer to Naming Fields in the text following this exercise. Press Enter to move to the Data Type column and click on the list button which displays the following list box.

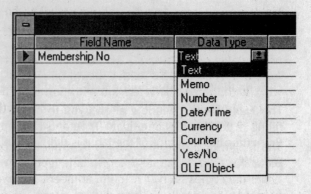

❐ Click on the data type Counter. Press Enter and you will be in the description field. Key in the description as shown in the table. Press Enter to move to the next field.

❐ Continue to enter the definitions for the fields as detailed in the table. Where there is no description press Enter to take you to the next field name. The table will be revisited later to set individual field properties.

❐ The next stage is to define the primary key. Click on the row selector for Membership No and click on the Primary Key button in the tool bar.

❐ Choose *File-Save*.

❐ In the **Save As** dialog box, in the **Table Name** box type the name **Membership.**

❐ Close the table using *File-Close*.

activity 6 moving around the table design window

Through the table design window you can enter the field name, the data type and a description of each field (the description is optional) into the grid in the upper part of the window. To move between cells you have a choice of pressing either Enter, Tab, ➡ or clicking in the required cell in the grid.

Row selector symbol

Along the left hand edge of the grid you will see the row selector symbols. By clicking in the row selector box you can select an entire row.

Selector Symbol

Current row

Primary key field

activity 7 naming fields

Fields need names, lengths and data types to be defined. Many database products limit you to about 10 characters for a field name which means that they often need to be abbreviated. Also the use of a space in a field name is not usually allowed. However, *Access allows field names to be up to 64 characters long with spaces.* Field names should be meaningful so that the data is easier to work with. Some characters are not allowed in field names, these are full stops (.), exclamation marks (!), and square brackets ([]). You cannot give the same name to more than one field. Why not?

The length of a field may be pre-determined according to the data type of that particular field. If the field is of a date type then it will have a standard length. Other data types such as text and number can have their lengths defined. If a text field is being used to hold the title of a song, for example, then you need to estimate the length of the longest song title and set the size of the field accordingly.

Adding field description

A description for a field may be added into the description cell in the table's design view, for any field. The maximum length for the description is 255 characters. It is not necessary to enter a description but it can be useful to provide additional information about a particular field.

Correcting mistakes in field name or description

Point and click in the cell containing the mistake. Correct the mistake in a normal fashion by inserting or deleting text at the insertion point. Click back in the current cell to continue working.

Correcting mistakes in the data type

Click on the data type cell concerned. Open the list box and select the correct data type.

activity 8 creating a primary key

The primary key is a field or combination of fields that uniquely identifies each record in a table. As the main index for the table, it is used to associate data between tables. Though not required, a primary key is highly recommended. All the tables used in our system will have a primary key defined. It speeds data retrieval and enables you to define default relationships between tables. In Figure 1.1 the primary field keys are shown in bold italics. If the membership table is considered then the membership number is the primary key, each record has a different number as every member's number will be different.

If the table does not include an obvious primary key field, you can have Microsoft Access set up a field that assigns a unique number to each record. This automatically numbers each record uniquely. See Activity 1.5 for more discussion of primary keys.

Setting or changing the primary key

To set or change the primary key

1   In the table's Design view, select the field or fields you want to define as the primary key. To select one field, click the row selector. To select multiple fields, hold down the Ctrl key, and click the row selectors for each field.

2   Click the **Primary Key** button on the tool bar, or choose Set Primary Key from the Edit menu. Microsoft Access places the primary key icon in the row selector column.

To have Access define the primary key

1   With the table's Design view displayed, save the table without specifying a primary key. Access asks if you want it to create a primary key field.

2   Choose Yes and Access creates a field in your table called ID with the Counter data type.

activity 9 saving the table definition

Once the structure of the table has been designed it needs to be saved. Access uses this information to set up templates through which you enter data into the table.

❏ Choose *File-Save*

❏ In the **Save As** dialog box, in the **Table Name** box type a name for the table. Note that the name that you choose may be 255 characters long and contain any alphanumeric text.

Note: the table is saved as part of the database file and its name distinguishes it from other tables in the database file. There may be more than one table in a database file and Access allows more freedom for naming tables. You will also find this true for naming queries, forms, reports and macros as all these are stored in one database file. Make use of this freedom to give meaningful names to tables as they will be used later in queries, forms and reports and it is important to be able to recognise the name of the table you require.

activity 10 closing and opening the table

To close a table, either

❏ Double-click on the table's control menu button, or

❑ Choose *File-Close.*

You can open an existing table in either Design view or Datasheet view. So far we have only considered the Design view of a table.

To open a table in Design view

1   In the Database window, click on the **Table** button.

2   Select the table you want to open, and then click on the **Design** button.

activity 11 defining field properties

You may have noticed that once you start to enter the field definitions, field name, data type and description, then the Field Properties are displayed in the lower left hand section of the design window. You have defined the basic data type for each field and by setting the Field Properties you can specify the data type in more detail, for example, if the data type is text you can define the length of the field.

Field Size	
Format	
Caption	
Default Value	
Validation Rule	
Validation Text	
Indexed	

Access 1

Field Size	
Format	
Input Mask	
Caption	
Default Value	
Validation Rule	
Validation Text	
Required	
Allow Zero Length	
Indexed	

Access 2

In the Field Properties section, you can set properties for individual fields. The available options depend on the data type you define for the field. In the lower right hand section of the window a description of the current column or field property is displayed.

Each field has a set of properties you use to specify how you want data stored, handled, and displayed. You set the properties in the bottom part of the Table window's Design view. The properties you can set for each field are determined by the data type you select for the field.

exercise 6 *defining field properties*

So far we have not changed any of the field properties. In this exercise the field properties of the **Membership Table** will be defined. First open the **Membership Table** in design view

❑ From the **Database Window** click on **Membership** and click on the **Design** button.

❑ Select the field **Category No.**

This field has a data type of Number and the Field Properties are preset as Field Size – Double, Decimal Places – Auto, Default Value – 0, Indexed – No and in Access 2, Required – No. In this field the data that will be entered is a number between 1 and 6 inclusive, as there are 6 categories. Refer forward to the section entitled Field Size to see a list of the different number properties that are available. The Byte number type allows whole numbers up to 255 so is a good choice for the number property of the **Category No** field.

❏ Click in the **Field Size** box, open its associated list and select Byte.

There are only six categories so a validation rule can be created.

❏ Click in the Validation Rule box and enter **<=6** and enter the text **Please enter a category number between 1 and 6** into the Validation Text box.

❏ Open the Required list box and select **Yes.** It is necessary for there to be an entry in this field.

❏ Select the field **Surname.**

❏ Click in the **Field Size** box, delete the default size of 50 and replace it with 25

❏ Alter the sizes of the other text fields as follows:

Forenames	30
Title	10
Street	30
Town	25
County	20
PostCode	10
Telephone No	12

❏ Select the **Post Code** field and put > in the **Format** property. This changes all text to uppercase.

❏ Select the **Town** field again and in the **Default Value** box type Chelmer.

❏ Select the **County** field and put Cheshire into its **Default Value** box. Why do think these defaults are set? (Refer to the section on defaults in the following text).

❏ Select the **Date of Birth** field and in the **Format** box put the format d/m/yy repeat this for the two other date fields. Alternatively, select **Short date** from the drop down list of the **Format** box.

❏ Select the **Sex** field and in the **Format** box put the format ;"Male";"Female" which will display Male for Yes and Female for No. Note it is important to put the first semi-colon.

❏ Select the **Smoker** field and in the **Format** box put the format ;"Smoker";"Non-Smoker" which will display Smoker for Yes and Non-Smoker for No.

❏ Save the changes using *File-Save* and close the table using *File-Close.*

activity 12 setting a field property

1   In the table's Design view, select the field whose properties you want to set.

2   Click the property you want to set in the bottom part of the window.

3   Set the property, as explained in the following table.

Property	Description
FieldSize	Maximum length of the text field or type of Number
Format	How data is displayed; use predefined formats or customise your own
DecimalPlaces	Number of places to the right of the decimal
Caption	Default field label in a form or report
DefaultValue	Value entered in a field when records are created
ValidationRule	Expression that defines data entry rules
ValidationText	Text for invalid data
Required	Whether or not an entry must be made
Indexed	Single-field indexes to speed searches

field size

This property sets the maximum size of data that can be stored in a field. If the DataType property is set to Text, enter a number less than 255. This number should be chosen by considering the length of the longest text data that is to be entered into the field. The default setting is 50.

If the DataType property is set to Number, the FieldSize property settings and their values are related in the following way.

Setting	Description
Byte	Stores whole numbers with values between 0 to 255.
Integer	Stores whole numbers with values between -32,768 and 32,767.
Long Integer	Stores numbers from -2,147,483,648 to 2,147,483,647 (no fractions). It occupies 4 bytes.
Single	Stores numbers with six digits of precision, from -3.402823E38 to 3.402823E38. It occupies 4 bytes.
Double	(Default) Stores numbers with ten digits of precision, from -1.79769313486232E308 to 1.79769313486232E308. It occupies 8 bytes.

defaults

Access will assign default values to the fields in your table. This default value is automatically entered in the field when a new record is created. These are values that are usually appropriate for the addition of new records to a table. The default value for Number, Currency and Yes/No fields is zero, in the case of

Yes/No fields zero means No. Text, Memo and Date fields are empty by default. You can save time by specifying your own default values for fields.

You can specify a default field using text or an expression. For example, in an address table you might set the default for the Town field to London, if the majority of records are London addresses. When users add records to the table, they can either accept this value or enter the name of a different town or city. If, for example, an Orders table contains the field Order Date then the expression =Date() can be used to put the current date into this field.

validation

The data entered into tables must be accurate if the database is to be valuable to the person or organisation that it serves. However, even the most experienced data entry operators can make mistakes. To try to detect mistakes you can test the data entered by creating validation rules. These are simple tests which are entered as short expressions into the Validation Rule text box.

If the data entered does not conform to your validation rule, a message box will be displayed to inform the operator that the data is incorrect. The message in the message box is defined by the text that you put in the Validation Text text box. The maximum length for both the Validation Rule and the Validation Text boxes is 255 characters. If data in a record is amended then the validation will still be performed. If a validation rule for a field hasn't been entered then no validation will be performed on that field.

Examples of expressions that can be used are often concerned with numeric fields, e.g. a credit limit that cannot be greater than a certain value. Field with other data types may also be validated, for example a date may only be entered in a certain time period, or a department code can be checked to see if it is a correct department code.

required entry (Access 2)

By setting the required property of a field to Yes then you will need to make an entry in that particular field for every record. Where it is not necessary to have an entry then this property can be left as it's default value. In the **Membership** the **Category No** field has been defined as required, a member cannot be enrolled without being given a category of membership. Revisit the **Membership** table and consider which of the other fields in this table are required entry and make the necessary changes.

activity 13 creating custom display formats

Custom formats will display the data in the format that is specified regardless of the format in which it is entered. For example a display format can be created which will show all telephone numbers using a particular format e.g. (0777) 565656 or 0777-565656. A custom format is created from an image of the format. To design the image a special set of characters, known as *placeholders* are used. To illustrate the creation of a custom format some examples are shown in the following table.

Numeric format	The # indicates the place for a digit but if the place is not used then leading and trailing zeros are not shown. The **0** indicates a place for a digit and if the place is not used then a 0 is shown. The comma may be used as a thousands separator.
##,###.00	56.98 6.90 5,890.07 100.00
#0.000	12.456 0.020
Date	The days placeholder is **d. d** displays 1, **dd** 01, **ddd** Mon, **dddd** Monday. The months placeholder is **m. m** displays 1, **mm** 01, **mmm** Jan, **mmmm** January. The years placeholder is **y. yy** displays 94, **yyyy** 1994. The / or - separates the day, month and year.
dddd d mmmm yyyy	Tuesday 26 April 1994
dd/mm/yy	26/04/94
d-m-yy	2-5-94 (this format does not display leading zeros)
Time	The hours placeholder is **h. h** displays 3, **hh** 03. The minutes placeholder is **m. m** displays 6, **mm** 06. The seconds placeholder is s. s displays 7, ss 07. The colon separates hours, minutes and seconds. **AM/PM** or **am/pm** displays time in 12 instead of 24hr format.
h:mm AM/PM	6:34 PM
hh:mm:ss	11:09:57
Text	@ indicates that a character is required in the particular position.
>	Changes all text in the field to uppercase.
<	Changes all text in the field to lowercase.
(@@@@) @@@@@@	(0777) 565656
Yes/No	;"Male";"Female" Displays Male for true and Female for false.

activity 14 creating input masks (Access 2)

Data entry can be made simpler by creating an input mask, which is a particular format or pattern in which the data is entered. An input mask is only suitable where all the data for that particular field has the same pattern, for example, stock numbers like ABM-372-4590-C. To illustrate the creation of an input mask some examples are shown in the following table.

Input Mask	Sample Values
\ABM-000-0000->L	ABM-372-4590-C
0000-000000	0777-567890
>L<???????????????	Jackson

A mask is created using special mask symbols and these are described in the following table.

Mask character	Indicates
0	a number (digit) must be entered
9	a digit may be entered
#	a digit, + or - sign or space may be entered
L	a letter must be entered

Mask character	Indicates
?	a letter may be entered
A	a letter or digit must be entered
a	a letter or digit may be entered
&	any character or space must be entered
C	any character or space may be entered
. , : ; - /	decimal point, thousands, date and time separators
<	characters to right are converted to lower case
>	characters to right are converted to upper case
\	character following is not be interpreted as a mask character

Revisit the properties of the **Surname** field and set the mask using the third example illustrated above. Check that you use the correct number of question marks, i.e. one less than the field width.

activity 15 creating table indexes

What is an index? You are probably familiar with the index at the back of a book, which helps you to find a particular topic quickly. A table index works in a similar fashion enabling Access to locate a particular record without having to search through all the records from the first until it locates the one you want. When you enter data into a table the records are in chronological order according to when you entered them, in other words they are in no particular order.

A useful order for the table to be in would be that of the primary key. The primary key uniquely defines one record from another so this is a logical order for the records to be in. If the records are not physically in primary key order then Access does not physically re-arrange them, rather it creates an index which it uses to locate the records in that particular order.

When a primary key is defined the indexed property is automatically set to Yes (No duplicates). No duplicates means that Access expects this field in each record to be unique, which it should be if it is a primary key field.

Indexes on other fields may be defined as an index helps Access find specific records faster. For example an index on surname and forename together is useful if the Membership table is often searched using the member's name. Another index could be set on the Date of Renewal field, useful when the table is used to provide projected cash flow of membership fees. Do not index every field in your table as this slows record updating, each time a record is added the indexes need to be modified to account for the new record. The fields you should choose for indexing are ones that are used repeatedly to search for data.

You can create indexes based on a single field or on multiple fields. For example, you can index just on a surname name field or on both the surname and the forenames fields. An index on surname will not distinguish between Liam Locker and Alison Locker but an index on the multiple fields surname and forenames will. Another example is a date and time in the Booking table. Multiple-field indexes enable you to distinguish records in which the first field may have the same value. Instead of finding nine booking records for Monday, you can find one record for Monday at 14:00.

Creating a single-field index

1   In the table's Design view, select the field you want to index.

2   In the Indexed property box at the bottom of the window, choose Yes (Duplicates OK) or Yes (No Duplicates).

Choose the Yes (No Duplicates) option to ensure that no two records have the same data in this field.

Creating a multiple-field index (Access 1)

1   In the Design view of the table, click on the **Properties** button in the toolbar. Access displays the property sheet for the table.

2   You can define up to 5 multiple field indexes per table. Click in the next available Index property box.

3   Type the field names that will make up the index, separating them with a semicolon (for example: Surname; Forenames).

Creating a multiple-field index (Access 2)

1   In the Design view of the table, choose *View-Indexes* or click on the **Indexes** button in the toolbar. Access displays the **Indexes** dialog box.

2   In the **Index Name** column enter the name of the index.

3   In the **Field Name** column open the list box and select the field you require, set the sort order in the **Sort Order** column.

4   In the next row select the next field name of the multiple index and set it's sort order. By leaving the Index name blank up to 9 subsequent rows may be used to create a multiple field index, with each field having its own sort order defined. Note that fields should be listed in order of priority.

exercise 7 setting indexes

❑ Open the **Membership** table in design view.

❑ Select the **Category No** field and choose Yes (Duplicates OK).

❑ Repeat for **Date of Birth** and **Date of Joining** choosing Yes (Duplicates OK) for the indexed property. Why can't Yes (No Duplicates) be chosen?

❑ *Access 1.* Display the table properties by clicking on the **Properties** button in the toolbar. In the **Index1** box enter **Surname; Forenames.**

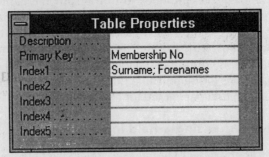

❑ *Access 2.* Display the **Indexes** dialog box. In the **Index Name** column enter the name Member. List the fields **Surname** and **Forenames** as illustrated below.

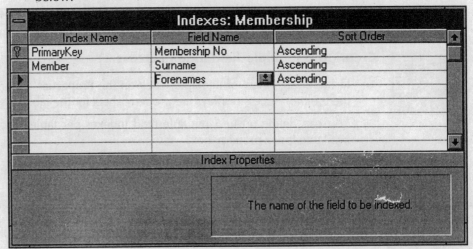

activity 16 making a printed copy of the table design

Access does not provide a command for printing the table structure. If you have software which enables you to capture the screen then this is a method you could adopt, however you may need to capture several screens in order to capture all the design definitions.

A better way is to create another table as a data dictionary. This requires more work but gives a more complete perspective and gives a chance to revise the work already done. Each data element in the database system will have an entry in this dictionary table.

exercise 8 *creating a data dictionary table*

The data dictionary records the definitions of the fields in the database tables. It is a reference document containing the design information of each field which is useful to have handy when the database is added to or revised. To produce a data dictionary for the Chelmer Leisure and Recreation Centre database, first create a new table. The fields in this table will be:

❐ Table Name

❐ Name of Field

❐ Data Type

❐ Description

❐ Length

❐ Format

❐ Default Value

❐ Validation Rule

❐ Validation Text

❐ Required Entry (Access 2 users only)

❐ Index Name.

Field Name	Data Type
Table Name	Text
Name of Field	Text
Data Type	Text
Description	Text
Length	Text
Format	Text
Default Value	Text
Validation Rule	Text
Validation Text	Text
Required Entry	Text
Index Name	Text

Use the default text setting for all the fields. Select the **Table Name** and **Name of Field** together and set these as the primary key. Other table dictionaries may be added later so this keeps the dictionary in **Name of Field** within **Table Name** order. Save the table with the name **Dictionary.** Enter the dictionary data for the **Membership Table.** Try to create the dictionary table yourself, use the table shown in Appendix 2 to check your work.

activity 17 *entering data*

The next stage is to enter data into the tables. Up until now the tables have been opened in design view. To enter data a table needs to be opened in the Datasheet view.

To open a table in Datasheet view

1. In the **Database Window**, click the **Table** button.

2. Double-click the table name or select the table, and choose the **Open** button.

Once a table is open it is possible to switch from the datasheet view to the design view and vice versa. If you make changes to the design you will be asked to save them if you switch back to the datasheet view. There are two buttons on the tool bar for switching between the views:

Design view   Datasheet view

In the datasheet view the headings of the columns are the field names you previously designed. Each row in the datasheet is a record and as you complete each record it is automatically saved into the table.

exercise 9 membership data

Open the Membership table in datasheet view. Notice that there are some fields already filled in these are the default values. A default value can be accepted or it can be overridden. Do not enter a value into the membership number but press Enter to move to the next field. This is a counter field and if you do try to enter data into it the entry will not be accepted. When you press Enter after entering data into the last field of the first record, Access saves the record. Notice what appears in the membership number field. Let Access number all the membership number fields.

The data for the **Membership** table is shown in Appendix 2. When entering the data for the logical fields enter either Yes or No and the appropriate word as defined by the format appears, e.g. Male or Female. Also while entering the data test the validation rules, those that Access applies and those that have been defined. Try the following

❐ entering text into a date-type field, Access expects the correct data type,

❐ entering a **Category No** greater than 6, this will test the validation rule set up in the field properties for **Category No.**

Skip fields that are blank. Validation, skipping fields and using Undo are described below.

validation

Data is validated as it is entered, if it does not conform to the data type set for that field an error message will be generated. If the data entered breaks the Validation rule that has been set as a property for that field, then if there is validation text, this appears as the error message.

skipping fields, null values

Sometimes not all the data for a record is available, for example, the telephone number may be missing. To skip a field simply press Enter or Tab to take you to the next field. It is acceptable to skip fields where the data is not vital but for data such as the Membership No it is not acceptable. Access automatically enters a membership number as the field was defined with a Counter data type.

Where a field is left without an entry it is said to be Null i.e. there is nothing there. If you perform mathematical calculations on numeric fields, then Access ignores fields containing Nulls. This can lead to error in statistical analysis, for example, you will meet a query in Session 2 that calculates the average age of the members. There are 20 member records and if a 21st record is added where there is no entry in the Date of Birth field, from which age is calculated, then the average of the 20 known ages will be calculated. However, if a count of members is requested based on Membership No then the result would be 21. If you intend to use a numeric field for calculation then it is good practice to try to ensure that each record has an entry in that field.

zero length strings (Access 2)

Nulls indicate that data may exist but is not known. To enter a null leave a field's Required property as No and leave the field blank. A zero length string can be used to indicate that there is no data for the field in that record, for example, a company without a fax machine doesn't have a fax number. To enter a zero length string check that the Zero length string property is set to Yes. In the datasheet type two double quotation marks without a space between i.e. "". Nulls and zero length strings may be distinguished when searching the data table.

using undo

Should you do anything wrong or if something unexpected happens always try *Edit-Undo* or click on the **Undo** button (Access 2) before doing anything else.

activity 18 editing data

Once the records have been entered into a table, this data is available to be used as is evident in the following sessions. However, the data in the data sheet can be viewed and if mistakes are spotted these can be rectified.

Moving between records

By using either *Records-Go To*, the Up and Down Arrow keys, Page Up and Page Down keys, or the vertical scroll bar you can move between records in the datasheet. However, the most efficient way to move between records in large databases is with the navigation buttons in the lower-left corner of the window.

Access record indicators

In the status bar of the datasheet window are the Access record indicators. These are record movement buttons and the record number of the currently selected record.

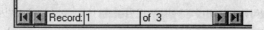

To move to	Click
First record	⏮
Last record	⏭
Previous record	◀
Next record	▶

Record: 1

Specific record   click in record counter box (or press F5), type the record number you want, and then press Enter.

Moving to specific fields (Access 1)

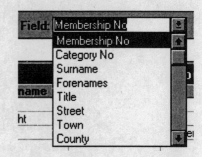

If the table contains records with many fields, as is the case with the **Membership** table, not all the fields will fit on the screen. To locate a specific field, first find the record you want and then open the field list box on the tool bar and select the field to move to.

Selecting data

Various parts of the datasheet can be selected, when an area is selected it appears in inverse colour, so if text is normally black on white, then selected text is white on black.

To select a single field

❑ Move the pointer to the left hand side of a cell, so that it changes shape into a right pointing arrow and click.

To select a word in a field

❑ Double-click on the word.

To select a record

❑ Click in the record selector at the left edge of the record, or choose *Edit-Select Record*

To select more than one record

❑ Click and drag in the record selector edge for the required number of records.

To select a field column

❑ Click on the column heading (the field name at the top of the column).

Moving and copying fields

A field may be moved, by selecting it, using *Edit-Cut*, clicking in the cell where the field is to be moved to and using *Edit-Paste*.

A field may be copied, by selecting it, using *Edit-Copy*, clicking in the cell where the copy is required and using *Edit-Paste*.

Buttons are available in Access 2, i.e. Cut, Copy and Paste.

Hiding and showing columns

If there are a lot of fields in a table as is the case with the **Membership** table then columns may be hidden. By using the Show command the columns may be re-displayed. To hide a column in a datasheet

1. Click on the column selector at the top of the column. Note only one column at a time may be hidden.

2. *Choose Layout-Hide Columns* (Access 1) or *Format-Hide Columns* (Access 2).

To re-display the columns

1. Choose *Layout-Show Columns* (Access 1) or *Format-Show Columns* (Access 2).

2. In the dialog box select the column(s) to be shown and click on **Show**. When finished click on **Close**.

Moving and copying records

You can copy a complete table or some records of a table to the clipboard. Records may be moved and copied using *Edit-Cut/Copy* and *Edit-Paste.* Generally moving isn't an operation you would need to carry out within the same table as the records can be displayed in any order chosen. Moving and also copying can be carried out between databases providing the table structures are similar. Importing and exporting data is considered in more detail in Session 8.

One instance where copying is useful is for making a backup of a table. Should you decide to revise the data types of fields in a table then it is advisable to make a backup of the table first in case mistakes are made which could result in the loss of data.

---

exercise 10 backing up a table

In this exercise a backup of the **Membership** table will be made.

❏ Click on the **Table** button in the **Database Window.**

❏ Select the table **Membership** and choose *Edit-Copy.*

❏ Next create a database to hold the backup by choosing *File-New Database* and typing **backup** in the **File** box and clicking on OK. This database is now active.

❏ Choose *Edit-Paste* and in the **Table Name** box of the **Paste Table As** dialog box type **Membership backup.**

❏ Check that the default option **Structure and Data** is selected before clicking on **OK.**

❏ Use *File-Close Database* to close the backup database.

25

If this backup is needed to restore a damaged file then open the backup database, select and copy the table, open the normal database (use *File-Open*) and paste as described above.

activity 19 deleting records

You can delete a record from a table using a datasheet or a form. (We shall meet forms in Session 3). Here we delete records using a datasheet.

To delete a record

1. Select the record or records you wish to delete.

2. Press the **Delete** key (or choose *Edit-Delete* from the menu).

3. Access prompts you to confirm the deletion. Choose **OK** to delete the record or **Cancel** to restore it.

activity 20 finding and replacing

To find a particular field

1. If you wish to find a particular entry in a certain field make that field current by clicking in that column.

2. Choose either *Edit-Find* or click on the **Find** button in the toolbar.

3. Key the string (set of characters) you wish to find into the **Find What** text box.

4. In the **Where:** box select whether your string should match the whole field, any part of the field or the start of the field.

5. In the **Search In** option group choose between **Current Field** or **All Fields.** The all fields option will search the entire table.

6. In the direction option group you may choose between searching up or down through the records.

7. If you wish to make the search case specific, i.e. the same case as the string in the **Find What** text box then click in **Match Case.**

8. To start the search click on either **Find Next**, which will search from your current position in the direction you have chosen, or **Find First** which will find the first occurrence in the field or table.

9. Each time a match is found it is highlighted. If either the top or the bottom of the table is reached Access displays a message asking whether you would like to continue the search from the bottom or the top of the table.

10. When you have found the desired field click on **Close.**

To replace a particular field, select *Edit-Replace* and the steps are the same as for finding a field, except that in the dialog box there is an additional text box, **Replace With**, into which the replacement string is entered. Strings can be replaced according to which button is clicked:

Find Next   Finds and highlights but does not replace. Use when you don't want to replace.

Replace   Replaces the highlighted string and finds the next occurrence of the **Find What** string.

Replace All   Replaces all occurrences of the string without stopping.

Close   Closes the dialog box

exercise 11 editing data

In this exercise we experiment with finding and replacing data.

❏ Open the **Membership** table. Move to the end of the table.

❏ Add another record, Category 3. Move to record 9, select the **Surname** field and copy it.

❏ Move back to the **Surname** field of the new record and use *Edit-Paste.* Finish the record as shown in the table below:

Forenames	Title	Street	Town	County	Post Code
Frances	Miss	70 Meir View	Chelmer	Cheshire	CH2 7BZ
Date of Birth	**Date of Joining**	**Date of Last Renewal**	**Sporting interests**	**Smoker**	**Sex**
5/5/80	1/3/92	1/3/94	Swimming, Judo	No	No

❏ Go to the first record. Click in the **Telephone No** field.

❏ Choose *Edit-Find* or click on the **Find** button in the toolbar.

❏ Key **0778** into the **Find What** box and select **Start of field.**

❏ Click on the **Find First** button. This should highlight the first occurrence. If the **Find in field** dialog box is in the way drag it out of the way.

❏ Click on the **Find Next** button to find other matches. Close the **Find in field** dialog box.

❏ Move to the top of the table again and click in the **Telephone No** field. Choose *Edit-Replace* and key 0777 into the **Find What** box and 0779 into the **Replace With** box. The current field should be selected to search in and the **Match Whole Field** check box should not be checked as shown below:

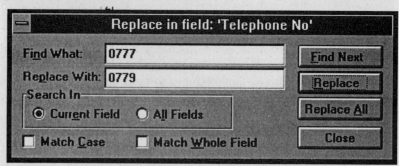

❏ Click on the **Replace All** button.

❏ Answer **No** to the continue searching from the beginning question.

❏ Choose **OK** to continue the replace action. It is at this stage that the replace could be cancelled.

❏ Replace all 0779 codes with 0777.

❏ Select the last record, which you have just created, and delete it.

activity 21 customising the datasheet layout

Adjusting column widths

To improve the datasheet display, it is possible to alter the widths of the columns. Usually columns are made smaller, as field widths often err on the large side, and this is easily achieved especially if you are familiar with Windows applications.

To alter a column width:

1. Move the pointer to the field name row (at the top of the table).

2. Move the pointer to the dividing line between the column you wish to change and the column to the right, it should change shape to a

3. Click and drag the column to the desired width.

Adjusting row heights

Another way in which more fields can be displayed across the screen is by making the row height larger.

To alter a row height:

1. Move the pointer to the row selector (at the left edge of table).

2. Move the pointer to the dividing line between the row you wish to change and the row below, it should change shape to a

3. Click and drag the row to the desired height.

Changing the font used in the datasheet

Choose *Layout-Font* (Access 1) or *Format-Font* (Access 2) and select the required font and size from the **Font** dialog box.

Changing fields

You may find it necessary to change a field data type as the design of your database develops or if you import data into it. Session 9 deals with importing data. Before you make any changes to field data types make a backup copy of the table in case you accidentally lose data because your changes were too great.

Before you make changes consider the following implications:

❐ **Numeric fields**

Changing to a data type to one that can hold a larger number is generally safe, for example changing a data type of Byte to that of Integer. If on the other hand you change to a data type that holds a smaller number, for example changing from Double to Integer, then your data will be truncated, in this case by losing the decimal part of the number. Truncation means reducing the number of digits in a number to fit the new field size property that you choose.

Note: You cannot convert any type of field into a Counter type field as Access provides automatic numbering in this field type.

❐ **Text fields**

The field size of text fields may be altered but if the alteration is to make the field size smaller text may be truncated. Text fields may be converted to Memo fields but if a Memo field is converted to a text field it will be truncated to 255 characters.

❐ **Conversion between data types**

It is possible to convert a field from one data type to another.

❐ **Primary key or fields used in relationships**

You cannot change the data type or field size property of these fields.

To change a field data type, make a backup copy of your table, display the design view of your table and make the necessary alterations.

Reorganising fields

If you consider that the order in which the fields are shown in the datasheet needs rearranging, then this can easily be achieved using a drag and drop method. First select the field column you wish to move, move the pointer over the selection so that it changes shape to a left-pointing arrow, click and drag the column to a new position. A darker column dividing line will indicate where the field will go when the mouse button is released.

When you close the table you can choose whether or not to make the rearrangement permanent by selecting **Yes** or **No** in the **Save Changes** message box.

exercise 12 *customising the membership datasheet*

The aim of this exercise is to see how columns of data may be re-arranged and also how to adjust their width.

❏ Display the **Membership** datasheet.

❏ Adjust the widths of the columns to accommodate the data displayed.

❏ Select the **Sporting Interests** column and drag it to between the **Occupation** and the **Date of Birth** columns.

❏ Close the table without making the rearrangement permanent by choosing **No** in the **Save Changes** message box when closing the table.

activity 22 *printing a table*

You can print a table from its datasheet. Access prints a datasheet as it appears on the screen. For large datasheets, Microsoft Access prints from left-to-right and then from top-to-bottom. For example, if your datasheet is three pages wide and two pages long, Microsoft Access prints the top three pages first, then the bottom three pages. You should preview your datasheet before printing by choosing *File-Print Preview* or clicking on the Preview button in the toolbar.

If you need to set up your printer, choose the **Setup** button in the **Print** dialog box.

To print a table datasheet:

1. Display the table datasheet.

2. If you intend to print selected records, select those records. To print all the records, select nothing.

3. Choose *File-Print Preview,* and if the preview is satisfactory click on the **PRINT** button to display the **Print** dialog box.

4. Under **Print Range**, choose one of the following:

❏ **All**, to print all of the records in the table.

❏ **Selection**, to print the selected records.

❏ **Pages**, to print specific pages from your table.

If you select **Pages**, specify the page numbers of the first and last pages you want to print.

5. Set other **Print** dialog box options if necessary.

6. Choose **OK**.

exercise 13 *printing the membership table*

❐ Display the **Membership** table datasheet.

❐ Choose *File-Print Preview*, and then click on the **PRINT** button to display the **Print** dialog box.

❐ Under **Print Range** select **All** and click on **OK**.

❐ Close the table.

activity 23 defining relationships between tables

If you wish to use only one table in your database you may omit this activity. You will find that you can complete most of Sessions 2 to 6 as many exercises are based on the **Membership** table. You should then return to this activity before moving on to Session 7.

The relationships between the tables are shown in Figure 1.1. Relationships are made between a field in one table and a field in another table. Relationships fall into three types,

❐ one-to-one relationships

❐ one-to-many relationships

❐ many-to-many relationships.

A one-to one relationship between two tables means that for a particular field in one table there is only one matching record in the other table and vice versa. A one-to-many relationship means that for one field in one table there are lots of matching records in the other table. A many-to-many relationship means that for one field in one table there are lots of matching records in the other table and vice versa.

Membership table		Bookings table
Membership No		Membership No
1		4
2		1
3		6
		8
		1
		17
		3

ONE   to   **MANY**

Membership table   **Youth club table**

Membership No
1
2
3
10
11
12

Membership No
3
11

ONE   **to**   **ONE**

The commonest type of relationship is that of one-to-many and it is the only type used in our system. Consider the relationship between a member and that member's booking. A member may make no bookings, one booking or several bookings. So one member can make several bookings, a one-to-many relationship, i.e. there is only one record with that person's membership number in the membership table, yet there can be several records with that person's membership number in the bookings table.

However, in our database these relationships do not yet exist because they have not been defined. You need to set up these relationships. The relationships can be set up before any actual data is entered into any of the tables. Before any relationships between tables can be defined the tables must be closed. It is important that when a link is make between a field in one table and a field in another table, the two fields have the same data type.

Referential integrity

When a relationship is created between two tables Access allows the choice of whether or not to enforce referential integrity. If the relationship between the **Membership** and the **Bookings** table is considered then what is to stop a membership number being entered into the **Bookings** table which does not exist in the **Membership** table. By enforcing referential integrity Access will check the membership number entered into the **Bookings** table against the membership numbers in the **Membership** table and will prevent non-existent membership numbers being entered.

exercise 14 *creating relationships*

As yet only one table has been created in the Chelmer database. Before relationships can be defined the other tables in the database need to be defined. For this exercise the **Bookings** table will need to be defined.

To create a **Bookings** table, click on the **New** button in the **Database** window to open the table design window (you may wish to refer back to Exercises 1.4 to 1.6). Define the field types as shown.

Define **Booking No** as the primary key. Save the table as **Bookings.**

Field Name	Data Type	Description
Booking No	Counter	
Room/Hall/Court	Text	
Member/Class	Yes/No	
Membership No	Number	
Class No	Number	
Date	Date/Time	
Time	Date/Time	

Amend the field properties as shown following. Save and close the table.

Bookings table

Field	Property	Setting
Room/Hall/Court	Field Size	20
	Required	Yes
Member/Class	Format	;"Member";"Class"
	Required	Yes
Membership No	Field Size	Long Integer
	Default value	=Null
Class No	Field Size	Long Integer
	Default value	=Null
Date	Format	d/m/yy
	Required	Yes
Time	Format	Short time
	Required	Yes

Make sure that both of the tables are closed, i.e. just the **Database Window** is left open. Now the relationship between **Membership No** in the **Membership** table and **Membership No** in the **Bookings** table will be created. The data type of the **Membership No (Bookings)** is a long integer number which is compatible with the data type counter of **Membership No (Membership)**. In one-to-many relationships the primary table in the relationship is the 'one' table, in this case the **Membership** table and the related table is the 'many' table, i.e. the **Bookings** table.

To define a relationship between tables:

Access 1

❑ Choose *Edit-Relationship* and the **Relationships** dialog box appears.

❑ Open the primary table list box and select **Membership.**

❑ Open the related table list box and select **Bookings.**

❑ In the **Type** section the **Many** option should be highlighted as shown below:

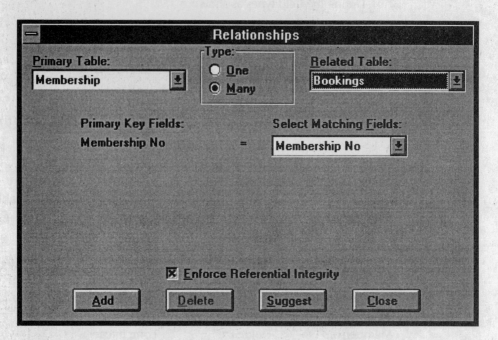

❑ Access will match a field from the bookings table with the **Membership No** from the **Membership** table, which should be **Membership No.**

❑ Click in the **Enforce Referential Integrity** to prevent non-existent membership numbers from being entered.

❑ Click on the **Add** button to include this relationship in the database.

❑ Click on the **Close** button to close the **Relationships** dialog box.

Access 2

❑ Choose *Edit-Relationships* and the **Relationships** dialog box appears with the **Add Table** dialog box within it.

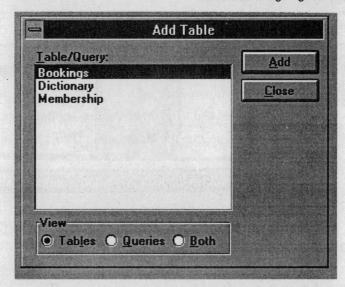

☐ Select **Membership** and click on **Add**. Select **Bookings** and click on **Add**. Click on **Close**. The two table windows should be displayed and you may re-size them if you wish.

☐ To create the relationship click on the **Membership No** field in the **Membership** table and drag to the **Membership No** in the **Bookings** table. This displays a **Relationships** dialog.

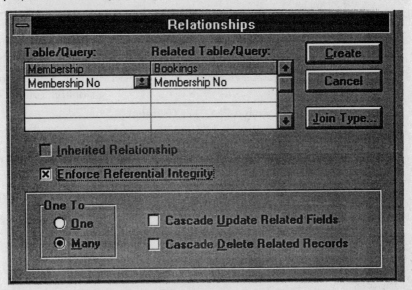

☐ Click in the **Enforce Referential Integrity** check box and click on **Create** and the relationship between the tables will be shown.

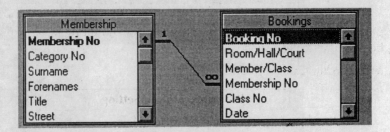

☐ Use *File-Save Layout* to close the **Relationships** box.

integrative exercises

exercise 15 *defining the other tables in the database*

Create the following tables. Click on the **New** button in the **Database** window to open the table design window. Define the field types as shown. For each table set the primary key, shown in bold italics, before closing the table.

1. *Membership Category*

Field Name	Data Type	Description
Category No	Number	A one digit identification number
Category Type	Text	Categories are Senior, Senior Club, Junior, Junior Club, Concessionary, Youth Club
Membership Fee	Currency	

Define Category No as the primary key. Save the table as Membership Category and close the table.

2. *Classes*

Field Name	Data Type	Description
Class No	Counter	
Class Day	Text	
Class Time	Date/Time	
Class Tutor	Text	
Class Activity	Text	
Male/Female/Mixed	Text	

Define Class No as the primary key. Save table as Classes and close the table.

In your database window you should see four tables listed.

exercise 16 *defining field properties for the other tables*

Open each table in turn, in design view. Amend the field properties as shown below. Save and close the tables.

Membership Category table

Field	Property	Setting
Category No	Field Size	Byte
	Required	Yes
Category Type	Field Size	15
	Required	Yes
Membership Fee	Required	Yes

Classes table

Field	Property	Setting
Class Day	Field Size	10
	Required	Yes
Class Time	Format	Short time (equivalent to hh:mm)
	Required	Yes
Class Tutor	Field Size	30
Class Activity	Field Size	20
	Required	Yes
Male/Female/Mixed	Field Size	10
	Validation Rule	"Male" or "Female" or "Mixed"
	Validation Text	Please enter Male Female or Mixed

exercise 17 *creating indexes*

In this exercise indexes for the **Classes** and **Bookings** tables are created.

❒ Open the **Classes** table in design view.

❒ Select the **Class Tutor** field and choose Yes (Duplicates OK).

❒ Repeat for **Class Activity** choosing Yes (Duplicates OK) for the indexed property.

❒ Open the **Bookings** table in design view.

❒ Select the **Room/Hall/Court** field and choose Yes (Duplicates OK).

❒ Set a multiple field index using the fields **Date** and **Time**.

exercise 18 *defining the other relationships*

There are two other relationships in the database, (see Figure 1.1) these are

❑ between the **Classes** table and the **Bookings** table

❑ between the **Membership Category** table and the **Membership** table.

Both these relationships are one-to-many-relationships. Using the **Relationships** dialog box, set these relationships up as follows:

Access 1

Primary Table	**Type**	**Related Table**
Classes	Many	Bookings

Primary key fields		**Select matching fields**
Class No	=	Class No

Before adding this relationship, check the **Enforce Referential Integrity** check box to prevent non-existent class numbers being entered into the **Bookings** table.

Primary Table	**Type**	**Related Table**
Membership Category	Many	Membership

Primary key fields		**Select matching fields**
Category No	=	Category No

Before adding this relationship, check the **Enforce Referential Integrity** check box to prevent non-existent category numbers being entered into the **Membership** table.

Access 2

❑ Add the tables **Classes**, **Bookings**, **Membership Category** and **Membership** using the **Add Table** dialog box. Display this dialog box using *Relationships-Add Table.*

❑ To create the relationship click on the **Class No** field in the **Classes** table and drag to the **Class No** in the **Bookings** table. Note the direction of dragging is one to many.

❑ Click in the **Enforce Referential Integrity** check box and click on **Create** and the relationship between the tables will be shown.

❑ If you try to create the relationship between **Category No** in the **Membership Category** table and **Category No** in the **Membership** table you will find that if you check the **Enforce Referential Integrity** check box, Access will not create the relationship because there is no data in the **Membership Category** table. When the data is added in Session 3 the relationship can be created. Close the **Relationships** box.

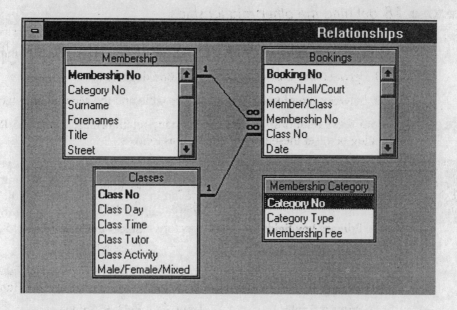

exercise 19 *completing the data dictionary*

Open the **Data Dictionary** table and add to it the definitions of the three tables created in these integrative exercises. When you have finished, save the table and refer to the data dictionary shown in Appendix 2.

exercise 20 *printing the data dictionary*

- ❑ Display the **Data Dictionary** table datasheet.
- ❑ Choose *File-Print Preview.*
- ❑ Click on **Cancel** and make any adjustments to column widths. Use **Setup** to choose a Landscape orientation if this would be preferable.
- ❑ Preview and then click on the **Print** button to display the **Print** dialog box.
- ❑ Under **Print Range** select **All** and click on **OK.**
- ❑ Close the table.

session two
designing queries to select data

objectives

This session explores the ability of databases to be able to answer questions asked of them. The information stored in a database is of no use unless it can be retrieved and only if it can be retrieved in a way so as to be useful. Data stored in a telephone directory can be retrieved, for example, by knowing the name and address of someone in the directory and using the database to find out the telephone number.

By the end of this session you should

❐ be able to question the database by creating a query

❐ be able to save a query so that it can be retrieved for later use

❐ print out your query

❐ sort the information shown in the answer to your query

There are many reasons for using queries, they have a very important role in database systems. Queries are used

❐ so that on-line search and retrieval of specific records can be made. For example, to look at particular set of members for editing, or to view the bookings for a given room on a certain day, or to find the class tutors who have a particular qualification.

❐ for creating forms and printing reports. Queries retrieve a particular set of records and fields and reports are used to print this information. A form based on a query can be used to restrict data entry to certain fields. Sessions 3 and 4 introduce forms and reports.

Queries may be based on more than one table but in this session all the queries will be based on the Membership table. You will see later in Session 7 how to create queries based on more than one table.

This session concentrates on basic query design and introduces you to a variety of queries that can be created using one table.

activity 1 the query design window

Creating a query involves two aspects. These are

❐ selecting the fields that are to be shown in the query. It is not usually necessary to retrieve all fields, for example, only the name and the telephone number of a member may be all that is needed for a telephone survey of a particular group of members.

❏ selecting the records that are to be shown in the query. For this Access provides a method of querying by which you can describe the characteristics of the data that you are looking for. This method is know as Query By Example (QBE) and is achieved by allowing you to give examples of the data that you are searching for in the form of criteria.

The Query Design Window (Figure 2.1) allows a query to be designed which will select the required fields and records that you ask for. This window is in two sections, the upper section is where the table windows of the tables used in the query are displayed. In the lower section is a grid for the query design. The two most important rows in the grid are Field and Criteria. Each column needs a field name and all the fields in the table may be chosen or a only few of them. In the criteria row an example of the data may be given. As you work your way through this session you will be introduced to the function of the other rows in the grid.

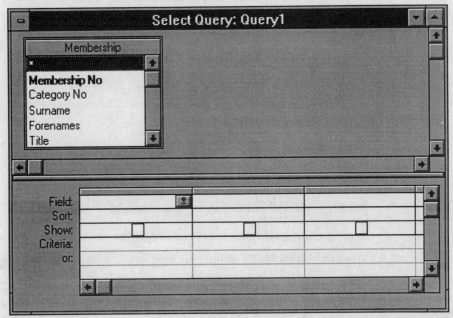

Figure 2.1 Query Design Window

Before asking questions of a database you must first decide which tables in the database are required to answer them. The following activities will describe how to ask questions of just one table, the membership table. You will see later, in Session 7 how to include more than one table in a query.

Displaying the query design window

1. Click on the **Query** button in the **Database Window** and click on the **New** button to create a new query. If you have not created any queries yet then the Open and Design buttons are not available.

2. Click on the **New Query** button in the **New Query** dialogue box (Access 2).

3. The **Add Table** dialog box appears. This dialog box allows you to select all the tables needed for the query. When the selection of table(s) is complete click on the **Close** button.

activity 2 adding fields to a query

After choosing the table for the query it will be displayed in the upper section of the query design window as seen in Figure 2.1. The next step is to decide which fields in that table you wish to include in the query, later we will explore query criteria which allow us to select specific records. The query is designed in the lower section of the query design window.

Adding all the fields in the table to the query

The simplest case is where we want to include all the fields in the table.

1. Double click on the title bar of the field list box of the table in the upper section of the window. This selects all the fields.

2. Click on any of the selected fields (not the *) and drag to the field cell in the lower section of the Query window. The pointer should look like a set of record cards.

3. When you release the mouse button all the field names will have been added to the query. Use the horizontal scroll bar to move to the right as all the columns will not fit on the screen.

Adding individual fields in the table to the query

There are three alternative ways of adding the fields one by one to a query.

The first method is by double-clicking, thus:

1. Double-click on the name of the field required in the field list box in the upper section of the window. It will appear in the next available column in the grid below.

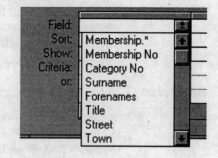

The second is to use the drop down list associated with each field cell, thus:

1. Click in the field cell in the lower section of the window. A list box button appears at the end of the cell.

2. Click on the list box button and a drop down list of field names will appear.

3. Select the name of the field required, if necessary scroll through the list, click on it and it will appear in the field cell.

The third way is to use the *drag-and-drop* method, thus:

1. Click on the name of the field required in the field list box in the upper section of the window.

2. Drag and drop this field into the required field cell in the lower part of the Query window. While doing this the pointer should look like one record card.

3. If you drop the field onto a column containing a field, then a column will be inserted to contain the new field.

Removing fields from the query

Fields may be removed singly or in blocks from the query. To remove the all the fields from the query.

1. Select the first column by clicking on the bar at the top of the column, (the pointer will change shape to a down arrow) drag to select all the columns.

2. Press the **Delete** key or choose *Edit-Delete*.

To remove an individual field from the query, just select the required column for deleting and use *Edit-Delete*.

activity 3 viewing or running a query

To see the result of a query, either click on the **Datasheet** button or the **Run Query** button in the toolbar. To return to the query design click on the **Design** button next to the Datasheet button in the toolbar.

Design button   Datasheet button   Run Query button

Access displays a datasheet containing the records which match the query with fields as defined in the query. This query result is what Access calls a dynaset. A dynaset is a temporary table and is not a permanent part of your database. If you modify your query the resulting dynaset will change accordingly.

exercise 1 selecting fields for a query

In this exercise the membership table will be queried, data from all records will be shown in the dynasets. Initially all fields will be shown and then you will see how to select only certain fields.

❏ Starting from the **Database Window,** click on the **Query** button.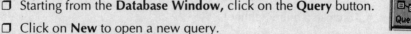

❏ Click on **New** to open a new query.

❏ Select the table **Membership** from the **Add Table** dialog box, click on **Add**, and close the dialog box.

❏ Add all the fields to the query, following the method for adding all the fields in the table to the query as described in Activity 2.

❑ Click on the **Datasheet** button in the toolbar, you should see the whole of the table forming the dynaset.

❑ Click on the **Design** button in the toolbar to return to the **Query** design window.

❑ Remove all the fields from the query, following the method for removing fields from the query as described in Activity 2.

❑ Add fields individually to the query, experimenting with the different methods described above in Activity 2. Add the fields **Membership No, Surname, Sex, Date of Joining.**

❑ Click on the **Datasheet** or **Run Query** button in the toolbar, you should see only these fields from all the records of the table forming the dynaset.

❑ Click on the Design button in the toolbar to return to the **Query** design window.

❑ By adding and removing fields alter the fields in your query so that they are **Surname, Sex, Category No, Sporting Interests.**

❑ Click on the **Datasheet** button in the toolbar, or the **Run Query** button and you should see only these fields from all the records of the table forming the dynaset.

activity 4 saving a query

Sometimes you may wish to ask the same question of a database over and over again, for example, is a membership subscription due. As time passes members need to renew their membership and it is useful to be able to send reminders. A query designed to do this would be saved so that it can be used repeatedly. To save a query

1. Choose *File-Save Query* or click on Save button on Access 2 toolbar.

2. In the **Query Name** box of the **Save As** dialog box enter a name that will remind you what the query is about. The name can be up to 255 characters. Click on **OK.**

3. If you close the **Query** window, you will see the name of your query in the Queries list of the **Database** window, from where it can be opened for use on another occasion.

Closing and opening a query

To close a query, either

❑ Double-click on the query's control menu button. or

❑ Choose *File-Close*, if you have made changes to the query and not saved then you will be prompted to do so.

You can open an existing query in either Design view or Datasheet view.

To open a query in **Design** view

1.   In the Database Window, click on the **Query** button.

2.   Select the Query you want to open, and then click on the **Design** button.

To open a query in **Datasheet** view

1.   In the Database Window, click on the **Query** button.

2.   Select the Query you want to open, and then click on the **Open** button.

exercise 2 *saving a query*

In this exercise the query created at the end of the previous exercise will be saved.

❑   Choose ***File-Save Query*** or click on the **Save** button.

❑   Give the name **Members sporting interests** to this query and click on **OK**.

❑   Close the query and you should see the name of the query in the Database Window.

activity 5 printing a query

Before printing the dynaset produced by your query it is advisable to preview it first. To preview a query table:

1.   In the datasheet view, click on the **Print Preview** button on the toolbar. You will be shown a preview which displays a miniature version of what is to be printed.

2.   The pointer becomes a magnifying glass and can be used to 'zoom-in' to part of the page. If you use other Windows applications you will be familiar with this. Clicking will 'toggle' between zoom-in and zoom-out modes. When 'zoomed-in' the vertical and horizontal scroll bars can be used to scroll around your previewed page.

3.   To adjust the column widths you need to return to the datasheet view. To do this click on the **Cancel** button (Access 1) or the Close Window button (Access 2). The column widths are adjusted in the same way as for table datasheets as described in Activity 9 of Session 1.

Once you are satisfied that the preview is correct, then from the Print Preview mode:

1.   Click on the **Print** button in the button or tool bar. The **Print** dialog box appears, if you want to print without changing anything then **skip the following three steps.**

2.   Click on the **Setup** button and the **Print Setup** dialog box appears.

3.   To change the margins click in the appropriate box and edit the default setting You can select the orientation of the page, the printer and the paper

size. The **Data Only** check box, if checked, will suppress the printing of the field names. Click on **OK** to return to the **Print** dialog box.

4. Click on **OK.** When printing is complete click on the **Cancel** button to return to the Query Datasheet.

exercise 3 printing

In this exercise the dynaset produced by the query created in Exercise 2 will be printed.

❏ From the Database Window open the query in datasheet view.

❏ Click on the **Print Preview** button on the toolbar.

❏ Some columns may need widening. Click on **Cancel** to return to the datasheet and widen the columns (see Session 1 Activity 9).

❏ Preview again, zoom in to check that the columns are wide enough, click on the **Print** button.

❏ Click on **OK** in the **Print** dialog box and the following dynaset should be printed.

❏ Click on the **Cancel** button to return to the datasheet view.

Surname	Sex	Category No	Sporting Interests
Walker	Male	2	Tennis, squash
Cartwright	Female	1	Aerobics, swimming, running,squash
Perry	Male	6	Judo, Karate
Forsythe	Female	2	
Jameson	Female	1	Aerobics, squash
Robinson	Female	3	Swimming, Judo
Harris	Male	5	Badminton, cricket
Shangali	Male	2	Weight training
Barrett	Female	1	Keep fit, swimming
Weiner	Male	1	Weight training, squash
Ali	Male	6	Judo, swimming, football
Young	Female	2	Keep fit, Aerobics, squash
Gray	Male	5	
Swift	Female	5	
Davies	Female	1	Aerobics, squash, swimming
Robinson	Female	1	Tennis, Aerobics
Everett	Male	2	Squash, Fitness training, football
Locker	Male	4	
Locker	Female	4	
Jones	Male	1	Weight training

activity 6 sorting the dynaset

The dynaset or result of a query can be displayed in different orders. If no sorting order is specified then the records in the datasheet will be shown in their natural order, i.e. the order in which they were entered into the table. Sorting is particularly useful, for example if the records are shown in order of date of birth then it is easier to see an age profile, if records are shown in order of town then geographical information becomes apparent. If a report is to be created from the query (see Exercise 4 Session 4) then the order of the records can be defined by the query.

You may wish to see your result in a particular order, for example, in last name alphabetical order or according to postal area etc. In the grid in the lower section of the query design window there is a sort row. To define the type of sorting:

1. Click in the sort cell for the field in which you are interested. A list box button appears at the end of the cell.

2. Clicking on the list box button will reveal the sorting choices.

   Ascending will sort from low to high, descending from high to low and not sorted will not apply any sorting.

   | Ascending |
   | Descending |
   | (not sorted) |

Note: There is an order of priority of sorting when more than one field is being sorted. The order of priority is determined by the order of the fields in the query, leftmost fields being of higher priority.

exercise 4 sorting

This exercise investigates the different orders in which the query created in Exercise 2 can be displayed.

❑ From the design view of this query, click in the sort cell for the Surname field.

❑ Open the list box and choose Ascending.

❑ Display the dynaset, by clicking on the Run Query button. Return to the Design view.

❑ Change the sort order of the Surname field to (not sorted).

❑ Choose Ascending as the order for the Sex field.

❑ Display the dynaset. Return to the Design view.

❑ Choose Ascending order for the Surname and Descending order for the Sex fields, respectively. What order do you expect the data for the twins to be shown? View the dynaset.

❑ Close the query without saving it, i.e. answer No when prompted to save changes.

exercise 5 sort order priority

For this exercise a simple query will be created to illustrate the effect that the order of the fields in the query has upon the priority of sort order. By choosing different priorities and viewing the resulting dynaset, the effect can be appreciated.

❐ Create a new query using the **Membership** table.

❐ Add the fields **Category No, Town** and **Surname** to this query.

❐ Choose Ascending as the order for both **Category No** and **Town** fields and view the resulting dynaset.

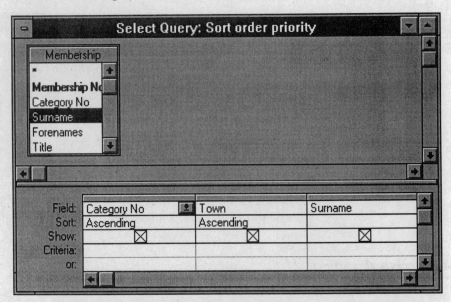

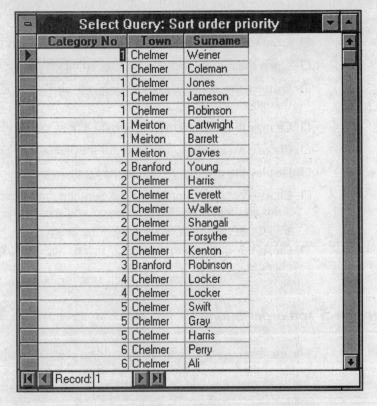

❒ Return to the **Query Design** window, select the **Category No** field, by clicking at the top of the column (while the pointer looks like a down pointing arrow). With the column selected point to the field header (pointer should be left pointing arrow shape) click and drag to reposition it *after* the **Town** field. Leave the sort order of **Category No** as ascending.

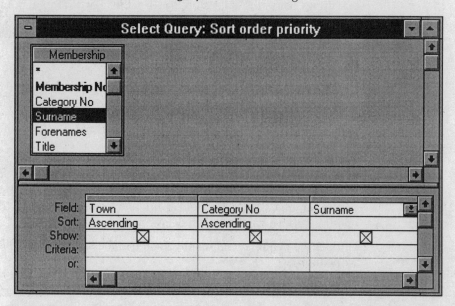

❒ View the resulting dynaset, which should be in a different order from the previous one.

❒ Close this query without saving it.

Town	Category No	Surname
Branford	2	Young
Branford	3	Robinson
Chelmer	1	Jameson
Chelmer	1	Weiner
Chelmer	1	Robinson
Chelmer	1	Coleman
Chelmer	1	Jones
Chelmer	2	Shangali
Chelmer	2	Everett
Chelmer	2	Forsythe
Chelmer	2	Kenton
Chelmer	2	Harris
Chelmer	2	Walker
Chelmer	4	Locker
Chelmer	4	Locker
Chelmer	5	Harris
Chelmer	5	Gray
Chelmer	5	Swift
Chelmer	6	Ali
Chelmer	6	Perry
Meirton	1	Davies
Meirton	1	Cartwright
Meirton	1	Barrett

Record: 1

activity 7 entering query criteria

Query criteria basically allow the enquirer to frame questions which enable specific records to be retrieved from the database. We might want to find out various things using the data stored in a table. For example, some questions that might be asked about the **Membership** table are

❑ Which members live in Chelmer?

❑ Which members smoke?

❑ Which members are over 60?

❑ Which members joined before 1/1/92?

❑ Which members are in categories 1 and 2?

There are many reasons for asking questions. In business questions are important in decision making and to be able to question data relating to, for example, marketing or management, can be very effective using a database management system. In the case of Chelmer Leisure and Recreation Centre the answers to the questions above can help with decisions regarding

❑ does the centre attract mainly local members, what is the effect of local competition;

❑ no-smoking areas being introduced;

❑ introduction of activities and facilities for the older members;

❑ introduction of discount scheme for loyal members;

❑ fees charged for various categories.

To ask questions, criteria need to be set and these criteria are entered into the criteria cells of the **Query** design grid. Querying is done by example, so an example of the answer to the question is entered into the criteria cell.

exercise 6 *query criteria for the membership table*

In this exercise the questions mentioned above will be formulated as queries for the **Membership** table. The queries use the datatypes Text, Number, Date and Yes/No. Each question will be dealt with in turn.

❑ Create a new query using the **Membership** table.

❑ Add all the fields to the query.

Which members live in Chelmer?

❑ In the Criteria cell of the **Town** field type **Chelmer**

❑ Click on the **Datasheet** or **Run Query** button and the resulting dynaset should only contain records for which the **Town** field is equal to Chelmer.

Town	C
	☒
"Chelmer"	

❑ Return to the design view, notice that Access puts quotes around your criterion if it thinks it is text. Delete the criterion 'Chelmer'. Select the cell by double-clicking and press **Delete** to clear the cell. Alternatively click in the cell and use the backspace key to delete the criterion.

Which members smoke?

❑ In the Criteria cell of the **Smoker** field type **Yes.** You may need to scroll to the right to display this cell on the screen.

❑ Click on the **Datasheet** or **Run Query** button and view the resulting dynaset.

❑ Return to the design view. Delete the last criterion.

Which members are over 60?

❑ In the Criteria cell of the **Date of Birth** field type **<1/1/34.**

❑ Click on the **Datasheet** or **Run Query** button and view the resulting dynaset. Return to the design view. Notice that Access has recognised your query example as a date and converted it to <#01/01/34#. Delete this criterion.

Which members joined before 1/1/92?

❑ In the Criteria cell of the **Date of joining** field type **<1/1/92.**

❑ Click on the **Datasheet** or **Run Query** button and view the resulting dynaset. Return to the design view. Delete this criterion.

Which members are in categories 1 and 2?

❑ In the Criteria cell of the **Category No** field type <=2.

❑ Click on the **Datasheet** or **Run Query** button and view the resulting dynaset. Return to the design view. Delete this criterion. Close the query without saving it.

activity 8 renaming and hiding fields in a query

When queries are printed it is sometimes necessary to widen the column so that the field name at the top of the column can be seen. This in turn can lead to unnecessarily wide columns, so it is useful to be able to rename the field. The field header can be renamed in a query with an alternative name. For example, **Last Renewed** instead of **Date of Last Renewal.**

Note: That renaming the field header does not affect the name of the field in the underlying table.

To change field header names

1. Switch to **Query Design** mode by clicking on the **Query Design** button. Move the insertion point to the column containing the field header name you wish to change.

2. Point to the beginning of the field header and click. The aim is to put the flashing insertion point at the beginning of the header name.

   If you accidentally select the header press F2 to de-select it. If the insertion point is not at the beginning, then press the Home key to move it to the first character position.

3. Type in the new name for the field, and follow the name with a colon. Do not put a space between the name and the colon.

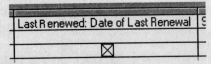

   The colon separates the name you type from the existing field name, which moves to the right to make room for your addition.

4. Click on the **Datasheet** button or the **Run Query** button and the query result with amended field header will be displayed.

In this session you have seen how to select the fields you want to see in the result of a query and how to impose criteria. These can be combined so that the dynaset is only the records that match the criteria and contains only the fields specified in the query. To be able to impose a criterion on a field, that field needs to be in the query grid, which means that it will form part of the dynaset. This may not always be desirable so Access offers the choice of whether or not the field forms part of the dynaset via the Show row. By default all fields in the query show in the dynaset i.e. the 'Show' cell is on, there is an X in the box. To hide a field click in the box in the Show cell, the X disappears and the field will not form part of the dynaset.

exercise 7 *renaming and hiding fields in a query*

Query 1

The following query lists the names and addresses of all the male members who are smokers.

❏ Create a new query using the **Membership** table.

❏ Add the following fields **Membership No, Title, Surname, Street, Town, County, Post Code, Smoker, Sex.**

❏ In the criteria fields of **Smoker** and **Sex** put Yes. Hide these fields by removing the X in the **Show** check box.

❏ Sort the **Surname** field in ascending order.

❏ Rename **Membership No** as Member No and display the dynaset.

Member No	Title	Surname	Street	Town	County	Post Code
13	Mr	Gray	4 The Parade	Chelmer	Cheshire	CH1 7ER
7	Mr	Harris	55 Coven Road	Chelmer	Cheshire	CH3 8PS
20	Mr	Jones	17 Mayfield Avenue	Chelmer	Cheshire	CH2 9OL
1	Mr	Walker	16 Dovecot Close	Chelmer	Cheshire	CH2 6TR

❏ Save the query as **Addresses of Male Smokers.** Close the query.

Query 2

In this exercise a query which looks at the occupations of the female members of the centre. The result of this query will be selected fields from selected records.

❑ Create a new query using the **Membership** table.

❑ Add the following fields to the query, **Category No, Forename, Surname, Occupation, Sex**.

❑ In the criteria cell of the Sex field type **No.**

❑ Click on the check box in the Show cell of the **Sex** field to hide it.

❑ Click at the beginning of the **Category No** Header and type Cat: (do not type a space before the colon).

❑ Click on the **Datasheet or Run Query** button to view the result of the query. The **Category No** field should have the header Cat and the **Sex** field should be hidden.

❑ Save the query as **Occupations of Female Members.**

activity 9 exploring types of query criteria

The queries that have been created so far in this session have only used criteria in one field. Criteria may be applied to all the fields that are included in a query. Each field may be sorted or hidden. By combining these more complex queries can be produced.

We have already used some of the operators used in criteria. The table following summarises them:

Mathematical operators

<	less than
>	greater than
<>	not equal to
>=	greater than or equal to
<=	less than or equal to
+	addition
-	subtraction
*	multiplication
/	division

Text operators

"J*"	text strings beginning with J
"*ton"	text strings ending with ton
"*k*"	text strings containing the letter k

activity 10 using logic in queries

The queries used so far are simple questions asked about a particular field. Queries can be asked which use queries on more than one field, for example, male smokers (Query 1 in Exercise 7). The question is 'Is the member male AND does he smoke?'. There is a logical AND between the two criteria; both criteria must be true for the record to be retrieved.

What if a logical AND is required on the same field, for example, members whose date of joining was after 1/1/92 AND before the 1/1/93 (Query 2 in Exercise 8). In the criteria cell the word 'and' is used between the two criteria, for example, **>=1/1/92 and <1/1/93**. More than two criteria may be specified but remember to put the word AND between them.

The other form of logic that is used in queries is OR. There is a row entitled or: in the query design grid. An example of this would be a query which requires as its answer the names and addresses of members that live in Chelmer OR Meirton. The way in which this query is set up is to enter 'Chelmer' into the criteria row of the Town field and underneath in the or: row to enter 'Meirton'. The example query below (Query 3) lists the names of the members who are likely to use the fitness suite as their sporting interests are Aerobics, Fitness training or Weight training.

exercise 8 using different types of query criteria

Query 1 – querying text fields

This query picks out people with particular sporting interests

☐ Create a new query using the **Membership** table.

☐ Add the following fields **Membership No, Surname, Category No, Sporting Interests**

☐ In the criteria fields of Sporting Interests type **"*Tennis*"**. Note that Access will convert this to read **Like "*Tennis*"**.

☐ Sort the **Surname** field in Ascending order.

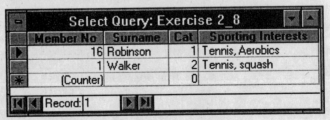

☐ Rename **Membership No** as **Member No** and **Category No** as **Cat.**

☐ Display the dynaset. Print the dynaset. Save the query giving it the name **Sporting Interest** and close the query.

Query 2 – logic, using AND

This query picks out members who joined in 1992.

❒ Create a new query using the **Membership** table.

❒ Add the following fields **Title, Forenames, Surname, Telephone No, Date of Joining**.

Select Query: Exercise 2_8			
Title	Forenames	Surname	Telephone No
Mrs	Sandra M	Davies	0778 891441
Mrs	Donna	Jameson	
Miss	Alison	Locker	
Mr	Liam	Locker	
Mr	Imran	Shangali	0777 561553
Mr	Andrew J	Walker	0777 569236
Mr	George W F	Weiner	
Ms	Aileen	Young	0778 894471

Record: 1

❒ In the criteria fields of **Date of Joining** type **>=1/1/92 and <1/1/93**. Note that Access will convert this to read **>=#01/01/92# And <#01/01/93#**.

❒ Hide the **Date of Joining** field.

❒ Sort the **Surname** field in Ascending order.

❒ Display the dynaset. Print the dynaset. Save the query giving it the name **When joined** and close the query.

Query 3 – logic using OR

This query picks out members whose sporting interests are either aerobics, fitness training or weight training and shows their home town so that local interest can be assessed.

❒ Create a new query using the **Membership** table.

❒ Add the following fields **Membership No, Category No, Surname, Town, Sporting Interests**

❒ In the criteria field of **Sporting Interests** type **"*aerobics*"**. Note that Access will convert this to read **Like "*aerobics*"**.

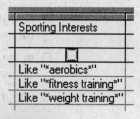

Sporting Interests
Like "*aerobics*"
Like "*fitness training*"
Like "*weight training*"

Select Query: Exercise 2_8			
Member No	Cat	Surname	Town
2	1	Cartwright	Meirton
15	1	Davies	Meirton
17	2	Everett	Chelmer
5	1	Jameson	Chelmer
20	1	Jones	Chelmer
16	1	Robinson	Chelmer
8	2	Shangali	Chelmer
10	1	Weiner	Chelmer
12	2	Young	Branford

Record: 1

- ☐ In the or: field of **Sporting Interests** type **"*fitness training*"**
- ☐ In the row below type **"*weight training*"**
- ☐ Hide the **Sporting Interests** field.
- ☐ Sort the **Surname** field in ascending order.
- ☐ Display the dynaset. Notice that when querying text Access is not case sensitive, **"*aerobics*"** will find **aerobics, AEROBICS** or **Aerobics.** Print the dynaset. Close the query without saving.

activity 11 more complex queries

Queries can perform calculations on the data in the table. Calculations may be to count the number of records, to add up or take the average of certain fields or to create new fields by calculation. In the exercise following a new field 'Age' is created and the average age of the members is calculated. A new field can be created from a calculation using existing fields in the table, for example, if there is a price field which doesn't include VAT then a VAT field can be calculated by multiplying the price by the rate of VAT.

There are a wide range of different applications where it might be appropriate to perform calculations as part of a query. Here we briefly explain some of the basic concepts and give a few examples.

To create a calculated field, in the next empty field cell, in the Query Design Window, enter an expression to calculate the new field. The expression takes the form **Name of calculated field:Expression.** The expression is the formula for creating the value of this field. An expression involves other fields and these are written enclosed in square brackets, for example, **Taxable pay:[Gross Pay]–[Free Pay]** or **VAT:[Cost]*0.175**.

Expressions may be used with date data types and there are several date functions available, the two that are used in the exercise following are

- ☐ Year() which returns the year of the date/time value enclosed in brackets as an integer number, for example Year([Date of Joining]) might result in 1992
- ☐ Now() which returns the date and time of the computer's system clock.

Sometimes it is useful to produce some summary statistics as a result of your query, for example the number of fields, the total of values in those fields or the average of the fields. These statistics may be for all the records in the table or just for the ones selected by the query. Click on the 'Sigma' button on the toolbar to gain access to the statistics functions, which can be entered into the Total row which appears in the Query Design grid when the **Sigma** button is depressed.

Each cell in the Total: row has its own drop down list. Various statistical functions are available as follows.

Count	will give the number of records
Sum	will give a total of all values in that particular field

Min, Max	will give the maximum or minimum value of that particular field
Avg, StDev, Var	the average, standard deviation, variance of a particular field
Group by	groups records according to this field producing summary statistics for each group
Where	allows criteria to be specified

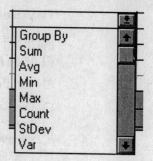

activity 12 editing and renaming a query

Once a query has been saved it can be used again and again. More records may be added to the table, each time a query is used it uses the data currently held in the table. However, as a database develops then a query may be changed to accommodate changing requirements. If the query is modified it may be advisable to change its name so that it remains as meaningful as possible.

exercise 9 creating a new field by calculation

❏ Create a new query using the **Membership** table.

❏ Add the fields **Category No** and **Surname.**

❏ Click in the next field cell and create a calculated field by typing **Age:Year(Now())–Year([Date of Birth])**

❏ Sort the **Age** field in descending order.

❏ Display the dynaset. Print the dynaset.

Age: Year(Now())-Year([Date of Birth])
Descending
☒

❏ Save the query with the name **Member ages.**

exercise 10 counting and averaging fields

❏ Continue with the query created in Exercise 9.

❏ Click on the **Sigma** button to display the **Total:** row.

❏ In the **Total** cell for the first three fields select **Count.**

❏ In the total cell for the **Age** field select **Avg.**

Field:	Category No	Surname	Age: Year(Now())-Year([Date of Birth])
Total:	Count	Count	Avg
Sort:			Descending
Show:	☒	☒	☒
Criteria:			
or:			

❏ Run the query.

The result of this query is different from the normal dynaset display. One row is displayed which contains summary information according to the specification in the **Total** row. Returning to the design view and clicking on the **Sigma** button will cause the **Total** row to disappear and the query reverts to that in Exercise 9.

CountOfCategory	CountOfSurname	Age
20	20	32

If you save this query, and close it, when you open it again, notice that Access will have changed the calculated field to **Age: Avg(Year(Now())–Year([Date of Birth]))** and put **Expression** in the **Total** row.

exercise 11 *grouping and averaging fields*

❐ Continue with the previous query, by returning to the query design.

❐ In the **Total** cell for the **Category No** field select **Group by** and chose Ascending as the Sort order for this field.

❐ Remove the sort order from **Age** and arrange the query as illustrated below:

Field:	Category No	Surname	Age: Avg(Year(Now())-Year([Date of Birth]))	
Total:	Group By	Count	Expression	
Sort:	Ascending			
Show:	☒	☒	☒	
Criteria:				

❐ Run the query.

Category No	CountOfSurname	Age
1	7	31.28571428571
2	5	36.4
3	1	10
4	2	11
5	3	60
6	2	13.5

This time a row for each category is displayed, containing in the **Age** field the average age of members in each membership category.

exercise 12 *using criteria in a summary query*

❐ Continue with the previous query by returning to the query design.

❐ In the Total cell for the **Category No** field select **Where.** Select Not Sorted in the Sort cell.

❐ In the **Criteria** row put **1 or 2** (this is equivalent to putting 1 in the **Criteria** row and 2 in the **Or** row).

❐ Hide the **Category No** field.

Field:	Surname	Age: Avg(Year(Now())-Year([Date of Birth]))		Category No
Total:	Count	Expression		Where
Sort:		Descending		
Show:	☒	☒		☐
Criteria:				1 Or 2
or:				

❏ Run the query. The result should be the total number of members in categories 1 and 2 and their average age.

❏ Try this for categories 3 and 4.

❏ Save the query.

CountOfSurnam	Age
12	33.41666666667

❏ Rename this query as **Average Ages.** With **Member Ages** selected in the Database Window, choose *File–Rename* and in the **Rename** dialog box change the name to **Average Ages.**

integrative exercise

exercise 13 additional queries

This exercise takes the form of a series of questions plus the rationale for the questions. All queries are created using the **Membership** table.

1. *What is the occupation of women members with sporting interests of aerobics?*

   If a large majority of women members whose sporting interests include aerobics have stated that they are housewives then a ladies aerobics class could be scheduled in the day rather than the evening. The fields that might be appropriate for this query, are **Membership No, Category No, Title, Initials, Surname and Occupation. Try sorting on Category No.**

2. *What is the home town of male members with sporting interests of weight training?*

   Does the centre offer better weight training facilities than the local competition and so attracts members from a wide area? The fields that might be appropriate for this query, are **Initials, Surname, Category No and Town**. Sort on the **Town** field in Ascending order.

3. *Which members joined the centre between 1/1/93 AND 1/1/94?*

   This query can easily be created by referring to the query in Exercise 8. Such queries can be used to assess the success of the centre.

4. *Which members are aged between 18 AND 25?*

   Should the bar consider holding social events targeted at this age group? Are there enough members locally in this age group to make this worthwhile? The fields that might be appropriate for this query, are **Name,** all address fields and **Sporting Interests.** Sort the query in **Post Code** order in Ascending order.

5. *Which members are either housewives OR unemployed OR retired?*

   Technically this query ought to include househusbands, although there are none listed in the data given for members! The centre may consider a range of daytime activities which would appeal to this group of members. The fields that might be appropriate for this query, are **Membership No, Category No, Date of Birth and Sex.** Sort the query in **Date of Birth** order.

6. *Which members have sporting interests of Keep fit AND aerobics?*

   The fields that might be appropriate for this query, are **Membership No, Surname, Category No, and Date of Birth**. Sort in Ascending order both the **Category No** and **Date of Birth,** with **Category No** having the highest priority.

objectives

In this session you will learn how to create a screen form. A screen form provides a more user friendly way with which to work with your data. Entering data can be made easier and less prone to error. At the end of the session you will be able to:

❏ create a form using Form Wizards

❏ use a form to enter data

❏ perform simple customising of a form

❏ save and print a form

In Session 1 the tables for the Chelmer Leisure and Recreation Centre were defined. Data was entered into the Membership table but as yet data has not been entered into the other tables. In this session the data will be entered into these tables. The data could be entered into these tables as it was for the Membership data, using the datasheet view of the table. The disadvantage of using the datasheet view is that the fields in a record often do not all fit on the screen. Also viewing and entering data in the datasheet grid can be somewhat tiresome.

When data is collected manually it is often by means of filling out a form. In a form there are boxes to fill in with, for example, name, address etc and there may be boxes that are ticked, for example Yes/No boxes. Access offers the facility to create a form on the screen so that data can be entered into a table by simply filling in the form. Filling in such a form should be more user–friendly than filling in the cells in a datasheet provided that the form has been designed carefully.

A form can be based upon a table or a view created from a query. A query can use more than one table so the form created from such a query can be used to enter data into several different tables. This will be explored in later sessions. In this session we will concentrate on designing forms to enter data into the tables in the database. It is usual to have a form for each table of data for the purpose of entering and editing data in that table.

Forms can be used to enter, edit, display and print data contained in your tables. They offer the advantage of presenting data, on screen, in an organised and attractive manner.

Standard forms are created for most applications or jobs, for example, a form for entering the details of a new member, as shown in Figure 3.1.

Access allows you to create forms to your own design, for which it provides a wide range of tools. If you are a new Access user or simply for convience the

Form Wizards provide a quick and easy way to create a basic form. This basic form can be customised later. To enable us to get started quickly on form design we will make use of the Form Wizards.

activity 1 creating a form with Form Wizards

There are four types of form that can be created using the Form Wizards, these are Single Column, Tabular, Graph and Main/Subform. This session will concentrate on the first two types as these are the types usually used in database applications. The form types we will investigate are Single Column and Tabular.

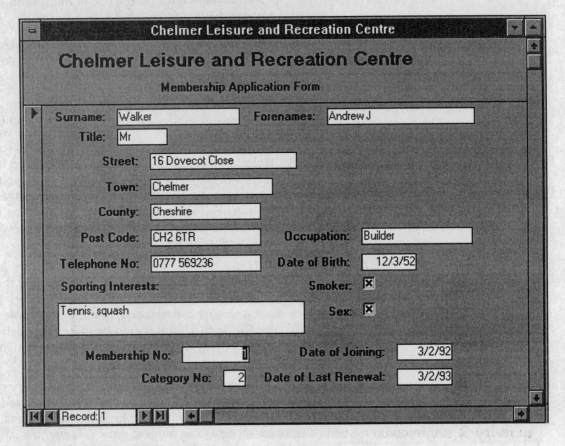

Figure 3.1 A form for entering membership data

1. Starting from the Database Window, either,
    - ☐ click on the **Form** button and then click on the **New** button, or
    - ☐ choose *File–New* and then **Form,** or
    - ☐ click on the **New Form** button in the toolbar and a **New Form** dialog box appears.

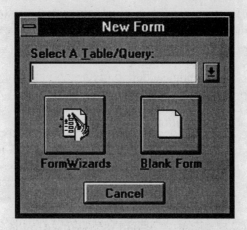

2. Click on the list box button of the **Select A Table/Query** box, to produce a list of tables and queries and select the table for which you wish to create a form.

3. Click on the **FormWizards** button.

Once you have selected the **FormWizards** button then the choices that will be considered are single column and tabular forms.

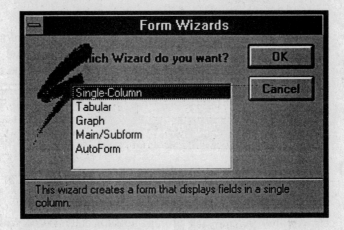

activity 2 single column Form Wizards forms

A single column form is one which allows the user to input one record at a time. The form shown in Figure 3.1 started as a single column form but has been modified slightly. A single column form has boxes to fill in for the fields of information required for that record, these boxes are arranged in a column. To create a single column form:

1. Perform the three steps as above, selecting the Single–column form, and click on **OK**.

2. The next stage is to choose which fields are to be on the form. The fields that you can have in the form are shown in the **Available fields** box.

   ❑ These can be transferred to the **Field order on form box** by means of selecting each field in turn and clicking on the > button.

   ❑ If you wish to add all the fields in the table to the form then click on the >> button.

   ❑ You may set the order in which the fields appear on the form by selecting them in the order you desire. The < button will remove a highlighted field from a form and << will remove all the fields from the form.

   Once you have added the required fields to the form continue by clicking on the **Next>** button.

3. You are then asked what kind of look you want for your form and are given a choice of:
   ❑ Standard
   ❑ Chiselled
   ❑ Shadowed
   ❑ Boxed
   ❑ Embossed

   An example of the look is shown in the top left of the dialog box. Click on each 'look' in turn to see what it would look like. On the first occasion a form is created choose **Standard,** the 'look' can be modified later. The next thing you are asked for is a title. Key in an appropriate title for your form into the text box. Now click on the **Open** button to display the form with data in it.

activity 3 saving and closing a form

Save a form by choosing *File–Save.* If this is a new form which you have not yet saved then Access will prompt you for a file name with a **File Save As** dialog box. If you wish later to save this form with a different name then use *File–Save As* and fill in the appropriate details in the dialog box.

Remember that there is a distinction between the name and the title of a form. The title is displayed at the top of the form window. The name you give when saving the form is the form's file name which you need to be able to recognise when you want to open the form for use again. These names appear in the Database Window when the **Form** button is depressed.

A form can be closed by using *File–Close* or by using the control menu button of the form window. If the form or the latest modification has not been saved you will be prompted to save. When a form is closed its name (the one you gave to it when saving) will be shown in the database window when the **Form** button is depressed.

To open a form from the Database Window, click on the **Form** button, select the name of the form required and click on the **Open** button.

exercise 1 *creating a single column membership form using Form Wizards*

In this exercise a single column membership form will be created which can later be modified to look like the form shown in Figure 3.1. The order in which the fields are selected for the form are important, as will become apparent when the form is used to enter data. To create this form:

❐ From the Database Window click on the form button and click on the **New** button.

❐ Display the list of tables in the **New Form** dialog box and select Membership from the list of tables. Click on the **FormWizards** button and choose a Single–column form.

❐ Select which fields are to be added to the form one at a time by selecting the field and clicking on the [>] button to add it to the table. Add them in the following order, **Surname, Title, Forenames, Street, Town, County, Post Code, Telephone No, Occupation, Date of Birth, Smoker, Sex, Sporting Interests, Membership No, Category No, Date of Joining** and **Date of Last Renewal.**

❐ Click on the **Next>** button and choose a **Standard** look for the form. Click on Next>.

❐ Key in the title **Chelmer Leisure and Recreation Centre** and click on the **Open** button (Access 1) or with the option **Open the Form with data in it**, selected click on **Finish** (Access 2).

❐ You should have created a form with a title and a list of field names in a column with a corresponding list of data for the first record in another column. Notice the difference between this form and the one shown in Figure 3.1. Customising the form will be considered later in this session.

❐ Choose *File–Save Form* and give the form the name **Membership.** Click on OK.

❐ Close the form.

activity 4 *creating a tabular form*

A tabular form is one which displays more than one record on the screen. The field names form headers for columns and the records are shown below in a table. The number of records displayed will depend upon the size of the window and the number of records in the table. If there are a lot of fields in a record is unlikely that you will be able to see the complete record on the screen and you will need to scroll to the right to display more of the fields. This type of form is suited to records with only a few fields, such as those in the **Membership Cate-**

gory table. The advantage of this form is that it displays more than one record at a time.

To create a tabular form:

1. Starting from the Database Window, either,

   ☐ click on the **Form** button and then click on the **New** button, or

   ☐ choose *File–New* and then **Form,** or

   ☐ click on the **New Form** button in the toolbar and a **New Form** dialog box appears.

2. Click on the list box button of the **Select A Table/Query** box, to produce a list of tables and queries and select the table for which you wish to create a form.

3. Click on the **FormWizards** button.

4. Select **Tabular** and click on **OK.**

5. Select the fields to be shown on the form as described for single column forms, step 5.

6. As described in step 6 choose a standard 'look' for the form and click on the **Open** or **Finish** button to display the form.

exercise 2 *creating the membership category form*

No data has been entered into the **Membership Category** table, this exercise will create a form which can later be used for this purpose.

☐ First close any open form.

☐ From the Database Window with the **Form** button depressed click on **New.**

☐ In the **New Form** dialog box select the **Membership Category** table from the drop down list.

☐ Click on the **FormWizards** button and choose **Tabular** and click on **OK.**

☐ Add all the fields to the form and click on the **Next>** button.

☐ Give it the title **Membership Category.** Choose the standard look and click on the **Open** or **Finish** button to display the form.

Figure 3.2 Membership Category Form

The difference between this form and the single column form is that the fields are arranged in columns. The top of the column is headed by the field name. There is no data in the underlying table so there is only one blank record to display. When records have been added, as we shall see later, then more than one record is shown in the form.

❑ Save the form as **Membership Category.**

❑ Close the form.

activity 5 using a form

To use a form, first display the available forms in the Database Window by clicking on the **Form** button in that window. Open the form either by selecting it and clicking on **Open** or by double-clicking on its name.

You can use the form to look at the data in the table (or query) upon which it is based. Whether it is a single column or tabular form use the record movement keys in the status bar or use the *Records* menu to move around the records in your form. Using the Page Up and Page Down keys with a single column form will display the next/previous record whereas with a tabular form they will either page up or down a screenful of records.

Using the form to enter a new record into the table

Forms should be designed with this purpose in mind as this is their primary function. Entering data is a labour intensive task and the design of the form is important as it may be used for long periods by a person entering data.

To enter a new record using a form:

1. Go to the end of your records using the go to end of records button on status bar. If your form is single column press the Page Down key and a blank form appears. If your form is tabular click in the first field of the blank record shown at the end of your records.

2. Enter data for another record by filling in the boxes for each field. When you have completed each text box (control) press Enter or Tab to move to the next one.

3. Check boxes are used for Yes/No fields. Checked is Yes, not checked No.

exercise 3 using a form to enter data into a table

In this exercise we shall enter data into the categories of membership table, using the tabular form just created.

❑ Open the **Membership Category** form.

❑ Enter data as shown following. As you enter each record it is saved to the **Membership Category** table.

❑ Close the form.

❑ (Access 2 users.) Now there is data in the form use *Edit-Relationships* to create the link between the **Membership Category** and **Membership** tables. Drag **Category No (Membership Category)** to **Category No** on the **Membership** table. Check in the Enforce Referential Integrity check box. Refer back to Session 1.

Membership Category		
Membership Category		
Category No	**Category Type**	**Membership Fee**
1	Senior	£25.00
2	Senior Club	£30.00
3	Junior	£10.00
4	Junior Club	£15.00
5	Concessionary	£18.00
6	Youth Club	£20.00
0		£0.00

Record: 1 of 6

activity 6 printing a form

Forms are designed primarily for screen use, i.e. they are intended for data to be entered via the computer and they display the data on screen. However, Access offers the facility to print from a form. Before printing a form always preview it first. A form can be previewed from either the run or design view mode.

Previewing

Previewing will display a miniature version of what is to be printed. This allows the layout to be assessed so that adjustments can be made before printing.

To preview a form

1. Click on the **Print Preview** button in the toolbar, and a miniature version of what is to be printed will be displayed.

2. To zoom-in and zoom-out simply click anywhere on the preview, or use the **Zoom** button.

3. Click on the **Setup** button to make adjustments such as the orientation, portrait or landscape, the choice of printer and the width of the margins. Click on **OK** when the required adjustments have been made.

Printing

When satisfied that the preview is correct, printing may be done from either the preview screen or the form screen. To print from the preview screen

1. Click on **Print** button in print preview bar – or on the Access 2 toolbar.
2. Select whether all or certain pages of the form will be printed and the number of copies. Click on **OK.**

To print from the form screen

1. Choose *File-Print* or click on Print button and follow step 2 above.

exercise 4 *printing the membership category form*

To print this form

❏ Open the **Membership Category** form.

❏ Click on the **Print Preview** button.

❏ Experiment with 'zooming-in' and 'zooming-out'.

❏ When ready to print click on the **Print** button and click on **OK** in the **Print** dialog box.

activity 7 customising a form

Forms are constructed from a collection of individual design elements which are called *controls*. If you are familiar with windows applications you will be familiar with dialog boxes and the controls that they contain. The controls that appear on the forms created so far are:

❏ labels, so that you know what each part of the form is for,

❏ text boxes, for entering data,

❏ check boxes, for yes/no type data

There are other controls which will be introduced in Session 5.

A form may be modified so that so that it is easier for inexperienced users to enter information into the database. To modify a form you need to display the form in design mode (see following section). **FormWizards** is a good way of quickly creating a form. However, the resulting form is rather standardised in terms of vertical spacing between controls, fonts, colours and the length of text that can be entered for the title of the form, so you are likely to wish to make modifications.

Components of a form in design view

Form Header	Contains text such as the form's title, but field headers and graphics may be put into a header section.
Detail	Contains the controls (field labels, text boxes and check boxes) that display data from your table for which the form has been designed.
Form Footer	Similar in function to the Form Header and may contain information such the date.

Right Margin The position of the right margin is indicated by a vertical line on the right edge of the form. This right margin can be moved by clicking and dragging it.

Bottom Margin A horizontal line that indicates the bottom margin of the form. This also can be positioned by clicking and dragging.

Scroll Bars Vertical and horizontal scroll bars enable movement of the form within its window.

If you have used a Form Wizard to create the form, only the header band and the detail band contain controls. The header band contains information which will always appear at the top of the form, usually the title of the form. The detail band contains the controls for displaying the data.

Form design view

So far in this session a form has only been opened in 'form run' or data view. This is the mode in which forms are usually run where they display and more importantly accept data. A form can also be shown in design view that allows modifications to be made to its layout. In design view data cannot be entered into the form, only the layout and appearance of the form can be changed. A form has a different appearance in design view as illustrated in Figure 3.3.

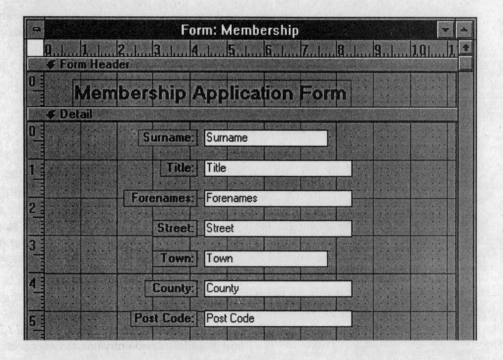

Figure 3.3 Part of the Membership form shown in Design mode

Instead of data appearing in the controls, the field names appear. Text or controls may be selected and moved to achieve the layout desired.

Label and text box controls

A field usually has two controls, a label control in which the field name appears and a text box control in which the data will appear when the form is run.

Extra windows

Other features of design mode are the availability of rulers and grid and design aids in the form of other small windows, the Toolbox, Field List, Properties Sheet and Palette.

The Toolbox offers a selection of tools by which controls and text may be added to the form. The Field List shows a list of fields in the table that the form was based upon and the Properties sheet is a list of properties. The list of properties will depend upon what part of the form is selected. The Palette allows colour selection to be made. You will become familiar with these as you progress through the exercises. To display the Toolbox use *View–Toolbox.* To display the **Field List** click on the **Field list** button or choose *View–Field List.* To display the **Properties** sheet click on the **Properties** button on the toolbar or choose *View–Properties.* To display the **Palette** click on the Palette button on the toolbar or choose *View–Palette.*

The buttons are (from left to right) the **Properties** button, the **Field List** button and the **Palette** button.

To open a form in design view, from the database window, click on the **Form** button, select the name of the form required and click on the **Design** button.

Once a form is open you may switch between the form run (data) view and the design view by clicking on the buttons on the toolbar.

Run form   Design form

Moving and sizing controls

Before you can move or size a control you must select it first. A control is selected by clicking anywhere on its surface. When selected the control is enclosed by an outlining rectangle with an anchor rectangle at its upper left corner and five smaller rectangles. These smaller rectangles are sizing handles. On single column forms text boxes often have associated labels and when you select one of these objects they are both selected together as a unit.

To	Do this
Select a text box control and its label (if it has a label)	Click anywhere on either the label or the text box
Move a text box control and its label (if it has a label)	After selecting, move the pointer over label until it changes shape to a hand. Click and drag label and entry box to new position.
Move label or text box control separately	After selecting, move the pointer over the anchor handle at the top left corner of either the label or text box control. The pointer should change shape to a pointing hand. Click and drag to new position.

Adjust the width and height of a selected control simultaneously	Move the pointer over one of the small sizing handles at one of the three corners. It should change to a diagonal two-headed arrow. Click and drag to size required.
Adjust only the height of the selected control	Move the pointer over one of the sizing handles on the horizontal surface of the outline. It should change shape to a vertical two-headed arrow. Click and drag to height required.

Selecting and moving a group of controls

You can select and move more than one object at a time. This is useful if you want to keep the relative spacing of a group of objects yet want to move them to another part of the form.

To select a group of objects, either:

❐ Imagine that the group of objects is enclosed by a rectangle. Use the pointer and by clicking and dragging draw this rectangle on the form. When you release the mouse button all the objects within this rectangle will be selected, or

❐ Select one object, hold down the Shift key whilst selecting the next and subsequent objects.

To move

❐ the whole group, with pointer as the shape of hand then drag.

❐ an individual control in the group, point to its anchor handle and drag.

To deselect

❐ one object in the group, click on it while holding down the Shift key.

❐ the whole group, click anywhere outside the selected area.

To move the group of objects click and drag the anchor handle of any of the objects in the group.

Using the ruler and the grid

The *View–Ruler* command will select whether or not the ruler is displayed. When a control is being dragged, indicator lines slide along both rulers to aid positioning of controls.

View–Grid will display or hide a grid of small dots which are also an aid to the positioning of controls. The spacing of the grid can be adjusted by adjusting the setting of the **GridX** and **GridY** properties on the form's property sheet. To display the form property sheet use *Edit–Select Form* and click on the properties button.

If a control is selected and *Layout–Size to Grid* is used (Access 1 only), then all sides of the control will be moved either in or out to meet the nearest points on the grid. Note that this works even if the grid is not displayed.

When *Layout–Snap to Grid* (Access 1), *Format - Snap to Grid* (Access 2) is on which is indicated by a tick by **Snap to Grid** in the menu, any new controls drawn on the form will have their corners aligned to points on the grid. When Snap to Grid is off the control can be placed anywhere.

Aligning a group of controls

Once you start to move controls around the form they can become untidy as they become mis-aligned. By selecting a group of controls together then they can be aligned. Select labels and text boxes separately for alignment purposes. To align labels:

1. Select the labels by drawing a rectangle which encloses part or all of all the labels you wish to select as illustrated. Alternatively click each label while holding down the Shift key.

2. Choose *Layout–Align* or *Format-Align* and as these are labels select **Right**. The selected group of controls should all align to the right.

To align text box controls:

1. Select the text box controls by drawing a rectangle which encloses part or all of all the text boxes you wish to select or click each text box while holding down the Shift key.

2. Choose *Layout–Align* or *Format-Align* and as these are text boxes select **Left**. The selected group of controls should all align to the left.

Changing the form's area

The area of each section of a form, the header, detail and footer sections may be altered individually. Also the position of the right and bottom edge of a form may be adjusted. To alter the depth of a section of the form:

1. Move the pointer to the bottom edge of the section where it will change shape.

2. Drag down to increase the depth of the section.

To alter the area of the form drag the right and bottom edges to the size that you require.

exercise 5 customising the membership form

Open the **Membership** form in design view. The aim of this exercise is to create the form shown in Figure 3.1. Exact instructions are not given as you can experiment with selecting and moving controls. You may find it useful to widen the form temporarily so that controls can be moved to temporary positions while you rearrange them on the form. If you wish to keep a group of controls together, select them as a group and then they can be moved as a group. Also try aligning groups of controls to achieve a tidy looking form.

If you inadvertently delete a field from the form see the following table for instructions on how to restore it. When you have rearranged the detail section save the form design using ***File–Save.***

Deleting or restoring fields from or to a form

To	Do this
Delete a label or label and text box	Select the control and press Delete or use ***Edit–Delete*** to delete both label and entry box. To delete only the label click on it again before deleting.
	Note: if you delete a field you won't be able to use the form to enter data into this field. Use ***Edit–Undo*** if you unintentionally delete a field.
Restore a label and field	Use ***View–Field list*** to display the list of fields available in the table. Click on the field name required and drag to required position on the form. If the form is a single column form then both label and field will appear, although the label will require editing. If the form is a tabular one then just the field will be restored.

Changing the text of a field name label

The text of a field name label may be edited and if required additional text can be added to the form.

To	Do this
Add a label	Click on the **Label** tool in the Toolbox window (see Figure 5.1) and click on the form in the required position and type the text required.
Edit a label	Double–click on the label to display an insertion point in the text. Edit the text as required. Press Enter or click on a blank part of the form when finished.

Altering the size, font and alignment of controls

To alter the size, font or alignment of controls in a form:

1. Select the control(s) to be altered.

2. Open the **Font** list box in the toolbar and select the font required.

3. Open the **Point Size** list box and select the point size required.

4. Click on left, centre or right alignment button in toolbar.

Note: If you increase the size of a font you may need to alter the size of the control and the size of the section.

exercise 6 *adding text to a form*

In this exercise additional text is added to the header section of the **Membership** form.

❏ Open the **Membership** form in design mode.

❏ Widen the header section, by dragging its lower edge downwards.

❏ Click on the **Label** tool in the Toolbox window. Select centre alignment.

❏ Click under the main heading of the form and key in the text **Membership Application Form**

❏ Move and size the heading as in Figure 3.1. If you wish you may alter the font of this text. Save the form.

exercise 7 *using the customised form to enter data*

To gain a full appreciation of the modifications made to the **Membership** form then it should be used to enter data.

❏ Open the form from the Database Window by clicking on the **Open** button.

❏ Move through the records and display a blank form.

❏ Compose data for a new member and using the form enter data into the next record.

❏ Close the form.

Reorganising the field order

When data is entered into each field, Enter or Tab takes you to the next field. The order in which the fields are entered is defined by the order in which they were selected in the **FormWizards.** Once the form has been modified then this order may need to be changed. To change the Tab order of the fields

1. Choose *Edit–Tab Order* in Design view to display the **Tab Order** dialog box. This dialog box displays the order of the fields in the **Custom Order** box. In the **Section** box normally the Detail section is selected.

2. To alter the order of the fields select the field or fields to be moved and drag to the new position to achieve the new order.

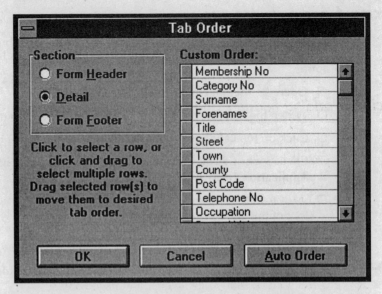

3.   When the new order has been selected click on **OK**.

The **Auto Order** button will set the Tab order according to the way in which the fields are set out on the form and they are ordered with the priority of left to right and then top to bottom.

Adding headers and footers

It is straightforward to add text into the header and footer sections of a form. Headers and footers are always displayed on the screen. Calculated text may be added to the header or the footer, for example the date can be shown.

If a form is to be printed the header section prints before the first record and the footer section prints after the last record. Extra sections, page header and page footer can be added which will print on each page of the printout. You can control whether to display or print these sections. Calculated text may be added to show the page numbers. Page breaks may occur in the middle of records, if the record is in single column format. This can be avoided by adjusting the **Keep together** setting of the **Detail** properties from **No** to **Yes**. To display the Properties sheet check that the **Properties** button is depressed and click on the detail bar.

exercise 8 adding the date

The aim of this exercise is to put the date in the **Membership Category** form footer.

❒   Open the **Membership Category** form in design view.

❒   Click on the Text box tool in the Toolbox.

❒   Position the pointer in the footer section at a point where the top left corner of the calculated text box should appear and click.

❏ Key the formula **=Date()** into the text box and press Enter.

❏ Switch to run mode by clicking on the **Form View** button to see the result. Close the form. Save the change.

exercise 9 *adding headers and footers to a printed form*

When a form is printed the header is printed at the beginning and the footer is printed at the end of the records. To add a header and footer that print at the top of each page of the **Membership** form when printed:

❏ Open the **Membership** form.

❏ Click on the **Print Preview** button.

❏ Cancel the preview and display the form in design view.

❏ Choose *Layout–Page Hdr/Ftr* or *Format–Page Header/Footer.* Two extra sections appear, Page Header and Page Footer.

❏ Select all the title in the Form Header and use *Edit–Copy.*

❏ Click on the Page Header bar and use *Edit–Paste.* Position the pasted copy.

❏ Click on the text box tool. Point in the Page footer section and click.

❏ Key the text **="Page"&Page** into the box. When you add text to a single column form the text box has an associated label. This is not needed so it can be deleted by clicking on it and pressing the Delete key.

❏ Click on Form Header bar.

Section	
Force New Page .	None
New Row Or Col .	None
Keep Together . .	No
Visible	Yes
Display When . . .	Screen Only
Can Grow	No
Can Shrink	No
Height	1.31 cm
Special Effect . . .	Color
Back Color	12632256

❏ In the Section properties box click in the **Display When** box. If the Section properties box is not displayed click on the **Properties** button on the toolbar.

❏ Open the list and select **Screen Only.**

❏ Click on the Detail bar and change the **Keep Together** property to **Yes** to prevent page breaks in the middle of records.

❏ Preview and print the form.

activity 8 Creating a blank form

If the single column or tabular layout is not suitable for the intended form, then it may be easier to start with a blank form and create a custom design.

Choosing the type of form

If a form is created using the FormWizards you are given the choice of the type of form. If a blank form is chosen then only a blank detail section is displayed. To choose the type of form

1. Display the Properties window by choosing **View–Properties** or clicking on the properties button in the toolbar.

2. Choose **Edit–Select Form** to display the Form Properties sheet.

3. Look for the **Default View** property. This is set at **Continuous forms** (Tabular form) to change to Single Column form open this box and select **Single form.**

Adding header/footer sections

1. Choose **Layout–Form Hdr/Ftr** or **Format–Form Header/Footer** to add the header/footer sections to the form. If you intend to print the form then page header/footer sections may also be added.

Adding a label to the form

A label is the simplest control that you can add to your form. Labels are unbound (see Activity 1, Session 5), they only display the text which you give to them. Labels may be added anywhere in the form, for example, as a title in the header section. To add a label to a form:

1. Click on the **Label** button in the toolbox. Position the pointer in the form at the point where the label should go. The pointer becomes a symbol with two parts, one the label symbol and two, the cross hair symbol used for box drawing.

2. Either click to put a small label box on the workspace which will expand as you add text, or by dragging draw a box of the desired size. If you drag below the bottom or to the right of the particular section, this part of the form will expand to accommodate the size of label you require.

3. The label is outlined and inside it a flashing insertion point appears, ready for you to enter text. If you don't enter any text and click the mouse button the label will disappear.

4. The size and font may be adjusted by selecting the label and formatting using the appropriate list boxes in the toolbar. Choose alignment using the appropriate button on the toolbar.

Adding a text box

A text box is the most common type of control that is found on forms. The fields to which text boxes can be bound will be found in the field list which is compiled from the source table or query. To add a text box:

1. To display the field list window, click on the **Field List** button on the toolbar or choose **View–Field list.** Choose **View–Grid** to put a series of dots on the form to help with positioning the controls. Note this grid is not visible when then form is run.

2. Click on the required field in the list and holding down the mouse button, drag to the detail workspace. Whilst pointing in the workspace the pointer becomes a field symbol. The position of the field symbol indicates the upper left hand corner of the text box *not* the label so position the top left corner to allow room for the label.

3. Click to place the label and field boxes. Position them by using the hand symbol to drag or by dragging the anchor handle and size by using one of the sizing handles.

4. If desired select the size and font of text in the control.

5. More than one field may be selected from the field list and they can be placed as a group. To select a contiguous selection click on the first field and hold down the Shift key while clicking on the last field in the group. To select a non-contiguous selection hold down the Ctrl key while making the selection.

6. The order in which the fields are selected determines the 'tab order' i.e. the order in which they will be filled in on the form. If this needs amending then from the form design screen choose **Edit–Tab order.** In the dialog box use a drag and drop method to re-arrange the fields.

Adding a multi–line text box

Multi–line text boxes are usually used to display memo fields. They are larger than the single line boxes. They also have a vertical scroll bar so that when there is too much text to be fitted into the text box then the scroll bar can be used to move through the text.

1. From the field list select a memo field. Drag the field list pointer to the lower middle part of the detail section and drop.

2. Adjust the size of the text box and position the label.

3. Scroll through the Text Box **Properties** window until you see the **Scroll Bars** property box appear. Click in this box and open its list and choose Vertical. This will add a vertical scroll bar to your text box. Note that the scroll bar will only appear when the form is run and you click in the text box, indicating to Access that you are using this control.

4. You may wish to print the form so to make sure that the whole memo field is printed, in the properties window change both the **Can Grow** and the **Can Shrink** properties to **Yes.** This will not affect the text box while it is being displayed on the screen.

exercise 10 *creating a blank form*

Although the **FormWizards** has been used to create forms for all the tables, this exercise will explore using a blank form which will duplicate one of the forms already created. The table that is to used is the **Membership** table.

❐ Click on the **Form** button in the Database Window, then click on the **New** button. Select the **Membership** table.

❐ Click on the **Blank Form** button. Access creates a new form, showing the detail section.

❐ In the Form Properties box change the **Default view** property to **Single form.**

❐ Add a header and footer section by choosing *Layout–Form Hdr/Ftr* or *Format–Form Header/ Footer.*

❐ You should see a grid of dots on the form's workspace, if not then select *View–Grid* to display it.

❐ Adjust the depth of the detail section by pointing to the top line of the Form Footer bar. The pointer should change shape to a horizontal bar with double headed arrow. Click and drag downward to expand the detail section area.

❐ Add all the fields, referring back to the previous 3 sections, considering the order in which you select them, to the form from the field list. Try selecting and placing a group of fields.

❐ Add a title to the form and save the form as **Membership2.** Remember that there is a distinction between the title of the form and the name it is saved under.

❐ Run the form and use it to add another record to the **Membership** table.

❐ If the order of field entry does not match the form design, for instance if the fields were not selected in the right order, then the order can be changed by returning to design view and choosing *Edit–Tab Order.* Save the changes.

integrative exercises

exercise 11 *designing and using forms*

There are two other tables which require forms to be designed, these are the **Classes** table and the **Bookings** table. Use the FormWizards to create single column forms for both these tables, saving them as **Classes** and **Bookings** respectively.

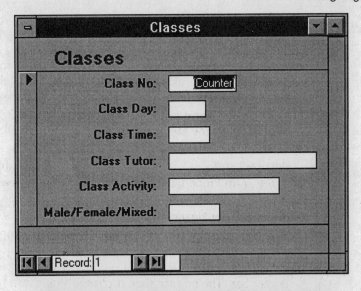

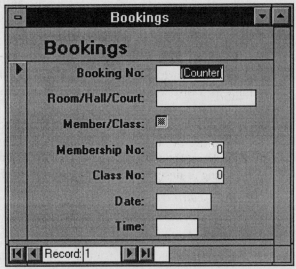

Use the forms to enter the data for these tables, shown in Appendix 2. Remind yourself of the validation rules set in Session 1 and try testing them validation while entering the data. Close the forms when the data has been entered.

exercise 12 *adding a new table and creating a form*

This exercise recaps on some of the activities met during these first three sessions. The aim of this activity is to create a new table and link it to the Chelmer database and create a form to input data into this table. The table to be created is the **Tutor** table.

The **Tutor** table could comprise of the following fields; **Surname, Initials, Title, Street, Town, County, Post Code, Telephone No, National Insurance No, Date of Birth** and **Qualifications.** Create this **Tutor** table, make all fields text and choose suitable lengths for each, except for Date of Birth and Qualifications. Use a short date for **Date of Birth** and a memo for **Qualifications.** Save the table as **Tutor.** Create a link between this table and the Classes table using ***Edit–Relationships.***

Access 1

Primary Table	Type	Related Table
Tutors	Many	Classes
Primary key fields	·	**Select matching fields**
Surname	=	Class Tutor

Access 2

Use ***Relationships–Add Table*** to add the **Tutors** table. Drag the field **Surname** from the **Tutors** table (the one side of the relationship) to the **Class Tutor** found in the **Classes** table (the many side of the relationship).

Consider the pros and cons of checking the **Enforce Referential Intergrity** check box.

To design a form for this table

❐ Click on the **Form** button in the Database Window, then click on the **New** button.

❐ Click on the **Blank Form** button. Access creates a new form, showing the detail section.

❐ In the Form Properties box change the **Default view** property to **Single form.**

❐ Add a header and footer section by choosing ***Layout–Form Hdr/Ftr*** or ***Format–Form Header/Footer.***

❐ You should see a grid of dots on the form's workspace, if not then select ***View–Grid*** to display it.

❐ Adjust the depth of the detail section by pointing to the top line of the Form Footer bar. The pointer should change shape to a horizontal bar with double headed arrow. Click and drag downward to expand the detail section area.

❐ Add all the fields to the form from the field list.

❐ Add a title to the form and save the form as **Tutor.**

❐ Select the text box for qualifications so that its properties sheet is displayed. Set the following properties for this text box; **Scroll bars – Vertical, Can Shrink – Yes, Can Grow – Yes.**

❐ Save the form and run it. Use it to enter the following tutor record: Evans, P J, Mrs, 25 Lyme Green, Chelmer, Cheshire, CH2 1ED, 0777 560935, XZ 32 99 06B, 17/7/70, Y.M. C. A. Dance to Music, Certificate in Aerobics, First Aid (Red Cross).

exercise 13 *adding text to a form*

Add some text to the **Membership** form next to the **Sex** check box to indicate that X indicates male and blank indicates female.

session four
designing a printed report

objectives

This session explores the basic design of printed reports which include data from an Access table. It explains how to quickly create a report using Report Wizards, and then explores some aspects of customising reports. Sessions 5 and 6 develop some of the themes in this session more fully. At the end of this session you will be able to:

❑ create a report using Report Wizards

❑ use a report to print data from an Access table

❑ save and print a report

❑ perform simple customising of a report

Reports are used to print information from a number of records. Reports can show the data from either a table or a query. In addition to records, they may show summary information relating to the records displayed. Graphs created using Microsoft Graph may be added to reports.

Reports, then, are intended to allow you to select the data to be printed and then to present that data in an acceptable format. To emphasis the distinction between reports and forms: reports are intended to be printed, screen forms are normally displayed on screen, although the facilities often also exist for printing them.

In most applications you will create a number of different standard reports. For example, a mailing list of clients may simply show customer name and address, but a list showing outstanding orders to specific clients will also show details of the items customers have ordered, their value and other associated information.

Access allows you to create reports either to your own design using its wide range of tools for customising reports, or to start by using Report Wizards which provide you quickly and easily with a basic report, which you can later format and customise. We use Report Wizards here because they allow you to understand the basic concept of what a report is and how it works, before you grapple with customising specific features of the report.

Since forms and reports share many design and creation features, you will re-use some of the skills that you acquired in Session 3 in designing a form to help you to design a report.

activity 1 creating a report with Report Wizards

There are three types of reports that can be created with Report Wizards: Single column, Groups/totals, and Mailing label. This session describes the creation of all of these, but first we deal with the Single column report which is used most frequently and is relatively simple to create.

1. To enter Report wizards starting from the Database Window, either:

    ❐   Click on **New** at the top of the Database Window when you are displaying reports; or

    ❐   Choose *File–New* and then Report; or

    ❐   Click the **New Report** button on the toolbar.

A **New Report** dialog box appears.

2. Click on the down arrow button of the **Select A Table/Query** list box, to produce a list of tables and queries and select the table for which you wish to create a report.

3. Click on the **Report Wizards** button to create a report using Report Wizards

Once you have selected the ReportWizards button, choose which Report Wizard report you wish to create as discussed below. Each Report Wizard asks a different set of questions.

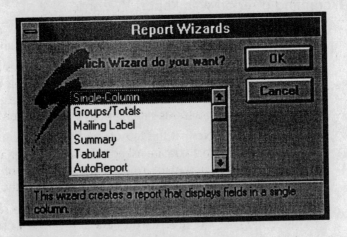

activity 2 single column Report Wizard reports

A single column report places all of the selected fields in a single column, with their field names to the left as shown in Figure 4.1

To create a Single column report:

❐ Perform the three steps as above, selecting the Single column report, and click on **OK**.

❐ The next stage is to choose which fields are to be in the report. The fields that you can have in the report are shown in the **Available fields** box.

❐ These can be transferred to the report by selecting each fields in turn and clicking on the [>] button.

❐ If you wish to add all the fields in the table to the report then click on the [>>] button.

❐ You may set the order in which the fields appear on the report by selecting them in the order that you desire. The [<] button will remove a high-lighted field from a report and [<<] will remove all the fields from the report.

❐ Once you have added the required fields to the report continue by clicking on the **Next>** button.

❐ The next dialog box asks you to select the order in which records will be sorted. Select the fields you want the records to be sorted by. If you have only a small set of records just one sort field will be adequate. If you want records to appear in the same order as in the table or query it is not necessary to indicate a sort field. Choose the **Next>** button.

❐ You are then asked what kind of look you want for your form. You are given a choice of:

- Executive Style,
- Presentation Style and
- Ledger Style.

❐ The look decides the appearance of the field names and field contents in the report. An example of the look is shown in the top left dialog box. Click on each look in turn to see what it would look like. On the first occasion a report is created choose Executive. The look can be modified later. Click on the **Next** button.

❐ The next thing that you are asked for is a title. Enter a report title. Report titles are particularly important in flagging the purpose of the report to the reader, so choose something that conveys the contents of the report.

❐ Choose **Print Preview** to display the report on the screen (Access 1) or with the option **see the report with data in it** selected click on **Finish** (Access 2). Note that Access has added a page number at the bottom of every page and the date at the top of the report.

activity 3 saving and closing a report

Save a report by choosing *File–Save.* If this is a new report that does not have a name, Access will prompt for a file name with a *File–Save As* dialog box. If you later want to save a report under another name use **File–Save As,** and enter the new name in the dialog box.

Note: Remember that there is a distinction between the name and the title of a report. The title is the text that is displayed at the top of the report when it is printed. The name you give when saving the form is the form's file name which you need to be able to recognise when you want to open the from for use again. These names appear in the Database Window when the **Report** button is depressed

exercise 1 creating a single column report using Report Wizards

We wish to create a Single column report which lists the records for all of the members that have records in the database, showing the following fields:

> **Membership No**
> **Category No**
> **Forenames**
> **Surname**
> **Occupation**
> **Date of Birth**

and **Sporting Interests.**

We wish to create a report which looks like the extract shown in Figure 4.1.

Chelmer Leisure and Recreation Centre Members

08-May-94

Membership No:	1
Category No:	2
Forenames:	Andrew J
Surname:	Walker
Occupation:	Builder
Date of Birth:	12/3/52
Sporting Interests:	Tennis, squash
Membership No:	2
Category No:	1
Forenames:	Denise
Surname:	Cartwright

Figure 4.1: The beginning of a single column report

☐ To enter **ReportWizards** starting from the Database Window, either:

☐ Click on **New** at the top of the Database Window when you are displaying reports; or

☐ Choose *File–New* and then **Report;**
   or

☐ Click the **New Report** button on the toolbar.

☐ A **New Report** dialog box appears.

☐ Click on the down arrow button of the **Select A Table/Query** list box, to produce a list of tables and queries and select the **Membership** table.

☐ Click on the **Report Wizards** button to create a report using **ReportWizards**

☐ Choose to create a **Single column** report.

☐ Select the fields to appear in the report by clicking on the field names above in the **Available Fields** list box, and then clicking on the ▶ button. The selected fields should appear in the **Field Order on Report** list box.

☐ If any fields are included by mistake, use ◀ to remove them. Choose **Next>**.

☐ Choose to sort by **Membership No** by clicking on the ▶ button so that **Membership No** appears in the **Sort Order** box. Choose **Next>**.

☐ Choose Executive Style for the Look of the report. Choose **Next>**.

☐ Enter the following report title: **Chelmer Leisure and Recreation Centre Members**

☐ Click on **Print Preview** to display the report on the screen.

☐ Choose *File–Save* to save the report with the name **Members.**

activity 4 using a report

To use a report, first display the available report names in the Database Window, then double click on the report name and the Print Preview window will appear showing a preview of how the report will appear when printed. To zoom in and out and to view a complete page on the screen, click on the report.

Note that a report picks up the table properties of the table or query the report uses when it was designed. Later, you change the properties of the table or query without changing the properties of the report.

activity 5 printing a report

Before printing any report always view the report in Print Preview first.

Previewing

To preview a report:

1. Click the **Preview** button on the toolbar, and a miniature version of what is to be printed will be displayed.

2. To zoom-in and zoom-out simply click anywhere on the preview, or use the **Zoom** button.

3. Click on the **Setup** button to make adjustments such as the orientation, portrait or landscape, the choice of printer and the width of the margins. Some of the options in the **Print Setup** dialog box will be familiar since you will have used them in printing tables and queries, but there are also special options for use when printing report, such as the number of items (records) across the page, item size, and item layout. Use the **Select More** button to expand the dialog box to display all options. Click on **OK** when the required adjustments have been made.

Printing

When satisfied that the preview is correct, printing may be done from either the preview screen or the design screen. To print from the preview screen:

1. Click on the **Print** button in the print preview bar or in Access 2 toolbar.

2. Select whether all or certain pages of the report will be printed and the number of copies. Click on **OK**.

Alternatively, to print from the design screen:

Choose *File–Print* and then follow step 2 above.

exercise 2 *using and printing a report*

To use the report **Members,** first select it from the report names displayed in the Database Window, by double clicking on its name. The Print Preview window will appear showing a preview of how the report will appear when printed.

Now print the report:

☐ Select the **Print** button, followed by **OK.**

☐ This displays the **Print** dialog box. Select **OK.**

Now experiment with different Setup options, for example:

☐ With the Print dialog box displayed click on the **Setup** button. Click on **More>>** in the **Print Setup** dialog box, to display the full range of options.

☐ Experiment with:

- Two items across the page by entering 2 in the Items Across box. You may need to adjust the Width in the Item Size section to less than half your page width.

- With 2 items across the page explore the effect of Horizontal and Vertical in the Item Layout section.

- Try making item Height larger.

☐ Close the **Print Setup** dialog box between each trial in order to view the new layout in Print Preview.

activity 6 *creating groups/totals Report Wizard reports*

Note: You may choose to omit this activity for the moment and return to it later when you are ready to design this kind of report.

A Groups/Totals report puts the fields you select into a row and groups the records according to the value of a fields in the table or query. This approach can also be used simply to create a report in a table form with fields shown in columns, if you do not specify groups. The advantage of this type of report is that it displays more records to the page. However, it does not display records with several long fields which therefore can not be accommodated next to each other on the page in parallel columns.

Records can be grouped by up to three different fields although we shall use only one field for grouping.

Apart from the need to define how records will be displayed in groups, the process of creating a Groups/Totals Report is similar to that for a Single column report. The process is basically:

1. Select the fields to appear in the report.

2. Select how the records in the table or query will be grouped for the report. Groups are divisions within a report that include all records that have a value for a specific field.

3. Select the order in which you want the groups created (if you are using more than one group), and choose **Next.**

4. Decide, for the selected fields, how the field values will be divided into groups. The best option will depend upon the fields data type. On a first run through use the default 'Normal'. Normal means that whenever the value for that group field changes, the report starts another group.

5. Select how the records are to be sorted for the report.

6. Select a Look for the report.

7. Add the report's title. Note titles are restricted to 50 characters long.

8. Select **Print Preview** to display the report on screen in the Print Preview window (Access 1) or with **see the report with data in it** selected, click on **Finish** (Access 2).

9. Save the report.

10. Print the report, as appropriate, and subsequently, close the report.

exercise 3 *creating a groups/totals Report Wizard report*

We wish to create a Group/Totals report which lists all the members for which there are records in the database, showing the following fields:

Category No

Surname

Forenames

Telephone No

The records are to be grouped according to **Category No,** so that, for instance, all records with a given **Category No** are grouped together. We wish to create a report which looks like the report shown in Figure 4.2.

Chelmer Members by Membership Category
08-May-94

Category No	Surname	Forenames	Telephone No
1			
	Barrett	Martha A	0777 557822
	Cartwright	Denise	0777 552099
	Davies	Sandra M	0778 891441
	Jameson	Donna	
	Jones	Edward R	0777 567333
	Robinson	Rebecca	0777 568812
	Weiner	George W F	
2			
	Everett	Alan	
	Forsythe	Ann M	0777 569945

Figure 4.2: An Extract from a Group/Totals Report created using ReportWizards

- ❏ Enter Report Wizards by clicking the **New Report** button on the toolbar.
- ❏ From the Select a Table/Query drop down list box select the **Membership** table.
- ❏ Click on the **ReportWizards** button to create a report in Report Wizards.
- ❏ Choose to create a Groups/Totals report.

Create the report thus:

- ❏ Select the fields to appear in the report by clicking on the fields names as indicated above, in the **Available Fields** list box, and then clicking on the ⊳ button. The selected fields should appear in the **Field Order on Report** List box.

- ❏ If any fields are included by mistake use ⊲ to remove them.
- ❏ Group the records by **Category No.** Click on **Next.**
- ❏ Select 'Normal' for grouping data with the same value. Choose **Next.**
- ❏ Sort records within groups alphabetically by the **Surname** field. Choose **Next.**
- ❏ Select Presentation Style for the Look of the report. Choose **Next.**
- ❏ Enter the following report title: Members by Membership Category.
- ❏ Click on **Print Preview** or **Finish** button to display the report on screen.
- ❏ Save the report: choose *File–Save* to save the report the name **Categories.**
- ❏ To print the report: select the **Print** button. This shows the **Print** dialog box. Select **OK.**

activity 7 mailing label Report Wizard reports

A mailing label report fits the fields you select into a rectangle that is designed to print labels. Unlike other Report wizard reports this type does not show field names. It does, however, make it easy to add text such as commas and spaces.

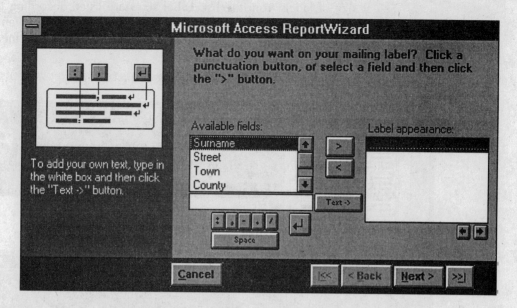

To create a mailing label report:

1. Select fields as with other report types, but remembering that more than one field can be added to a line.

2. Add text, fields and punctuation to a line and then advance to a new line by clicking on the ⏎ button (Access 1) or Newline (Access 2).

3. Add any text by entering it in the text box below the field names box and then clicking on the **Text** button.

4. Add punctuation by clicking on the colon, comma, hyphen, period, slash or space buttons.

5. Select how the records are to be sorted, or in other words the order in which mailing labels are to be printed.

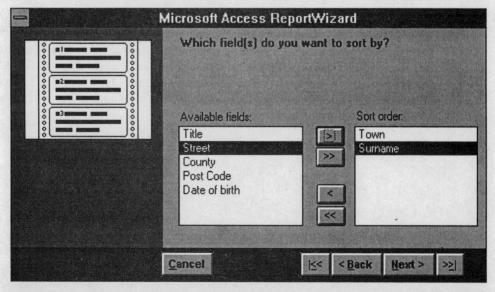

6. Select size of labels from the list. **Label sizes** are listed according to the Avery number. If you do not know the Avery label number for a given label size, look at the Dimensions and Number Across columns to find the label size that matches your labels.

7. In Access 2 select the size, font and weight of the label text.

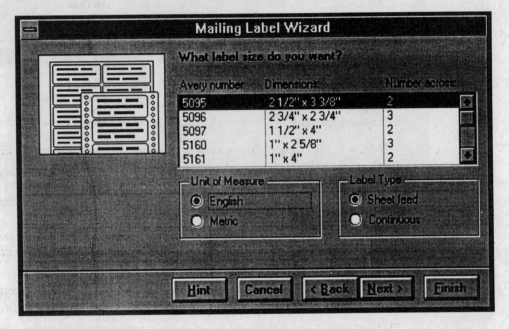

8. Use Print Preview (Access 1) or with **see the mailing labels as they will look printed** selected click on **Finish** to display labels on screen.

9. Save the report.

10. Print and close the report as appropriate.

exercise 4 *creating a mailing label report wizard report based on a query*

We wish to create a mailing label report which lists all members who joined in the last year, i.e. since 1/4/93. An extract from such a report is shown in Figure 4.3. First we need to define and execute a query to select the appropriate records, and then we need to define the mailing label report that is to be used to display this set of records.

Mr Ali	Mrs Barrett
35 Meirton Road	7 Oldcott Way
Chelmer	Meirton
Cheshire, CH4 5KD	Cheshire, CH9 3DR
Mr Everett	Mr Gray
12 Stanley Street	4 The Parade
Chelmer	Chelmer
Cheshire, CH3 3CJ	Cheshire, CH1 7ER
Mr Harris	Mr Perry
55 Coven Road	59 Church Street
Chelmer	Chelmer
Cheshire, CH3 8PS	Cheshire, CH1 8YU

Figure 4.3 An Extract from a mailing label report created using Report Wizards

Query design and execution were introduced in Session 2, and you may wish to review Session 2 at this point.

To define the query:

❑ Starting from the Chelmer Database window, click on the **Query** button, and click on the **New** button to create a new query. In Access 2 select the **New Query** button.

❑ The **Add Table** dialog box appears. Select the table **Membership** and click on the **Add** button and then click on the **Close** button.

❑ Next choose to include all fields in the query by double clicking on the title bar of the field list box of the table in the upper section of the window. Click anywhere in the selected area and drag to the field row to transfer all of the fields to the lower section.

❑ In the **Date of Joining** criteria cell enter the query criteria >1/4/93.

❑ To view the result of this query click on the Datasheet icon on the toolbar.

❑ Save the query by choosing *File–Save Query.*

❑ In the **Query Name** box of the **Save As** dialog box, enter the Query Name: **New Members.**

❑ Close the query.

Now that you have defined a query, you need to design a report to display the records retrieved by the query.

❑ Click on the **Report** button in the Database Window and click on **New.**

❑ From the **Select A Table/Query** drop down list box select the Query **New Members**.

❑ Click on the **Report Wizards** button to create a report using Report wizards.

❑ Choose to create a Mailing Label report

Create the report thus:

❑ Select the fields to be included. These are, in the order that follows:

Title
Surname
Street
Town
County
Post Code.

❐ Add the field **Title** followed by a space and then the field **Surname** to the first line. Click on the **Enter** or **Newline** button to move onto the next line.

❐ Add **Street** to the next line.

❐ Add the remainder of the fields, each to a separate line, with the exception of **County** and **Post Code** which should be on the same line separated by a comma and a space. Click on **Next.**

❐ Choose to order the records in alphabetical order according to **Surname.**

❐ Select the size of the labels. You may need to experiment with different label sizes. Try Avery number 5095 first. Click on next.

❐ In Access 2 leave the font as default and click on Next.

❐ Use Print Preview or Finish to display the report on the screen.

❐ Save the report: choose *File–Save As* to save the report with the name **Mailing.**

❐ To print the report select the **Print** button. This displays the **Print** dialog box. Select **OK.**

activity 8 customising a report

Although Report Wizard produces a useful basic report, eventually you may wish to design or create your own design from scratch, so that you can exercise greater control over the report design. If you examine the Report Wizard reports that you have created recently you will note that they have the following limitations: the title length is restricted; the spacing is fixed horizontal spacing that makes it difficult to distinguish between records; and, the fixed format gives the same standard appearance time and time again.

This activity explores some of the simple tools for customising a report. These may be applied either to a report created initially with Report Wizards, or to create your own report independently. Before attempting to create or modify a report it is useful to identify the components of a report. These are listed and described below. If you examine the reports that you have just created using Report Wizards, you should recognise that they have these components

Components of a report

Page header	Contains headings that will appear at the top of each page, such as a running title and page numbers.
Report header	Contains any headings or other introductory text that might appear at the beginning of the report.

Detail	Shows data from the records in the database. Sets up the format for records in general which is then used for every record to be included in the report
Report footer	Contains information at the end of the report, such as a final summary or a statement such as; 'this is the end of the report'.
Page footer	Appears at the bottom of the page.
Group header	Marks the beginning of a group, usually introduces the group that the report will display.
Group footer	Marks the end of a group and often contains sections that summarise the records that are part of a group.

Working with report design allows you to adjust the contents, size and position of everything that appears on the report. As with forms, each small piece of a report is called a control. Controls include a fields data, text, picture and calculations. Again, many of the features relating to forms that you experimented with in Activity 7 of Session 3 also apply to reports.

exercise 5 examining the components of a report

Examine one of the reports that you have created with Report Wizards. With the Database window displayed, click on Report, and then Design. Note that Report Wizards creates reports with default settings in many areas of the report. Examine the report that you have displayed. What are the default settings for:

> Page header
> Report header
> Detail
> Report footer
> Page footer
> Group header, and
> Group footer

Modifying an existing report

To customise an existing report it must be selected in Design mode thus:

❑ Select the report in the Database Window and then select the **Design** button; or

❑ Double click on the report name using the right mouse button. (Not Access 2 clicking the right button gives a shortcut menu).

Creating a new blank report

To create a new report, without the aid of Report Wizards:

❑ Click on the **Report** button in the Database Window; or

❏ Choose *View–Reports* and then click on the **New** button in the Database window, or

❏ Choose *File–New–Report*, or

❏ Click the **New Report** button on the toolbar, then Select the table or query from the **Select a Table/Query** drop–down list box, and then select the **Blank Report** button.

Extra windows

When you create a new blank report the Toolbox window will be displayed. This is useful for adding controls to the report. There are a number of such windows which you will encounter as you advance in report design. These are:

Palette window	to change colours
Properties sheet	to change different features of the report's contents
Field list	to add controls bound to fields

All of these windows can be moved or closed in the same way as any other window. They can also be opened and closed from the *View* menu or by clicking on the appropriate button in the toolbar.

exercise 6 *creating a blank report*

Create a blank report for the **Classes** table, showing all of the fields in the table, thus:

❏ Click the **Report** button in the Database Window, and then click the **New** button in the Database window. Select the **Classes** table from the **Select A Table/Query** drop down list box.

❏ Select the **Blank Report** button.

❏ Save as **Classes** and close.

activity 9 moving and sizing controls

Moving and sizing controls is the basic activity for improving the appearance of the report.

In order to move a control, the control must first be selected and then it can be moved by dragging it. The different types of controls can be selected in the same way as controls are selected and moved on forms. If you need a reminder, see Moving and sizing controls in Activity 7 of Session 3.

exercise 7 *moving and sizing controls on an existing report wizards report*

We wish to improve on the design of the report **Members,** so that the final report looks as shown in Figure 4.4.

❑ First open the existing report. Select the report **Members** in the Database Window and then select the **Design** button.

❑ Now move the controls on the report until it resembles the Design screen in Figure 4.4, using the instructions above for selecting and moving controls. If the toolbox is in the way, remove it by using ***View–Toolbox.***

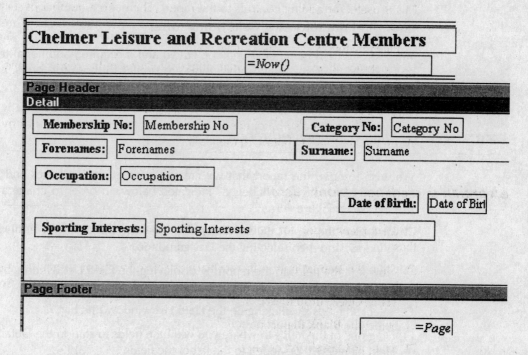

*Figure 4.4 Design screen for **Members2***

Note: You may get into a muddle in your first attempt to move controls. Remember that controls can be deleted by selecting them and using the Delete key. If all else fails close ***without saving*** and start again.

❑ View the new report on screen using Print Preview

❑ Save the report as **Members2** using ***File-Save As.***

Changing the reports area

The area of each section of a report, the header, detail and footer sections, may be altered individually. Also the position of the right and bottom edge of a report may be adjusted. To alter the depth of a section of the report:

Move the pointer to the bottom edge of the section where it will change shape. Drag the pointer to a new location.

To alter the area of the report drag the right and bottom edges to the size that you require.

Deleting, adding and restoring fields to and from a report

When you create a report from scratch it is necessary to add appropriate fields from a selected table or query. You may also wish to add or delete fields when changing an existing report. Again, procedures are similar to those for deleting, adding and restoring fields to or from a form. If you require a reminder consult the section headed Deleting, Adding, Restoring Fields from or to a Form in Activity 7 of Session 3.

Changing the text of a field name label

The text of a field name label may be edited and if required additional text can be added to the form. Again procedures are similar to those for forms, and are detailed in Activity 7 of Session 3.

---

exercise 8 creating a customised report

We wish to open the report that we created in Exercise 6, **Classes** and to add fields and to modify field labels as indicated below, in order to create a report like the one in Figure 4.5:

☐ First open the report called **Classes** by selecting the report in the Database Window, and then selecting the **Design** button.

☐ Now add the fields to the report by displaying the **Field List** window by clicking on the **Field List** button.

☐ Select all fields by clicking on the **Field List** window title bar.

☐ Drag one of the fields to where you want the fields to start in the Detail band. Field names will be added to the left of the fields.

☐ Click on the fields and their labels and move them into a more satisfactory position. Rearrange them as necessary. You may wish to use *Layout–Align–Left* to align a group of controls. (Select them as a group first.)

☐ When all fields are added satisfactorily, close the **Field List** window, by, for example, double clicking on its control box.

☐ Edit the field label **Class No** so that it reads **Number,** by selecting the field label control, clicking where the text editing is required and modifying the field name label. Modify other labels as necessary in the same way.

☐ Press Enter or click on another part of the report to complete changes.

☐ Try aligning groups of controls to achieve a tidy looking form.

☐ Next create a report header and a report footer by choosing *Layout–Report Hdr/Ftr* or *Format-Report Header/Footer.* so that a tick is placed beside this option.

❏ Next create a control box into which you can insert the text, thus:

❏ With the toolbox displayed click on the **Label** tool (See Figure 5.1). Place the pointer in the Report Header box and drag it to create a box large enough to accommodate text.

❏ Type the following text into the report header band: Chelmer Leisure and Recreation Centre – Sports, Fitness and Exercise Classes.

❏ Repeat these steps to insert text in the report footer, page header and page footer bands.

❏ Print Preview the report, save the report as **Classes** and close the report.

Chelmer Leisure and Recreation Centre. Sports, Fitness and Exercise Classes

Classes

Number:		1	Activity:	Ladies' Aerobics
Day:	Monday		Time:	10:00
Tutor:	Evans			Female

Number:		2	Activity:	Weight Training
Day:	Monday		Time:	11:00
Tutor:	Franks			Male

Figure 4.5 A customised report

You have now created a basic report showing all of the basic information, but clearly there is much scope for improvements in its format. A few of these are explored in the last Exercise in this Session, but the majority are the subject of the next two chapters.

Altering the size and font of controls

To alter the size of font of the controls on a report:

1. Select the controls to be altered.

2. Open the **Font** list box in the toolbar and select the font required.

3. Open the **Point Size** list box and select the point size required.

Note: If you increase the size of a font you may need to alter the size of the control and the size of the section.

Adding headers and footers

Page headers and footers can be easily added to a form. With the Toolbox displayed click on the **Label** tool. Place the pointer in the appropriate header or footer section and drag it to make a box large enough to accommodate the text.

exercise 9 reformatting a report

This exercise reformats the report created in Exercise 8 using a number of additional features that have been introduced above.

❏ Open the report called **Classes** in Design mode.

❏ Select the controls in the Report Header and open the Point Size list box and select an appropriate larger point size. Click on the **Bold** button to make the text bold. Click on the centre justify button to centre the text within the control.

❏ Move the field labels into the page header band by first selecting them as a group. Choose **Edit–Cut** and click any where in the page header. Then choose **Edit–Paste.**

❏ Rearrange the labels in the page header to make column headings. Select these as a group and format them by making them bold and italic and of a slightly larger point size.

❏ Adjust the size of the page header so that it just accommodates the labels by dragging the bottom of the page header.

❏ In the Detail band, re-arrange the controls to align with the labels in the Page Header. If necessary expand the boxes to accommodate the longest field value. For example make sure that the control box for Activity accommodates Badminton.

❏ In turn select the text boxes for **Class No** and **Time** and left justify them by clicking on the left justify button. Select the **Male/Female/Mixed** control box and delete it by pressing the Delete key.

❏ Select and format the report footer in bold and italics. Note Access 1 screen is shown, refer to Appendix 4 for the Access 2 toolbar.

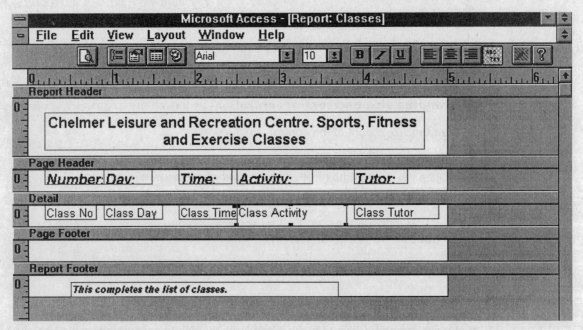

❑ Note that it will probably be necessary to move back and forth between Print preview and Design mode a few times as you make changes and would like to view the results of those changes.

❑ Print Preview, Save as **Classes2,** Close and Print as required.

Chelmer Leisure and Recreation Centre. Sports, Fitness and Exercise Classes

Number	Day:	Time:	Activity:	Tutor:
1	Monday	10:00	Ladies' Aerobics	Evans
2	Monday	11:00	Weight Training	Franks
3	Monday	15:00	Body Conditioning	Latham
4	Monday	19:00	Step Aerobics	Wheildon
5	Tuesday	10:00	Men's Multi-gym	Jackson
6	Tuesday	14:00	Ladies' Multi-gym	Adams
7	Tuesday	19:00	Family Multi-gym	Jackson

This completes the list of classes.

Figure 4.6 Sample print-out from the customised report

Note: tools

The report design window has a number of tools that you have been benefiting from in designing a report. These are described in more detail in Activity 7 Session 3. It is useful to briefly review these:

1. **Ruler** measures the distance from the top and left corner of the ruler. The Ruler can be removed or replaced by choosing *View–Ruler.*

2. **Grid** is an organised layout of dots. Access automatically aligns moved or sized controls with the grid. The Grid can be moved or replaced by choosing *View–Grid.* To deactivate the Grid choose *Layout–Snap to Grid* or *Format-Snap to Grid.*

3. **Alignment** option. Use *Layout–Alignment* to position controls relative to each other. Select controls, choose *Layout-Align* and the appropriate alignment e.g. Left. In Access 2 use the alignment buttons on the toolbar.

integrative exercises

exercise 10 *creating a single column report using report wizards*

Report

You require a report, based on the **Membership** table, which lists the following details for all members who are smokers:

Membership No

Category No

Title

Forenames

Surname

Occupation

Date of Birth

Sex

First define a query which allows you to select the records for the members who are smokers. Save this query and then use it in the design of a report using Report Wizards. Don't forget to save the report, as **Smokers** and print preview it on screen before seeking to print it.

exercise 11 *creating a groups/totals report using Report Wizards*

You wish to create a report that lists all of the classes offered by the centre, based on the **Classes** table. The report is to be organised in groups according to Class Activity. All fields in the Classes table are to be included in the report.

Produce a second Groups/Totals report, based on the **Classes** table, which details all the information in the Classes table. Sort the report in classes order. Save this report as **Classes List.**

exercise 12 *creating a customised report*

Instead of using Report Wizards to create the report in Exercise 4.10, attempt to create the same report independently of the Report Wizards tool, i.e. as a customised report.

further customising forms and reports

objectives

This session focuses on the additional features which you can add to forms and reports. It also looks at ways in which you can organise your data for display or printing. At the end of this session you should be able to

❑ add other types of control to a form and report

❑ display the records in a form in the order you wish them to be displayed using filters

❑ print records in a report in the order you wish using Sorting and Grouping

❑ convert a form into a report

So far you have met forms and reports created by the Wizards, these tend to use limited controls. In this session we will start to explore the range of controls that can be added to both forms and reports. The level of sophistication that can be given to controls adds to the professionalism of the database application that is being created.

Controls on forms can be made more versatile by the use of list boxes, option buttons, option groups etc., features encountered in dialog boxes. If the entry for a control can be selected from a list, for example, rooms in a leisure centre, then data entry can be made more efficient by providing a list box. The person entering the data simply selects from the list rather than having to key in the entry. This has the advantages of reducing error and maintaining consistency.

Calculated controls may be added to either forms or reports. They display information that can be calculated from existing data. The example that is used in this session is of calculating which members have not renewed their membership.

Filters are used in forms as a means of displaying the records in a particular order. They also allow criteria to be imposed to 'filter' records that meet these criteria. Filters are created temporarily and can quickly allow the user to view their data using a variety of sequences and criteria without having to resort to creating a query. Trends in data may be identified using this transient method of data filtering. Information concerning, for example, poor membership in a certain category, or room usage can easily obtained. If the filter created is felt to be useful then it can easily be converted into a query which can be saved.

Note: In Access 2 filters may be used with tables and the methods for filtering forms described in this session are the same for filtering tables.

In reports ordering is achieved by using the **Sorting and Grouping** button on the toolbar. Sorting and Grouping enhances the presentation of data in reports. The addition of group header and footer identifies the group within the report. The field that is being used for grouping usually has its control in the group header acting as a heading. Calculated controls can be added to group footers to produce sub-totals or averages for the group. Records may be displayed in different orders within groups, for example, members may be listed alphabetically by surname within category grouping, bookings may be listed in time and date order within room grouping.

activity 1 types of form controls

In creating forms and reports you will have met labels and text box controls. If you are familiar with Windows applications you will be aware that there are other types of control, which you will have met when using dialog boxes. These include list boxes, check boxes and option buttons.

There are three categories of control.

1. *Bound controls.* A bound control is associated with a field in the table or query that was used to create the form. We have met text boxes, these are the most common type of bound control. Through a bound control data can be displayed or altered.

2. *Unbound controls.* An unbound control is independent of the data in the form's table or query. Labels used as titles are examples of unbound controls.

3. *Calculated controls.* A calculated control is an expression. Usually the expression performs a calculation upon data in the form's table or query.

The toolbox

The Access Toolbox allows you add control objects to forms and reports. The Toolbox only appears whilst you are in form or report design mode. If it is not visible in design mode then use **View–Toolbox** to make it visible. The Toolbox is composed of a set of buttons and by clicking on a button that particular tool becomes available. Each button gives access to a different tool, the icon on the button indicates the function of the tool, as outlined in Figure 5.1. In Access 2 there is an additional button, Control Wizards, next to the Tool Lock button.

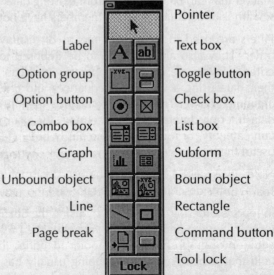

	Pointer
Label	Text box
Option group	Toggle button
Option button	Check box
Combo box	List box
Graph	Subform
Unbound object	Bound object
Line	Rectangle
Page break	Command button
	Tool lock

Figure. 5.1 Toolbox window

Tool	Function
Pointer	This is the default tool when the Toolbox is displayed. Click on this tool to deselect a previously selected tool and return the mouse pointer to its normal function
Label	Allows you to draw a rectangle (frame) on the form into which text can be inserted.
Text box	Creates a frame in which text is displayed or edited. This is the most common form of control.
Option Group	Creates a frame of adjustable size into which controls can be placed. Only one of the controls within the frame can be selected. Usually the controls are of the same kind e.g. option buttons or check boxes. When a control within an option group is selected all others in the group are deselected.
Toggle Button	Creates a button that switches between on and off when clicked with the mouse
Option Button	Creates a round button that switches between on and off when clicked with the mouse. Option buttons are most commonly used within option groups to select between values in a set.
Check box	Creates a check box that toggles on and off. Multiple check boxes can be used in groups, but not within an option group, so that more than one check box can be selected.
Combo box	Creates a combination box which is a combination of a text box and a drop down list box. This allows the choice of either selecting from a list or keying in an entry.
List box	Creates a drop–down list box from which an item or value can be selected.
Graph	Launches the GraphWizard which can create a graph based on a query or table.
Subform	Adds a subform or subreport to a main form or report. Don't use this unless the subform or subreport already exist, see Session 7 for more detail about subforms and subreports.
Unbound object	Adds an OLE object, that is something created by another application which supports OLE, for example, graphics created by Microsoft Word's Graph and Draw. An example of this would be a company logo which is added to a report or form.
Bound object	Where the data table contains OLE objects, for example, digitised photographs in a personnel table, this tool is used to create an object control in a similar way to the text box control.

Line	Creates a straight line that can be sized and relocated. The colour and width of the line can be changed using the properties and palette.
Rectangle	Creates a rectangle which can be sized and relocated. Select width, colour and fill from the properties and palette.
Page Break	Causes the printer to start a new page at the location of the page break on the form or the report.
Command button	Creates a command button. A macro can be assigned to the button which will execute when the button is clicked.
Tool Lock	Maintains the currently selected tool as the active tool. Without lock Access defaults to the pointer after a tool has been used. To remove the lock click on another tool.
Control Wizards	Provides Wizards when adding controls.

activity 2 adding controls to forms

This activity uses the Toolbox to add controls to forms. If the Toolbox isn't visible in form design mode choose ***View–Toolbox*** to display it. Move it by dragging its title bar to a suitable place on your screen. As the best way to see how to add controls is by experimentation so this activity will comprise entirely of exercises. By completing these exercises you should acquire the skills with which to attempt a form design of your own. To experiment with controls we will start with a blank form.

exercise 1 creating a calculated text box

In this exercise the calculated control that is to be created is one which flags members whose renewal is due. This control will be added to the **Membership** form created in Exercise 1 of Session 3. Before continuing with the exercise it will probably be necessary to review and amend the dates of joining and the dates of renewal to make this exercise realistic.

When people join Chelmer Leisure and Recreation Centre they pay for one years membership from that date. They renew their membership annually. To calculate whether the member's subscription is overdue then the renewal date is compared with today's date. If the renewal date is before today's date then the fee is overdue. To create a realistic number, say, three members overdue, amend or add records to the **Membership** table with appropriate dates for renewal.

❐ Open the **Membership** table using the **Open** button to display the data.

❐ View each record in turn and look at the **Date of Last Renewal** field.

❐ Make amendments, if necessary, to the **Date of Last Renewal** fields so that some members have a date of renewal before exactly one year ago from today and others after that date.

To add the calculated text box

❏ Open the **Membership** form in design view.

❏ Click on the **Text box** tool in the Toolbox.

❏ Click on a suitable place on the form for the text box and its label.

❏ Edit the label to read **Subscription:**

❏ Click in the Text box and key in the expression

=iif(DateAdd("d",365,[Date of Last Renewal])<Date(),"Overdue","Up to date")

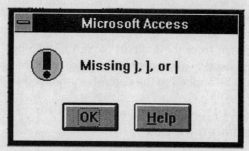

❏ If you miss out a bracket, when you press Enter Access will display an information box. Click on **OK** and you will be returned to the control so that you can edit the expression.

❏ If you have trouble seeing this expression you can display it in a Zoom box by clicking on the Control Source property in the Text Box properties sheet and pressing Shift+F2 to open the Zoom box for editing.

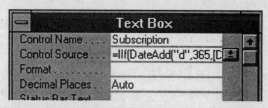

❏ Edit the Control Name (Name in Access 2) in the Text Box property window to read Subscription.

❏ Run the form. If you have errors return to the design view and check that you have keyed in the expression correctly. For example if you have misspelt the control name, then the message **#Name?** appears in the control. Check all control names carefully and correct them. Check there is an = sign at the beginning of the expression.

Note: If you rename a control in an underlying table then this kind of error may result and the names in the expression will need to be amended accordingly.

The expression is an in–line IF....THEN.....ELSE statement. DateAdd adds one year to the date of the last renewal. This is compared to today's date. IF the result is less than today's date THEN the subscription is overdue ELSE it is up to date.

❑ Save the form.

If you wish to create your own expressions refer to the Access manual for lists of functions available.

Formatting displayed values

Font and size formatting have already been discussed in sessions 3 and 4. Type-font (bold, italics, underlining) and alignment (left, centre, right, general) can be chosen from the toolbar. Note: underlining  and general alignment buttons not available on Access 2 toolbar. Formatting can also be applied to the controls introduced in this session.

exercise 2 adding a list box

List boxes are useful for picking values from a static list of options that you create. You may define a list or use a table as a source of the list. The example that will be considered is that of adding a list box to the bookings form. The list box will be defined for the **Room/Hall/Court** field and use a static list. This static list is a list of rooms at the leisure centre. At Chelmer Leisure and Recreation centre there are six bookable rooms, the Fitness Suite, Sports Hall 1 and 2, and three courts.

To add a list box to the **Bookings** form, first open the form in design mode.

❑ Select and delete the **Room/Hall/Court** text box.

❑ Open the **Field List** Window and check that the Toolbox is displayed.

❑ Adjust the controls on the form so that there is room to have a list box approximately deep enough to show all the six rooms. If the list box is made smaller it will be shown with a vertical scroll bar. You may wish to try a slightly different layout as illustrated later in this exercise.

❑ Click on the **List Box** tool in the Toolbox.

❑ Click and drag the **Room/Hall/Court** field from the Field List window to the former position of the **Room/Hall/Court** text box.

Access 1

❑ If the **Properties** dialog box is not displayed click on the **Properties** button in the toolbar. Click on the **Room/Hall/Court** list box to show its property sheet.

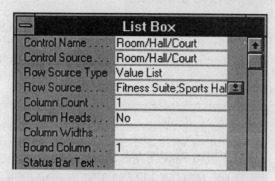

☐ Open the source type list box and choose Value List. Key into the Row Source property the following: **Fitness Suite; Sports Hall 1; Sports Hall 2; Court 1; Court 2; Court3.** Press Shift+F2 to use the zoom box to make the entry easier.

☐ Enter **1** for the Column Count property.

Access 2

☐ The List Box Wizard dialog box displays. Select the option **I will type in the values that I want** and click on **Next>**.

☐ Enter 1 into the **Number of columns** box. Click in the first cell and Type Fitness Suite. Complete the column with Sports Hall, Sports Hall 2, Court 1, Court 2 and Court 3 so there are six rows in column 1. Click on Next>.

☐ Choose the option **Store that value in the field** and click on Next>.

☐ Accept the label for the list box which should be Room/Hall/Court and click on **Finish.**

Note that if you elect not to use the Wizard by clicking off the Control Wizards button in the Toolbox then create the list according to the steps described for Access 1.

Testing the form

☐ Click on the **Form View** button on the toolbar to display the form. If adjustments to the position of controls are needed then return to the design mode to make them. The form could look something like:

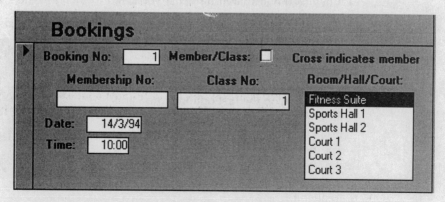

❑ Save the form as **Bookings2.** Try using the form to enter a booking. You may wish to amend the tab order depending upon your design.

exercise 3 adding option groups

Option buttons are commonly employed in Windows applications to select one option from a set of choices. They are best used where the value of the option is numeric, for example, the categories of membership. To illustrate this an option group will be added to the **Membership** form. Open the form in design mode. Adjust the area of the form to allow room for the option group at the bottom or side of the form.

To create an option group

❑ Click on the Option Group frame tool in the Toolbox.

❑ Choose **Category No** from the **Field List** and **drag** to the form. Dragging is important as it links the control with the field. Release at a suitable position.

Access 1 (without Wizard)

❑ Resize the option group frame so that it will be able to accommodate option buttons for the six categories. Note that the label is part of the border, as is standard in Windows option groups.

The option frame binds together the controls that are within it and for this reason the field list is not used when putting controls inside the frame. Adding multiple copies of controls is made easier if the **Lock** tool is used. To add six option buttons

❑ Click on the **Lock** tool in the Toolbox.

❑ Click on the **Option button** tool.

❑ Using the cross hair symbol of the pointer as a guide to the top left corner of the control, click to drop the option button at the top right of the frame. When the option button symbol is placed in the option group, the frame and everything within it appears in inverse video.

❑ Repeat the previous step 5 more times to include a total of six Category buttons inside the option frame. If you need to increase the size of the option frame, drag the corner handle.

❑ Click on the **Lock** button in the Toolbox to unlock and select the **Pointer** tool.

❑ Edit the labels as illustrated.

❑ If you click on the first option button and look at its **Option Value** property in the **Properties** list you will see it is set to 1. The next button is 2 and so on. This is the default setting and as it corresponds to the category numbers there is no need to alter it.

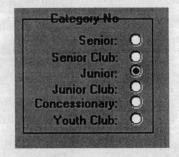

Access 2 Control Wizard

❐ Enter the label names as shown in the illustration and click on Next>.

❐ Select the option **No, I don't want to select a default** and click on Next>.

❐ The default values are correct so click on Next>.

❐ Choose the option **Store that value in this field: Category No** and click on Next>.

❐ Choose the Normal style and Option buttons and click on Next>.

❐ Give the option group the title Category and click on **Finish**.

Testing the form

❐ To test the form click on the **Form View** button. The already existing **Category No** text box control should serve to confirm the entry in the option group. Data could be entered into this field using either of the controls. Experiment by entering a new member's record. You may wish to revise the Tab order and edit the name of the new control in the properties sheet.

❐ Save the form as **Membership**.

exercise 4 *adding a combo box*

In this exercise a combo box will be added to the **Membership** form for the choice of county. Three counties will be listed but the text box will accept an alternative which may be keyed in.

❐ Open the **Membership** form in design view.

❐ Select and delete the **County** text box.

❐ Check that both the Field List window, the Properties window and the Toolbox are displayed.

❐ Click on the **Combo Box** tool in the Toolbox. Click and drag the **County** field from the field list onto its former location on the form.

Access 1

❐ Open the Source type list box and choose **Value list.** Key into the **Row Source** property, the following: **Staffs; Derbyshire**

❐ Enter 1 for the Column Count property.

Access 2

❐ Using the wizard, opt to type in the values, set the number of columns to one.

❐ Enter the list of counties, Staffs, Derbyshire.

❐ Choose the store in county field option and edit the label if required. Click on **Finish**.

Testing the form

❒ Click on the **Run** mode button on the
toolbar to display the form. The **County**
text box should have a list box button,
which when clicked will display the list
of counties. Notice that when entering a

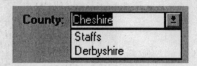

new record Cheshire is still the default county. If adjustments are needed
return to design mode to make them. When complete save the form. Experiment with entering data.

---

activity 3 using filters to sort and select records on a form

A common business need is to present the same information in a variety of
orders, e.g. a list of customers either in name or town order. At the moment our
database is in an unordered sequence but by using filters the records may be displayed in the order desired.

Note that Access 2 allows additional sorting. By clicking in a field, say, Date of
Birth in either the Membership table or form and clicking on either the Sort
Ascending or Sort Descending button all records are displayed in the order
chosen. To remove the effect click on the Remove Filter/Sort button.

As we have already seen queries can display selected data in the desired order.
The advantage that filters offer is that they can be designed whilst viewing a form
or table. If records are being amended then it can be useful to select certain
records and to view them in order, for example, to change a room for a particular activity. After the amendments are made the filter may be discarded. If the
filter is useful it may be saved as a query.

Filter window

Through the filter window you can set up the filters which will sort the records
into the order you require. To display the filter window:

1. Click on the **Edit Filter/Sort** button in the toolbar. The filter control buttons
   are shown below:

    Edit Filter/Sort

    Apply Filter/Sort

    Remove Filter/Sort (Show all Records in Natural Order)

The filter window is shown in Figure 5.2. This window is very similar in design
to the query window. As filters can be saved as queries this is not surprising.

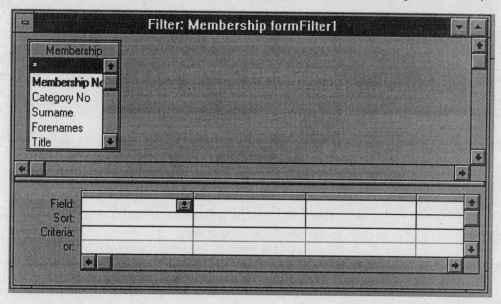

Figure 5.2 The Filter Window

Sorting data with a filter

To sort the data using one field:

1. Either, click in the field cell and open its list box and select the field required, or, click and drag the field required from the table window to the Field cell.

3. Click in the Sort cell and click on its associated list box button and choose Ascending or Descending.

4. To see the effect of the filter click on the **Apply Filter/Sort** button in the toolbar.

You may wish to sort a list of names into alphabetical surname order and within surname order you wish to sort the forenames in alphabetical order. You may add more than one field to your filter, however, the order in which you add them is important, the fields should be arranged in order of highest priority left-most. In the example mentioned the surname order is a higher priority than the forename order so surname should be in the first column and forenames in the second column. To sort the data using more than one field:

1. Add the fields to the filter as described for single fields above. For each field select the sort order required. You may have some fields that are ascending and some that are descending.

2. To see the effect of the filter click on the **Apply Filter/Sort** button in the toolbar.

exercise 5 *sorting with a filter*

This exercise will use the **Membership** form and apply a filter to it. Open the **Membership** form in **Form View**. The filter buttons should be in the toolbar. To apply a filter

❏ Click on the **Edit Filter/Sort** button and the filter window appears.

❏ Choose **Surname** from the table in the upper part of the filter window and drag it to the first field cell. Select the sort order as Ascending.

❏ Click on the **Apply Filter/Sort** button to see the records displayed in the form in ascending order of Surname.

❏ In Access 2 this may be achieved by clicking in the **Surname** field and clicking on the Sort Ascending button.

Editing a filter

When you view the result of your filter, if it is not quite how you expected it or you wish to add additional fields then you can edit it. To edit a filter:

1. Click on the **Edit Filter/Sort** button in the tool bar.

2. You may add fields as described previously, you may edit the filter, for example, by changing from an Ascending sort to a Descending one. You may delete a field from the filter. To delete a field select it by clicking on the column selector bar (the grey bar at the top of the column) and pressing the **Delete** key.

3. Fields in the filter window can be rearranged by dragging and dropping in the same way as in a query.

exercise 6 *editing a filter*

This exercise follows on from Exercise 5.

❏ Click on the **Edit Filter/Sort** button to re-display the filter window.

❏ Add a second field **Forenames** and select the sort order as Ascending.

❏ Click on the **Apply Filter/Sort** button to see the records displayed in the form in ascending order.

❏ Click on the **Edit Filter/Sort** button to re-display the filter window.

❏ Edit the window so that the field **Category No** is added so that it is in the first column.

❏ Click on the **Apply Filter/Sort** button. Experiment with different forms of sorting on different fields.

Selecting records with a filter

In the same way as criteria are used for queries, criteria can be used in filters to select certain records. One or more fields can be queried. To use criteria in a filter:

1. Add the fields to the fields row of the filter and set the sort order if this is required. You need not sort the records.

2. In the criteria cell you can enter criteria in the same manner as that for creating a query.

3. To see the effect of the filter click on the **Apply Filter/Sort** button in the toolbar.

exercise 7 *selecting records with a filter*

Using the **Membership** form the filter created in this exercise will select those members in category 1 and display them in name order.

❐ Click on the **Edit Filter/Sort** button to re-display the filter window.

❐ Set the fields in the columns to **Category No, Surname, Forenames.** Set the sort order for **Surname** and **Forenames** to ascending.

❐ In the criteria cell of **Category No** key in **1**.

❐ Click on the **Apply Filter/Sort** button.

❐ Repeat for the other categories by editing this query.

Saving the filter as a query

A filter can be saved as a query for later use. The sort order and criteria that are entered into the filter window can be saved as a query in the following way:

1. From the Filter Window choose *File–Save As Query.*

2. Type a name for the Query in the **Save As** dialog box and click on **OK.**

The new query will appear in the Database Window.

exercise 8 *creating a query from a filter*

Open the **Bookings2** form created in Exercise 2. Set a filter with the criteria "Fitness Suite" for the **Room/Hall/Court** field. Sort on the **Date** in Ascending order. Sort on the **Time** in Ascending order. View the result. To save this filter:

❐ Open the filter window and choose *File–Save As Query.*

❐ Type the name **Fitness Suite Bookings** and click on **OK.**

❐ Close the form and display the Database Window to see the new query listed.

activity 4 saving a form as a report

If you change a form to a report then you have more control over the variety of ways in which the data can be formatted for printing, for example, you can create a Group/Totals report from the data. To save a form as a report:

1. From the form design choose *File–Save As Report.* A dialog box appears with the name of your form as the default report name. If you wish you may rename the report.

2. Close your form and click on the **Reports** button in the Database Window.

3. Select the report and preview it. Make any adjustments to the design before printing. Note if the **Keep Together** property of the detail section is set to **Yes** then page breaks will not occur in the middle of records.

exercise 9 saving a form as a report

In this exercise the **Bookings** form will be saved as a report.

❑ Open the **Bookings** form in design view.

❑ Choose *File–Save As Report.* A dialog box appears with **Bookings** as the default name. Accept this.

❑ Close your form and click on the **Reports** button in the Database Window.

❑ Select the **Bookings** report and preview it.

❑ Use **Sorting and Grouping** to group by room and to sort in date and time order.

❑ Make any adjustments to the design before printing.

activity 5 adding controls to reports

Calculated controls

Calculated controls are useful in reports. If a report has been produced from a table which contains data about stock in the form of quantity sold and price then the sales revenue can be calculated by multiplying the quantity sold by the price. Another example is a logical field where instead of printing Yes or No you wish to print Male or Female.

exercise 10 adding a calculated control to the members2 report

Use the report **Members2** customised in Exercise 7 of Session 4. The aim is to add the fields **Sex** and **Smoker** but in such a way that Male or Female and Smoker or Non-Smoker are printed.

❑ Display the report in design mode. Rearrange the controls as illustrated below making space to insert the calculated controls.

❑ Click on the **Text box** tool and click in a suitable place for the information about sex to go.

❑ Edit the label to read Sex:

❑ Into the text box key in the expression **=IIF([Sex],"Male","Female")**

IIF is short for IF...THEN...ELSE, i.e. IF the field Sex is true THEN print Male ELSE print Female.

❑ Click on the Text box tool and click in a suitable place for the information about whether the member is a smoker or not.

❑ Delete the label part of this control.

❑ Into the text box key in the expression **=IIF([Smoker],"Smoker","Non-Smoker")**

IF the field Smoker is true THEN print Smoker ELSE print Non-Smoker.

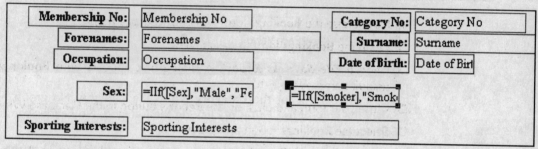

❑ Save the report, preview and print it.

Membership No:	1	Category No:	2
Forenames:	Andrew J	Surname:	Walker
Occupation:	Builder	Date of Birth:	12/3/52
Sex:	Male	Smoker	

activity 6 controls in grouped reports

The most usual way of grouping records is by category. An example that was used in Session 4 was that of the categories of membership. To group by category the best way is to choose to group by a particular category when constructing the report using the ReportWizard.

To alter the grouping properties once into design mode of the report use the **Sorting and Grouping** dialog box. This dialog box can be used to add group headers and footers. Calculated controls can be added so that, for example, group sub-totals or averages can be added to the report.

exercise 11 *adding calculated controls to a grouped report*

❏ Display the **Members2** report in design mode.

❏ Click on the **Sorting and Grouping** button in the toolbar and set the sorting and grouping as illustrated below. This report sorts the members into alphabetical order within the category number groups. For **Category No** set the **Group Header** and **Group Footer** to **Yes**.

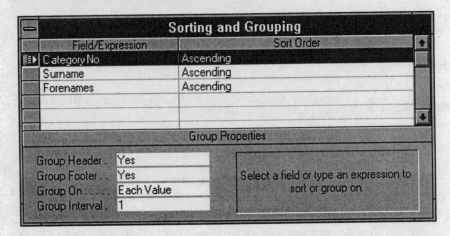

❏ Move the control for the **Category No** to the Category No group header. Select the control use *Edit–Cut* click on the Category No header bar and use **Edit–Paste**.

❏ In the Category No group footer add a text box control and key into it the expression **=Count([Membership No])** which will display the total number of members in each category.

❏ Add a label which says Number of Members.

❏ Add a line at the bottom of the Category No footer.

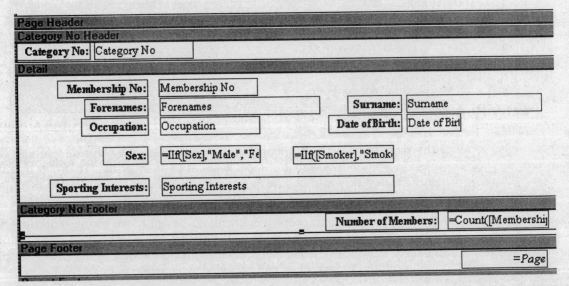

❏ Preview the report, save and print it. A selected part of the print-out is shown following.

Membership No: 10

Forenames: George W F   Surname: Weiner
Occupation: Electrician   Date of Birth: 10/2/58

Sex: Male   Non-Smoker

Sporting Interests: Weight training, squash

Number of Members: 7

exercise 12 *groups within groups in a report*

Continue with the previous exercise. The aim is create a report which groups by town within each category group. Display the report in design view and display the sorting and grouping dialog box.

❏ In the fourth row add the field **Town.** Select this row and drag it to below the First row. Priority of grouping can be changed by rearranging the rows in the **Sorting and Grouping** dialog box. Select **Yes** for **Group Header** and **Group Footer.**

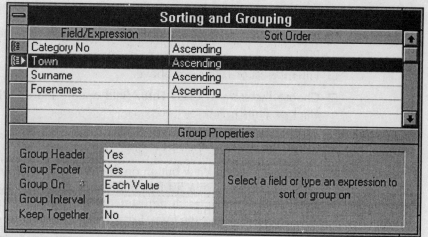

❏ In report design mode move the control for **Town** to the **Town Group Header.**

❏ Copy the calculated control for number of members from the **Category No** group footer and paste the copy into the **Town** group footer. Amend the labels for both these controls so that you know which is which.

❏ Preview the report, save and print it.

❏ Experiment with different sorting and groupings.

integrative exercises

exercise 13 adding a combo box to the classes form

In this exercise a combo box will be added to the **Classes** form for the choice of tutor. Six tutors will be listed but the text box will accept an alternative which may be keyed in.

❑ Open the **Classes** form in design view.

❑ Select and delete the **Tutor** text box.

❑ Check that both the Field List window, the Properties window and the Tool-box are displayed.

❑ Click on the **Combo Box** tool in the Toolbox. Click and drag the **Tutor** field from the field list onto its former location on the form.

Access 1

❑ Open the **Source type** list box and choose **Value list.** Key into the Row Source property, the following: **Adams; Evans; Franks; Jackson; Latham; Wheildon**

❑ Enter **1** for the **Column Count** property.

Access 2

❑ Using the Wizard, opt to type in the values and set the number of columns to one.

❑ Enter the list of Tutors (see above).

❑ Choose the store in **Class Tutor** field option and edit the label if required. Click on Finish.

Testing the form

❑ Click on the **Form View** button on the toolbar to display the form. The Tutor text box should have a list box button, which when clicked will display the list of tutors surnames. If adjustments are needed return to design mode. When complete save the form. Experiment with entering data.

If you complete the **Tutor** table (compose the records yourself) then the tutors' surnames are held in this table. This table could be used as the source for the combo box. This has the advantage that as tutors leave or new ones are employed the list in the combo box reflects the tutor surnames in the **Tutor** table. To make this change:

Access 1

❑ Alter the **Source type** property to Table/Query.

❑ Alter the **Row Source** property to be **Tutor.**

❑ Leave 1 in the **Column Count** property as this indicates that the first field is to be used for the list.

Access 2

❑ Choose I want the Combo box to look up the values in a table or query.

❑ Select the table **Tutors** and select **Surname** from the available fields list.

❑ Adjust the width of the column and continue with the wizard usual.

exercise 14 *Creating queries from filters*

Open the **Bookings** form and set a filter with the criteria "Sports Hall 1" for the **Room/Hall/Court** field. Sort on the **Date** and **Time** in Ascending order. Save the filter as Sports Hall 1 bookings. Repeat this exercise to create queries for Sports Hall 2 bookings, Court 1 bookings, etc. for all six rooms.

exercise 15 *Adding a calculated control to a report*

Use the **Classes** report created in Exercise 8 Session 4 and group it by **Tutor.** Save the report as **Classes3.** Move the Tutor control to the Tutor group header. Add a calculated control in the Tutor group footer which will **count** the number of classes. Hint: count the **Class No** field.

Within the **Tutor** grouping try to group by activity and count the number of classes of each activity held by each tutor.

having fun with reports and forms

objectives

This session focuses on features that allow you to adjust the appearance of the information on a report or form, and to make their presentation more exciting. Access offers a wide range of tools for formatting both screens and reports and supports the imaginative creation of interesting screens and reports. Whilst all of these features can be applied to both forms and reports, some features are used more often with forms and others are used more often with reports. At the end of this session you will be able to:

❏ add lines and boxes

❏ use different alignments and fonts

❏ add colour and shading

❏ set dimensions and borders of controls

❏ create form and report templates

❏ insert graphs and pictures into a report or a form.

This session focuses on those tools that are concerned with screen and report design. You will already have used some of these features briefly in the last three sessions. Forms and reports created using Wizards use some of these features to a limited extent, but by the time you have completed this session you should be able to improve on Wizards designs.

Although the tools we explore in this session allow you to be very adventurous with your designs, remember that good design hinges on the appropriate and sparing use of objects such as boxes and lines, and upon the use of only a limited number of different fonts. In addition most organisation will wish to establish a house style which might be applied to all screens and groups of similar reports. We are not this consistent in the forms and reports that we generate in this book, because the range of forms and reports used here have been used to demonstrate the wide range of features and designs that can be adopted. When, however you do need to create a House style, form and report templates are one means of doing this and we introduce these briefly later in this Session. The tips below act as a reminder of good deign features:

design tips – forms

1. Keep the form simple and easy to read. Don't use unnecessary text and graphics, but do use fonts and font sizes that are easy to read on the screen.

2. Use colour sparingly, to make forms interesting, but choose colours that are comfortable for those working at the screen for a long period of time.

3. Design the form taking into account how it will be used i.e. where data needs to be entered and ease of movement between data entry boxes.

4. Maintain a consistent appearance for related forms. This looks more professional and makes it easier for a user to acclimatise to a series of forms.

design tips – reports

1. Keep the report simple. Make the data easy to read by choosing font sizes and types that print well. Use fonts and graphics to help to convey important messages in the report.

2. Design in the knowledge of the capabilities of the printer. In particular, laser printers can produce much more intricate detail than a dot matrix printer.

3. Consider the application of the report. Who are the readers and why will they be using the report?

activity 1 adding lines and rectangles to forms and reports

Lines and rectangles can be added to reports and forms to emphasis portions of the form or report or to separate one part of the form or report from another.

Lines are added thus:

1. Select the **Line** tool in the toolbox

2. Point to where you want the line to start

3. Drag the pointer. The **Line** tool draws a line from where you start dragging the pointer to where you release the mouse.

Rectangles are added thus:

1. Select the **Rectangle** tool in the toolbox

2. Point to where you want the top left corner to be

3. Drag the pointer to where you want the opposite corner

activity 2 changing control layers

When you add boxes to a form or report, they are initially placed on top of any other controls, and will, for example, cover text boxes so that their details are obscured.

In order to display controls that have been covered, you can take one control and put it behind another. For example, you may move controls hidden by a rectangle so that they are on top of the rectangle.

1. To move a control from the front to below other controls, select it and choose *Layout–Send to Back* or *Format–Send to Back.*

2. To move a control from behind other controls and to put it on top, choose *Layout–Bring to Front* or *Format–Bring to Front.*

exercise 1 *adding lines and rectangles*

Open the form **Classes.** Experiment with adding lines and rectangles to the form as suggested above, until it looks similar to the form shown in Figure 6.1. More specifically:

❑ Move and size the controls so that they are in the position shown in Figure 6.1.

❑ Edit the text of the labels appropriately.

❑ Place a box around the text in the form header.

❑ Select the box by clicking on it and practice deleting it by pressing the **Delete** key. You are likely to need to delete lines or boxes that you have placed in the wrong place before you have finished!

❑ In order to view the text you will need, with the box selected, to choose *Layout–Send to Back* or *Format–Send to Back*

❑ Place a box around the controls in the Detail band. Again use *Layout–Send to Back* or *Format–Send to Back* to display the text.

❑ Insert a line underneath the controls for Day and Time.

❑ Save the form as **Classes3.**

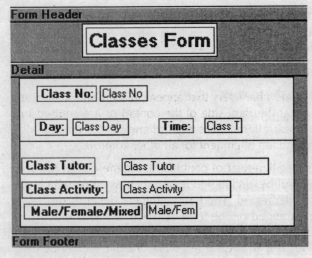
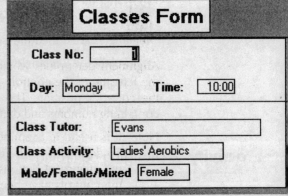

Figure 6.1 Form using lines and rectangles

activity 3 setting alignment and font

Style enhancements include alignment, colour, 3-dimensionality, fonts and borders. These properties are listed in the bottom half of the Property sheet window and may also be set using buttons on the toolbar. When a control is selected that uses any of the style enhancements described in this activity, the middle and right section of the toolbar change to show the buttons in the table listed below.

This activity explores the use of this toolbar to set alignment and font. Other enhancements are dealt with in Activity 6.5.

To set alignment or font:

❒ First select the control to which you wish to add style and then click on an appropriate icon on the toolbar as required below:

Alignment

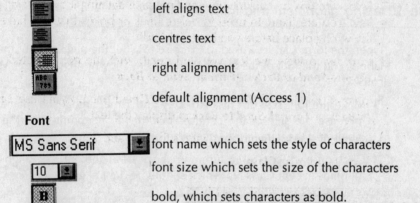

left aligns text

centres text

right alignment

default alignment (Access 1)

Font

font name which sets the style of characters

font size which sets the size of the characters

bold, which sets characters as bold.

italics, which sets characters as italic

underline, which sets characters as underline (Access 1)

Alignment determines whether the characters that appear in the control start at the left side of the control, end at the right side of the control or are centred in the control's position. The default alignment is right alignment for data fields containing numbers and dates and left alignment for all other controls.

Note: It is useful to examine the alignment of controls during the design phase. To do this select the control by clicking on it, and then examine which of the alignment buttons is depressed. The best alignment depends on how the controls have been arranged on the form or report. For example, in a report showing data in columns with field labels in the Page Header, set the alignment of the headers to the same as that for the entries below them in order to align the headings with the data.

Font. A font is a collection of features that describes how the text appears. Using two or three different fonts, and using a larger font size or bold or italics can emphasise parts of a report, and make your form or report more interesting.

Note: Although it is possible to set every control to a different font good design requires that you be selective in the use of a range of fonts. In particular you might consider the following:

❏ Do not use more than two or three fonts on one report or form.

❏ Select a font that is appropriate for the application For example, script and other fancy fonts are not often used in business applications, and where they are used they are used deliberately for effect.

❏ It is usual to use screen fonts for screen display and printer fonts for printing. If you use, for example, a screen font for printing a report, Windows makes the closest possible substitution and there will be a difference between what you see on the screen and what is printed on paper. If you have True type fonts, use them. They appear the same printed as on the screen.

❏ Access remembers the printer that is currently selected when you create a form or report and uses fonts specific to the selected printer.

exercise 2 *setting alignment and fonts on forms*

Open the form **Classes3** used in Exercise 6.1. Set the alignment of the text of the labels, and the font of the text of the labels as shown in Figure 6.2. More specifically:

❏ Make the font size of **Class No, Day** and **Time** larger. You may also need to increase the size of the controls in order to accommodate the text of the labels and the data in the larger size.

❏ Click on each control in turn and check its alignment. Left align controls for all fields except **Class No** which should be right aligned.

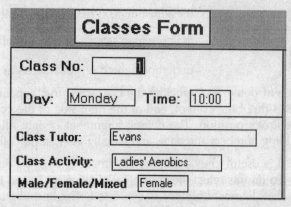

Figure 6.2 Setting alignment and fonts on forms.

exercise 3 *borders, lines alignment and fonts on reports*

The last two exercises have involved forms. In this exercise you are required to apply borders, lines, alignment and fonts to a report.

Create a new report **Classes4** based on the **Classes** report created in Exercise 8 Session 4. Format the report so that it looks like Figure 6.3. View the report on screen using Print Preview and, Save the report as **Classes4**. More specifically:

❏ In the Report Header insert two controls and type in the text shown in Figure 6.3. Move the controls to centre them. Centre align the text in the controls. Format the text to an appropriately large size and bold. Insert a box around the text. Use *Layout–Send to Back* or *Format–Send to Back* to re-display the text.

❏ In the Detail band, first add the controls using the **Field List.** Click on the Field List window title bar to select all fields, and then drag one of the fields to where you want the fields to start within he Detail Band. Fields and their field names will be added to the Detail Band.

❏ Edit the field names so that they match those shown in Figure 6.3

❏ Move the controls to match the arrangement in Figure 6.3.

❏ Format the text in the controls to a slightly larger size and size the controls appropriately.

❏ To align a group of controls select the group and apply *View–Align–Left/Right* or *Format–Align–Left/Right.* Most of these controls are Left aligned with respect to each other.

❏ Next examine the alignment of text within the controls. Ensure that all controls are left aligned, and, in particular, remember to left align **Time.**

❏ Insert a box around the **Class No** controls. Insert a further box to enclose all text in the Detail band.

❏ In the Page Header band type in 'Classes'. Format this text and place a line underneath it.

❏ At the top of the page footer band insert a line.

❏ Examine the report in Print Preview, noting especially that no text in truncated by too small controls.

❏ Make any necessary adjustments, Print Preview again, and save the report as **Classes4.**

Report Header

Chelmer Leisure and Recreation Centre
List of Classes

Page Header

Classes

Detail

Class No: | Class No

Day: | Class Day | Time: | Class Time

Tutor: | Class Tutor | Activity: | Class Activity

Male/Female/Mi

Page Footer

Report Footer

This is the end of the class list

Chelmer Leisure and Recreation Centre
List of Classes

Classes

| Class No: | 1 |

Day:	Monday	Time:	10:00
Tutor	Evans	Activity:	Ladies' Aerobics
			Female

| Class No: | 2 |

Day:	Monday	Time:	11:00
Tutor	Franks	Activity:	Weight Training
			Male

activity 5 setting dimensions, colours and borders

You can make a control look 3–dimensional, add colour or set borders to different widths, to make reports and forms look more exciting. Remember that since most printers do not print colours, colours are most likely to be useful for on-screen forms and do not normally need to be set for reports. Equally, three dimensional controls are particularly useful on forms, where they may be used to highlight labels or to mark out a button.

Dimensions, colours and borders can be set using the Palette, thus:

❑ choose *View–Palette* or select the **Palette** button.

❑ the following dialog box is displayed:

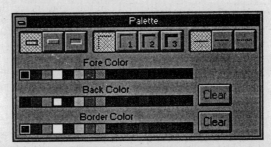

An alternative way to set these properties is through the **Property Sheet** window. Generally, it is easier to use the Palette so we shall restrict ourselves to its use here.

Dimensions

Dimensions can be set as one of three types: Normal, Raised and Sunken using the 3 buttons at the top left of the palette window. Normal is the default for most controls.

Notes

1. When you select Raised or Sunken, the control uses the same colours as buttons on the toolbar and command buttons. These colours are set by the Control Panel program. It is only possible to change the text colour.

2. When a control is shown as Raised or Sunken, changing the border has no effect.

Colours

A control can have separate colours for text, fill and border. To set a colour:

1. Select the control

2. Click on the appropriate colours in the Text, Fill and Border rows of the Palette

3. Use the Clear check box to clear earlier settings. This makes the control transparent so that the control shows whatever controls are behind it.

Note: Experiment with different colours until you have chosen a colour combination that is legible and draws attention to appropriate parts of the screen.

Borders

All controls have adjustable borders. Some controls, such as the labels for check boxes, option buttons and text boxes have as a default not to display any border. Other controls such as option groups, list boxes, and combo boxes, have as a default to display a thin black border.

1. To select whether a border appears around a control, clear or select the **Clear** button to the right of the colours for Border in the **Palette** window.

2. To select the border's width use the buttons at the bottom of the **Palette** window. In Access 2 use the buttons at the top of the window.

3. To set the border colour, use the Border colour row in the **Palette** window

exercise 4 *setting dimensions and borders*

Open the form **Classes3** and use the form to experiment with setting dimensions colours and borders. For example, try:

❒ Setting all of the field labels as Raised.

❒ Setting the Form Header as sunken

❒ Select the line in the Detail band and make it wider

❒ Apply some colours to different parts of the screen to make it look interesting.

activity 6 *setting the default properties of a control*

In earlier activities within this session we have set the properties of controls after we have added them to the form. It is also possible to set defaults for controls, which then apply to all of the controls of that type that you add to the current form or report. If you want to use a set of default control properties for multiple forms or reports, you can create templates that store default settings, and then use these templates whenever you create forms and reports.

Note: Whilst it is useful to note that it is possible to modify the default settings for a number of different types of controls, we do not recommend that you attempt this until you are sure that you understand which settings you are changing. There is immense potential for getting into an irretrievable muddle once you start to modify default settings. Proceed with caution!

To set property defaults for a form or report you follow similar steps to those for property setting (see Sessions 3 and 4):

1. Click the tool in the toolbox, whilst the Property Sheet window is displayed. Use *View–Properties* to display the Property sheet.

2. The Property Sheet window changes to show only the properties that you can set as the default for controls of the selected type e.g. text, date or number.

3. The title bar changes to Default and the name of the object. Most of the properties listed you should recognise from earlier Activities when you were setting the properties of the individual controls.

4. Change the properties in the Property Sheet window as you would change the properties for specific parts of forms or reports.

5. Any control of that type that you subsequently add to the form or report uses the new settings you have made for the control.

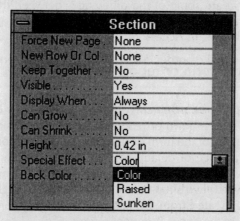

Figure 6.3 The Default Properties Box for a section in a form, showing the Special Effect property drop down list box.

Default text box

Clicking on the Text box button in the Toolbox will display the Default Text Box window.

Most of the property setting in the Property Sheet window will be familiar, but there are five new properties which are specific to default control setting.

These are:

Auto Label   Causes labels to appear with, for example, text boxes.

Add colon   Causes colons to appear at the end of labels

Label X and Label Y   Set the relative distance from the upper left hand corner of the selected control.

Label Align   Sets the position of the text in the label

exercise 6 *examining the default properties of a control*

Note: In order that there is less danger of you modifying the default settings in ways in which you did not intend and thereby finding it difficult to follow later activities in this book, this exercise concentrates on examining the existing default settings rather than modifying them. **Note that adjustments to default settings will apply thereafter until they are again changed.**

❑ Open any form or report.

❑ Select a section control by clicking on it. Click on the label button in the Toolbox. Open the **Property sheet** window. Examine the default properties for this tool.

❑ In a similar way, examine the **Property sheet** window for a text box control

❑ Again, similarly, examine the **Property sheet** window for a box or a line.

❑ What are some of the differences between the defaults that are set for these different types of controls?

activity 7 creating a form or report template

A template for producing reports or forms can be used in order to maintain a house style in form or report design, or, more simply, to avoid having to format all sections of the form or report on each occasion. For example you may choose to set a range of default settings for specific parts of a form. Alternatively, you may have an earlier version of a report design which you need to upgrade and from which two similar, but different reports might be created. A report template can be created from the first report, and that template used as the basis for the design of the two subsequent reports.

A template determines the default settings for form, report, section and control properties, section sizes and whether the form or report includes headers and footers.

To create a template:

1. Create a form or report on which the settings for controls are as you want them to be.

2. Display the form or report header and footer and page header and footer, if you want these to be included in the default

3. Set section sizes to determine their default size, if you want these included

4. Save this form or report

5. To use the form or report as a template, choose *View–Options*

6. In the **Category List** box, select **Form & Report Design**

7. After Form Template or Report Template in the bottom of the dialog box, enter the name of the form or report you want to use as a template

8. Select **OK.**

When you next create a new blank report the selected report or form will be used as a template.

Note: The default form template and report template are **Normal.**

exercise 7 *creating and using a report template*

In this Exercise we use a report that you have previously created to define the properties of a template. The most obvious properties that will be set are the section sizes (e.g. the size of the Page Header) and the presence or absence of various Headers and Footers. Other section and control properties have also been set.

First create a report template by:

❏ Opening the report **Classes4.**

❏ Display the report header and footer, and page header and footer, to include these in the default.

❏ Save this report as **Classes4.**

Next to use the report as a template:

❏ Choose *View–Options*

❏ In the **Category List** box, select **Form & Report Design.**

❏ After **Report Template** in the bottom of the dialog box, enter the name of the report **Classes4.**

❏ Select **OK,** and this will be used as the default report template.

❏ Now, create a new blank report.

❏ Note that the report has the same headers and footers and section sizes as the template.

activity 8 *adding graphs to reports and forms*

Analysis of the data in a database can often be effectively performed, and subsequently displayed with the aid of a graph. For example, it might be useful to examine the membership of the Leisure Centre by Membership Category or to look at the distribution of bookings and to display this data as a graph.

Graphs can be created by using Microsoft Graph which is a component of both Access and Word. Here we introduce a few exercises that make use of Graph in order to demonstrate how Graph can be used to insert Graphs into a report or form. These exercises first take you step-by-step through the creation of a simple graph, and then demonstrate how that graph can be inserted in a report or form. If you require more detailed help on the use of Graph, consider using Help in Access or work through the relevant exercise in *S J Coles and J E Rowley Word for Windows: An Action Learning Guide, DP Publications, 1993.*

Graphs are often most appropriate in reports where some summary data can be displayed pictorially. As such they will often be included in the footer for a report.

Graphs can also be added to forms. We start to demonstrate the process by creating a graph in a simple form, which we could display on the screen as a quick summary which displays the Prices for the various different membership categories. This is about the only sensible graph that we can create relating to the data in the Chelmer database which does not involve the use of a query. Later we experiment with some simple graphs that make use of queries to show counts of the occurrences of specific field values, for example to show the bookings by the room, hall or court that has been booked. We also experiment with moving graphs between forms using the clipboard.

Adding a graph to a form

Graphs can be used on forms to display data on screen at a glance. The simplest use of graphs is where the data comes from the tables, but the same data is shown on each screen. This is the type of graph that we shall explore here.

You may also create a graph that changes with each record. For example a simple graph may show the inventory information for one product. When another product is displayed another graph will be displayed. In this case it is likely that basic information about the product, such as its name and supplier may be called from one table, and data concerning inventory levels may be drawn from another table which stored order records. Such a graph involves the use of multiple tables, such as are dealt with in more detail in Session 7.

To use a graph to display summary data from a table:

❒ Insert a heading in the Form Header

❒ Prepare to insert a graph in the Detail band by ensuring that it is open.

❒ If necessary, display the Toolbox. Click on the Graph tool in the Toolbox.

❒ Click in the Detail band.

❒ When you release the mouse button, Access presents a series of dialog boxes to help you define your graph.

❒ Go through the dialog boxes making appropriate selections for fields to chart and label for the graph, and inserting a graph title.

❒ To complete the graph, choose the **Design** button.

❒ Access now inserts a control in the Detail band which accommodates the graph.

❒ Save and close the form. The graph is saved as part of the form

exercise 8 adding a graph to a form

In this exercise we wish to add a graph to Detail band in a form.

❒ First open a new form in **Design** view. Choose to use the table Membership Category.

❒ Insert the following heading in the Form Header:

❒ Prepare to insert a graph in the Detail band by ensuring that it is open.

❒ If necessary display the Toolbox. Click on the Graph tool in the Toolbox.

☐ Click on the Detail band.

☐ When you release the mouse button, Access presents a series of dialog boxes to help you define your graph.

☐ Select a data source for your graph i.e. the table **Membership Category.**

☐ Choose a graph type. This occurs later in Access 2.

☐ Select **Category Type** and **Membership Fee** as the fields to be graphed.

☐ When asked 'Link the graph to the report?', choose No. In Access 2 select a graph type.

☐ Give your graph a title e.g. Membership Fees.

☐ To complete the graph, choose the **Design Finish** button.

☐ Access now inserts a control for the graph in the Detail band.

☐ To see the graph on the form click on the Datasheet button.

☐ Save the form as **MemCatGraph** and close the form. The graph is saved as part of the form

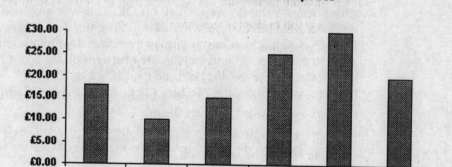

Editing a graph

Graphs can be edited in order to change the data that is displayed, or the way in which it is displayed. For example in the Graph displayed above. the column labels are not all displayed. Graph is a powerful graph creation tool which allows you a wide range of different options for creating and designing effective graphs. In the exercise below we demonstrate how to use Graph to make a few simple alterations to a graph.

To edit a graph:

1. In **Design** view, double click on the graph.

2. Access starts Graph and displays the graph in the **Graph** application window.

3. Make any changes that you require.

4. Choose **File–Exit and Return to Microsoft Access.**

5. When **Graph** prompts you to update your graph in Access, choose **Yes.**

6. Save and close the form or report. The graph is saved as part of the form or report

exercise 9 *editing a graph*

This exercise edits the form that you created in Exercise 6.8. We experiment with some basic editing techniques in order to demonstrate the principles. More specifically, we shall format the graph title, and tick mark labels, and place a border around the graph.

❑ Open the form **MemCatGraph** in **Design** view and double click on the chart.

Access 1

❑ Choose a different type of chart, by selecting *Gallery–Bar,* and selecting type 3 of the bar chart options available.

❑ Remove the gridlines by choosing *Chart–Gridlines*–**Value(Y) Axis– Major Gridlines**. Click on the appropriate check box to remove the major gridlines.

❑ Insert an axis label for the horizontal axis (y axis here), by choosing *Chart–Titles*–**Value(Y) Axis**. Click on **OK**. This will give you a small area demarked by boxes into which you can enter text. Enter Membership Price(£). Next click on this to display the text that you have entered. Double click on this label again to call the **Area Patterns** dialog box. Choose a larger font size and make the text bold and italic. Click on **OK**.

❑ Click on the Title, so that white boxes appear which indicate that it is selected. Press Delete to delete the title.

❑ Click on the vertical axis to select the tick mark labels and choose *Format–Text.* This displays the Axis Text dialog box Make the font size larger and choose bold and italic.

To remove the dollar signs on the y axis it is necessary to re-format the data using the Datasheet in Graph. Click on the Datasheet (the other window displayed in Graph in addition to the Chart window).

Click on the black bar at the top of the column 2. Choose *Format–Number,* and the **Number** dialog box will be opened. Choose 0.00 as a format. Click back on the Chart window and you should see the labels changed. Use *Format–Text* as you did with the other axis to format and size the labels appropriately.

❑ Choose *File–Exit and Return to Microsoft Access.*

Access 2

❑ Choose a different type of chart, by selecting *Format–Chart* type and selecting Bar or by clicking on down arrow of Chart Type Button.

❑ Add or remove gridlines by clicking on the Horizontal or Vertical Gridline buttons in the toolbar or using *Insert–Gridlines.* Further gridline formatting may be achieved by selecting a gridline and using *Format–Selected Gridlines.*

❑ Insert an axis label as described in Access 1 above. To edit label click on it and choose *Format–Selected Axis Title* and alter font and typeface as described above.

❑ Click on Title to select it and press Delete to remove it.

❑ Click on the vertical axis, choose *Format–Selected Axis.* Make axis text larger and bold italic.

❑ Choose *File–Exit & Return to Form.*

Access 1 & 2

❑ If necessary size the control by selecting it and dragging its border in order to display the edited graph.

❑ Save the form as **MemCatGraph.** Close the form.

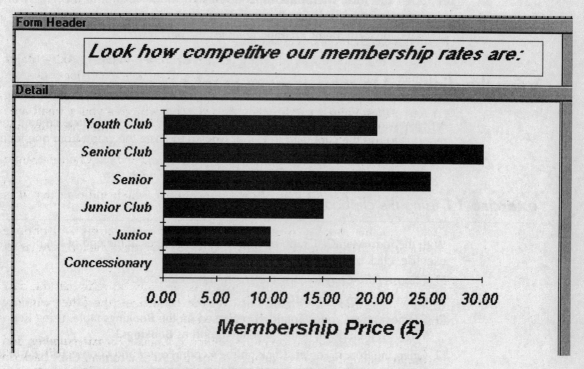

Demonstrating that graphs are linked to the database

The graphs that you create in Access and that use data in the database are updated when you update the data in the database. So for example, the graph that we have just created should be automatically updated if we change the values in the **Membership Category** table.

---

exercise 10 *testing links between the database and associated graphs*

In this exercise we wish to demonstrate how the graph changes to display new data in the **Membership Category** table. Suppose that we change the fees:

☐ Open the **Membership Category** table in datasheet view

☐ Edit the values in the **Membership Fee** column to:

Category No	Membership Fee
1	£30.00
2	£35.00
3	£15.00
4	£20.00
5	£23.00
6	£25.00

☐ Close **Membership Category.**

☐ Open the form **MemCatGraph** in Design mode. Examine the graph and check that it is displaying the new data.

☐ Leave the form **MemCatGraph** open for the next exercise

using the clipboard to copy or move graphs

An easy way to insert a graph in a from or a report, once you have created the report is to use the clipboard to Cut or Copy and Paste the graph from one location to a second location.

exercise 11 *using the clipboard to copy a graph*

With the form MemCatGraph open in Design mode as at the end of the previous exercise, click on the graph to select it.

☐ Choose *Edit–Copy* to copy the graph to the clipboard

☐ Close the form **MemCatGraph**

☐ Create a new Groups/Totals report based on the **Bookings** table, using Report Wizards. Include all fields. Save the report as **Bookings3.**

☐ Open the Report Footer. Click on the Report Footer and choose *Edit–Paste* to insert the graph into this report from the clipboard.

☐ The graph should now be inserted in the report.

adding a graph to a report, with the aid of a query

The basic approach to creating a graph for a report is the same as that for creating a graph in a form. The above exercise demonstrates how to copy a graph into a report footer, but this is not a very useful report to have in the Report Footer of a report which lists bookings. A more useful graph for such a report would display bookings according to some category such as Room, hall or court, or the category of membership. In order to create such a graph it is first necessary to create a query. Why?

If you think about the stages that you went through to create a graph in Exercise 8 you will remember that you needed to specify the two fields that were to be displayed on the graph. Suppose we wish to display the number of bookings for each room, hall or court. We need to display the values in the **Room/Hall/Court** field against the number of bookings for each of these. In order to do this we need a field called, say, CountofBookings. To create this field we need a query. Exercise 12 demonstrates how we might approach this.

Another interesting graph that we might add to a report which lists bookings is one which displays bookings by Category Type i.e. How many bookings are made by each category of member. The creation of this graph would be more complex than the graph which we create below. Why? Because here we need to show CountofBookings by Category Type This would involve creating a query which uses more than one table, and then basing the graph on that query. Which tables would you need to use in the query? Queries which use more than one table are introduced in session 7.

First it is useful to record the steps for adding a graph to a report.

To add a graph to a report footer:

1. Make 2 to 3 inches (5 to 8 cm) of space in the Report Footer section.
2. Click on the Graph tool in the Toolbox.
3. In the grey area below the Report Footer section, draw a control that is about 2in(5cm) deep and 6 in (15 cm) wide. Drag the Toolbox out of the way if necessary.
4. When you release the mouse button, Access presents a series of dialog boxes to help you define your graph.
5. Go through the dialog boxes making appropriate selections for fields to chart and label for the graph, and inserting a graph title.
6. To complete the graph, choose the **Design** or **Finish** button.
7. Access now inserts a control in the Report Footer for the graph an resizes the footer to make room for the new control.
8. To view the graph on the report, choose *File–Print Preview* and move to the last page of the report.
9. When you have finished looking at the graph choose **Cancel.**
10. Save and close the report. The graph is saved as part of the report.

The same principles apply for adding a graph to any other part of the report, such as the Report Header.

exercise 12 *adding a graph to a report using a query*

In this exercise we wish to add a graph to the report footer in the report **Bookings3**. First we need to create a query to use as the basis for the graph (you may find it useful to review Exercises 2.9–2.11):

❏ Create a new query using the **Bookings** table.

❏ Add the fields **Booking No** and **Room/Hall/Court**.

❑ Click on the **Sigma** button to display the **Total:** row.

❑ In the **Total** cell for the Booking No field insert Count

❑ In the **Total** cell for the Room/Hall/Court field insert **Group By** and in the **Sort** row insert **Ascending.**

❑ Display the dynaset and check that the query counts booking in categories as you would expect it to.

❑ Save the query as **Bookings by Hall**

Field:	Room/Hall/Court ⬩	Booking No	
Total:	Group By	Count	
Sort:	Ascending		
Show:	☒	☒	
Criteria:			
or:			

CountOfBooking	Room/Hall/Court
2	Court 1
1	Court 2
1	Court 3
8	Fitness Suite
1	Sports hall 1
9	Sports hall 2

Now we want to use this query to create a graph:

❑ Open the **Bookings3** report.

❑ To remove the existing graph, click on it and press **Delete.**

❑ Display the Toolbox, and click on the Graph tool. Click in the Report Footer.

❑ Access takes you through the creation of a graph using Graph Wizards.

❑ Choose **Bookings by Hall** as the data source for your graph.

❑ Choose a graph type.

❑ Select both fields to be displayed on the graph.

❑ When asked 'Link the graph to the report?', choose No.

❑ Give your graph a title e.g. Bookings by Room/Hall/Court

❑ To complete the graph, choose the **Design** or **Finish** button.

❑ Access now inserts a control in the Report Footer for the graph an resizes the footer to make room for the new control.

❑ To view the graph on the report, choose *File–Print Preview* and move to the last page of the report.

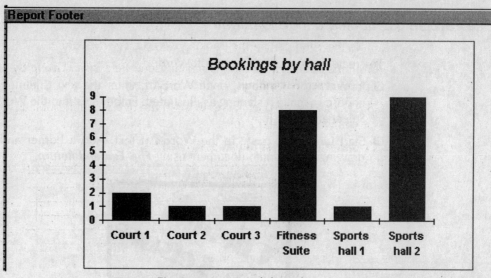

Figure 6.4 : A graph based on the Query Bookings by Hall

Note: If you made the control too small to display a graph effectively, you can not size the Graph in Print Preview You need to re-size the control that contains the graph in Design view, and to re-size the graph in Graph.

❏ When you have finished looking at the graph in Print Preview choose **Cancel** to move back into Design view.

❏ Double Click on the graph to take it into Graph and edit it as you choose. The graph in Figure 6.4 has been sized so that the tick mark labels display effectively, and the title has been formatted. Choose *File–Exit and Return to Microsoft Access* when you have finished editing.

❏ Save the report as **Bookings3** and close it. The graph is saved as part of the report.

activity 7 adding pictures and objects to forms and reports

We have just experimented with adding graphs to forms and reports. These are one type of object that can be added to forms and reports. You can also insert a picture from Windows version 3.1 Paintbrush, a worksheet object from Microsoft Excel, or any object from an application that supports what is known as object linking and embedding (OLE).

Here we briefly explore inserting a picture into a form or report. A picture can be created in Microsoft Draw (part of Microsoft Word), or with Windows Paintbrush. We can use Microsoft Draw to create a picture and insert this picture both into a report and into a form. If a field on a form, for instance, uses an OLE object data type it is possible to display that object on the form. For example, in Membership we might have a field which accommodates a photograph of the member. This could be displayed on a form or printed on a report. Another application of a picture might be to insert a logo into the Form Header on a form and the Report Header on a report. Since typically the same logo may be used on all forms and reports used by one organisation, in the exercises below we first create the logo for Chelmer Leisure and Recreation Centre, and then add it first to a form and then to a report.

exercise 13 *adding a logo to a form*

To create the logo using Microsoft Word:

❑ In Word for Windows, open WordArt. Enter the text Chelmer Leisure and choose to make it slanting as illustrated. Embed this into the Word document. Select and copy it.

❑ Start Draw and paste in the Word Art text. Add a border and a stickman drawing. Embed into document using ***File–Exit and Return.***

❑ Select the logo and copy it to the clipboard.

To add the logo to the form:

- Open the form Membership in Design view.
- Click on the Form Header section.
- Choose Edit–Paste, size the Header section and position the logo.

❑ Save the form. Close the form.

Integrative exercises

exercise 14 *creating a graph for the categories report*

The **Categories** report was created in Report Wizards as a Groups/Totals report. It shows members grouped in categories. It might be interesting to create a simple graph which counted the members in each category and displayed the number of members in each category. It would be even better if the category labels were not shown as **Category No,** but as **Category Type,** but this would involve the use of a query which used multiple tables, but these are not introduced until Session 7. To create this graph:

First create an appropriate query to count members by **Category No.** You will have created such a query in Exercise 2.11 but probably did not save the query. Revisit Exercise 2.11, to discover how to create a query which shows **Category No** and **CountofSurname.** Save this query as **Categories.**

To create a graph in the report **Categories:**

❑ Open the report **Categories**

❒ Go through the steps necessary to create a graph in the Report Footer, choosing the query **Categories** as the data source.

❒ Edit the graph as appropriate.

exercise 15 *adding a logo to reports*

In order to start to create some kind of house style to our reports, we would like to add the Chelmer Leisure logo to some of the reports generated form the Membership table. The easiest way to do this is to copy and paste the logo that we created in Exercise 13 into the clipboard, and then to paste the logo into the Report Header of the report.

❒ Open the form **Membership.**

❒ Click on the Chelmer Leisure logo to select it. Choose *File–Copy.*

❒ Close the form.

❒ Open the report **Members**. Click on the Report Header, and Choose *Edit–Paste.* The logo should appear in the Report Header. Size the section and position the logo.

❒ Repeat this operation for the other reports you have created.

objectives

This session introduces queries which use more than one table. Tables are linked by their relationships and through these links can act as if they are one large table. Subforms, subreports and action queries will be introduced. At the end of this session you should be able to

☐ add and delete tables from a query

☐ create queries using multiple tables

☐ use Subforms in forms and Subreports in reports

☐ perform an action query

In Session 1 you saw how to set up relationships between tables yet these relationships have not yet been used. The intervening sessions have introduced tables, queries, forms, and reports. In the interests of simplicity these are based on one table or a query generated from one table. In this session using more than one table will be explored. Queries can use more than one table and these queries can produce forms or reports.

Through constructing queries using more than one table you should appreciate how versatile a relational database is. By keeping data in a series of linked but separate tables the need to duplicate data is reduced and it is simpler to update data. To illustrate this point, if the **Membership** table contained a Fee field, if the fee changed then every record would need amending rather than just the records in the **Membership Category** table.

Subforms and subreports are another way of making use of the links between tables. An example of this would be keeping academic information about students. A student may study several modules and for each one a performance record is kept. The details about the student, for example, Student No, Title, Surname, Forenames, Date of Birth, Date Enrolled, Personal Tutor could be kept in a Student table. The module results for all students could be kept in a Results table, with fields Student No, Module No, Coursework Grade, Exam Grade, Overall Grade, Date Completed module. The tables Student and Results would be linked through the Student No.

A link between the Student and Results tables enables a main/subform to be designed for entering module results. By designing a form based on the Student table and another form based on the Results table the two forms can be combined into one known as a main/subform. This form would display the student details as heading information and results records for that student. A report can similarly be constructed. A Student report would be the main part of the main/subreport and a Results report would be the 'sub' part of the main/subreport.

Usually queries are passive in nature that is they do not change any of the data, they only retrieve it in response to criteria. However special queries known as action queries can be designed to change the data. An example of this could be a bank amending its customer credit limits. The bank wishes amend the credit limit of customers whose present limit is £200 or less and who have been with the bank for six months or more. First a query which selects the appropriate customer records would be constructed. By converting this search query to an action query the values in the Credit Limit field, for each selected record, would be updated with the new credit limit.

activity 1 multiple tables in a query

When you use more than one table in a query there should be links between those chosen for the query. This is a good opportunity to review the relationships between the tables in the Chelmer Leisure and Recreation Centre database. The **Membership** table is linked to the **Bookings** table through **Membership No**. The **Membership Category** table is linked to the **Membership** table through the **Category No.** The **Bookings** table is linked to the **Membership** table through the **Membership No.** The **Bookings** table is linked to the **Classes** table through **Class No. Tutors** table is linked to **Classes** table through **Surname.**

If tables are added to a query and there is no relationship defined between them then Access will try to link them and this could be a time-consuming and unproductive process.

Joins between tables

Before you can use joins between tables, you must know the contents of the fields of the tables and which fields are related by common values. Assigning identical names to fields in different tables that contain related data is a common practice. This has been adhered to in the Chelmer Leisure and Recreation Centre database, for example, **Membership No** which is the link between the **Membership** and **Bookings** tables. There is an exception which is **Class Tutor** (**Classes** table) and **Surname** (**Tutors** table), which could be remedied by using **Tutor No** as a field in both tables.

Knowing the contents of your tables will help when you need to add tables to a query so that you add the tables containing the data you wish to access and also any additional tables which are necessary to create links between the tables. This is discussed in more detail at the beginning of each multiple table query used in this activity.

Joins are indicated in Access query designs by lines between field names of different tables as illustrated in Figure 7.1.

Access allows different types of joins between tables, but only one type, the most common, will be considered here. This type of join is called an equi-join and this has already been created when the relationships were defined. Equi-joins display all the records in one table that have corresponding records in another table. This correspondence is determined by identical values in the fields that join the tables. In the case of the Chelmer Leisure and Recreation Centre database all joins are based on a unique primary key field in one table and a field in the other table in a one-to-many relationship (see Activity 23 Session 1).

Adding tables

When creating a query this is simply a matter of selecting more than one table from the **Add Table** dialog box. Tables are shown in the Query window with lines between them indicating the relationships. If you omit a table then choose *Query-Add Table* or click on the **Add Table** button to display the **Add Table** dialog box again.

Deleting tables

This a simply a matter of clicking on the title bar of the particular table and pressing the Delete key. However, check that the table was not providing an indirect link between two tables and also make any amendments to the query.

exercise 1 *adding tables to the query window*

In this exercise all the tables in the Chelmer Leisure and Recreation Centre are added to a query.

❐ Starting at the Database Window, click on the **Query** button and click on **New**. Click on **New Query** (Access 2).

❐ From the **Add Table** dialog box add all the tables, these are **Membership, Membership Category, Bookings, Classes** and (if you have created it) **Tutors**.

❐ By rearranging the tables, your query window will appear as illustrated following. If there are no lines (indicating the relationships) or some missing, abandon the query and check the relationships using *Edit-Relationships*. Refer to Activity 23 Session 1.

Note that Access 2 may display a link between **Surname** in the **Membership** table and Surname in the **Tutors** table. This illustrates that the significance of field names should be considered when designing a table. However, the link can be removed by clicking on it to select it and pressing the Delete key.

❐ Delete the **Tutors** and the **Membership Category** tables. Why is it dangerous to next delete the **Bookings** table?

❐ Close the query without saving it.

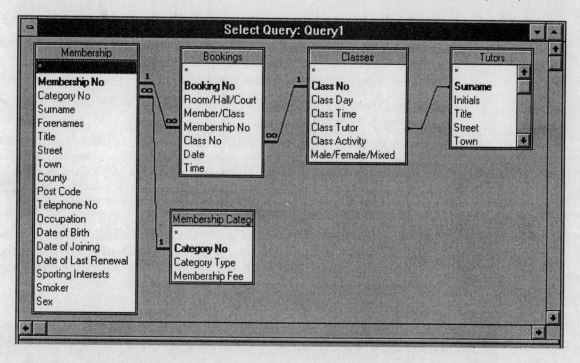

Figure 7.1 Joins between tables in the Query Window

Using multiple tables

This section will comprise of a series of exercises in which questions are asked of the database and queries containing multiple tables are devised in order to answer the question posed.

exercise 2

Q. *How much membership fee money has been collected in the last six months?*

A. First decide which tables are needed. The data needed is the members who renewed their membership in the last six months, their membership category and the amount of the fee. This data can be found in the **Membership** table and the **Membership Category** table. Is there a link between these two tables? Yes, between **Category No** (primary key **Classes** table) and **Category No** (**Membership** table), so only these two tables will be required.

Creating the query

❏ From the Database Window click on the **Query** button and click on **New**.

❏ From the **Add Table** dialog box select the **Membership** table and the **Membership Category** table. These two tables should be shown in the query window with a link between the fields **Category No.**

❏ Add the fields **Membership No** and **Membership Fee** to the query.

❏ Create a calculated field which works out the length of time between the date of last renewal and today's date. In the first field cell enter the expression

Rejoin: DateDiff("d",[Date of Last Renewal],Date())

This calculates the number of days from the date of the last renewal to today. Run this query to see the result.

❏ Return to the query design. Add the criteria <182 to the calculated field **Rejoin** (you may need to check your records to see if this query will work) to find those with renewal dates less than six months old. Run this query to check the dynaset and then return to design mode.

❏ Click on the **Sigma** button for totals.

❏ In the **Rejoin** field select **Where** in the total cell and hide this field. In the **Membership No** field select **Count** and in the **Membership Fee** field select **Sum**. Run the query. The result should be the numbers of members who rejoined in the last six months and the total of fees paid.

❏ Save the query as **Recent fees paid.**

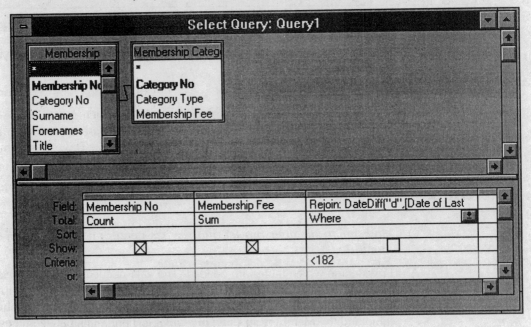

Creating the report

❏ From the Database Window click on the **Report** button and click on **New**.

❏ In the **New Report** dialog box select the query **Recent fees paid** and use **ReportWizards** to design a report similar to the one below. Save the report as **Recent fees paid.**

```
┌─────────────────────────────────────────────┐
│  ═══════════════════════════════════════     │
│                                               │
│  Fees paid in last six months                 │
│                                               │
│  15-May-94                                     │
│  ═══════════════════════════════════════      │
│                                               │
│  Total Of Members joining:              5     │
│                                               │
│       Total of Fees paid:          £91.00     │
│                                               │
└─────────────────────────────────────────────┘
```

exercise 3

Q. *What class activities are being held in the fitness suite?*

A. The tables that are needed to answer this question are the **Bookings** table and the **Classes** table. There is a direct link between these tables through **Class No.**

Creating the query

❑ From the Database Window click on the **Query** button and click on **New** (and **New Query**).

❑ From the **Add Table** dialog box select the **Classes** table and the **Bookings** table. These two tables should be shown in the query window with a link between them.

❑ Add the fields **Member/Class, Room/Hall/Court, Class Day, Class Time** and **Class Activity** to the query.

❑ In the **Member/Class** column set the criterion to No to select only classes and hide this field.

❑ In **Room/Hall/Court** put "Fitness Suite" in the criteria row and hide this field. Run the query.

❑ Save this query as **Activities in Fitness Suite.**

Creating the report

❑ From the Database Window click on the **Report** button and click on **New.**

❑ In the **New Report** dialog box select the query **Activities in Fitness Suite** and use **ReportWizards** to design report similar to the one illustrated. Save the report as **Activities in Fitness Suite.**

Activities in Fitness suite

Member/Class	Class Day	Class Time	Class Activity
class	Monday	10:00	Ladies' Aerobics
class	Monday	11:00	Weight Training
class	Tuesday	10:00	Men's Multi-gym
class	Tuesday	14:00	Ladies' Multi-gym
class	Tuesday	19:00	Family Multi-gym
class	Wednesday	10:00	Ladies' Aerobics
class	Thursday	15:00	Multi-gym
class	Friday	14:00	Men's Multi-gym

exercise 4

Q. *Which members are attending which classes?*

A. Our database is unable to answer this question. Why? The data needed has not been recorded. The database could be modified so that this data can be added. What would be the best way to go about this? One method could be to introduce an extra field, class, which is added to the **Membership** table. However, this leads to problems if the member attends more than one class or a class is cancelled. A better alternative is to create another table which keeps lists of members in classes. This table would be linked to both the **Membership** table and the **Classes** table. **Class List** would be a suitable name for this table.

Creating the *Class List* table

❑ From the Database Window click on the **Table** button and click on **New.**

❑ Create a table with two fields, **Class No** and **Membership No.** Make both fields numeric of type long integer. This is so that they are of a type which will correspond to the counter types used by the fields **Membership No** (**Membership** table) and **Class No** (**Classes** table) to which they will be related.

❑ Each record is unique, that is the entire record not a field on its own. There-fore the primary key must be both fields. To set both as the primary key select both before clicking on **Primary Key** button in the toolbar.

❑ Define two relationships as shown in the following tables. In both relation-ships click in the **Enforce Referential Integrity** check box. This will prevent a class or membership number being entered which does not exist in the **Classes** or **Membership** table, so a non-existent member cannot join a class nor can a member join a non-existent class.

Access 1

Primary Table	**Type**	**Related Table**
Classes	Many	Class List

Primary key fields		**Select matching fields**
Class No	=	Class No

Primary Table	**Type**	**Related Table**
Membership	Many	Class List

Primary key fields		**Select matching fields**
Membership No	=	Membership No

❐ Check Enforce Referential Integrity.

Access 2

❐ Click on Relationships button and click on Add Table button. Add the **Class List** table.

❐ Drag **Class No** from the **Classes** table to **Class No** in the **Class List** table. Check Enforce Referential Integrity.

❐ Drag **Membership No** from the **Membership** table to **Membership No** in the **Class List** table. Check Enforce Referential Integrity.

❐ Save the layout and close the Relationships box.

Access 1 & 2

Before a form can be created, first a query which links the members name to the class activity needs to be created. A form can be created from this query which lists the names of members in each class (this form will later become a sub-form in a main/sub form in the next activity):

❐ From the Database Window click on the **Query** button and click on **New** (and **New Query**).

❐ From the **Add Table** dialog box select the **Class List** table and the **Membership** table. These two tables should be shown in the query window with a link between them.

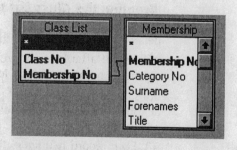

❐ Add the following fields to the query **Class No, Membership No** (it is important to add this field from the **Class List** table as this is the table receiving the data), **Forenames** and **Surname**. As there is no data in **Class List** running the query will produce an empty dynaset. Save the query as **Class Member List.** Close the query.

❑ From the Database Window click on the **Form** button and click on **New.** In the **New Form** dialog box select the **Class Member List** query just created and use the FormWizards to create a tabular form.

❑ Display this form in design view and display the properties window. Click on each control in turn, except for the **Membership No,** and set the **Locked** property to **Yes** and the **Enabled** property to **No.** This prevents data being entered into these controls and as this form is intended to be a sub-form then you will see that it will not be necessary to enter data into these controls. By setting the Enabled property to No this prevents the focus (the insertion point displayed in a control) going to these controls. Save the form as **Class Member List.**

❑ See the next activity for the creation of the Main/Sub form.

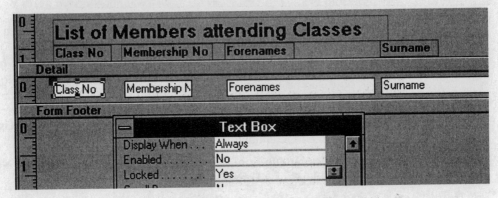

activity 2 creating and using main/subform forms

What is a sub-form? A main form is usually created from one of the primary tables in the database and a sub-form is a table which is related to it. This is best described by means of an example. Consider a wholesaler's database, where there is a table of customer names, addresses, etc. and there is a table of purchase transactions made by customers. A form which shows the customer's details plus a list of transactions made by that customer can be created using a Main/Subform.

The customer table creates the Main part of the form and that customers transactions comprise the subform part. This type of form is useful for all areas of transaction processing, such sales made by salesmen, or bookings made by members of a leisure centre.

A main/subform can be created using the Form Wizard or it can be created by inserting one form into another. The subform needs to be created first and if the main form does not exist then the Form Wizard can be used and the dialog boxes will guide you through the creation of the form and the addition of the subform.

If both main and subforms already exist then create a main/subform by inserting the subform into the main form:

1. Create both the main form and the subform separately. Ideally these should be linked through an existing relationship. The main form should be created in single column format and the subform in tabular format.

2. Open the main form in design view.

3. Choose the **Window** menu to display the Database Window (shortcut key F11). If necessary click on the **Form** button to show the list of forms.

4. Click and drag the name of the subform from the Database Window on to the main form.

exercise 5 *creating and using a main/subform*

This exercise creates a main/subform for the **Class List** table. This form shows the class details and lists members enrolled in the class in subform. This form can be used to book members into a particular class. Open the **Classes** form and use *File-Save As* to save the form as **Class Lists** which is a copy of the **Classes** form that can be modified. Display this form in design view and set the **Locked** property for all the controls to Yes. This is the reason for making a copy of the form. The original **Classes** form can be used to enter classes data but this new form cannot.

❑ Choose *Window-Tile* to display the **Class Lists** form window (in design view) and Database Window side by side.

❑ Click on **Class Member List** (the sub-form created in Exercise 4) and drag to **Class Lists** form.

❑ A sub-form box appears on the form. You may wish to reposition and resize this sub-form box.

❑ Run the form and it should appear similar to the one illustrated. Save the form. Try using the form to enter data. A class list can be created by entering the membership numbers of those members who are attending the class.

❑ So that a report can be generated later enter data for 3 class lists as follows:

Class No	Membership No
1	2
1	5
1	16
4	4
4	6
5	7
5	10
5	1

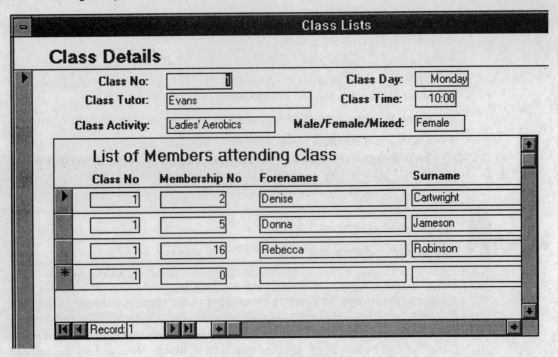

activity 3 creating and using main/subreport reports

Like forms, reports can include subreports. An example of such a report is one in which a customers details are shown in the main report and purchases made by that customer in the subreport. However, there is a difference, unlike the FormsWizards the ReportWizards does not offer the option of automatically creating a report that includes a subreport. To insert a subreport into a main report:

1. Create both the main report and the subreport separately as reports. Ideally these should be linked through an existing relationship.

2. Open the main report in design view. Use **Sorting and Grouping** to add a group footer, for example group by customer or group by company depending upon the nature of the subreport.

3. Choose the ***Window*** menu to display the Database Window (shortcut key F11). If necessary click on the **Report** button to show the list of reports.

4. Click and drag the subreport to the required section in the main report.

exercise 6 *adding a subreport to a report*

For this exercise check that you have a **Classes2** report created in Exercise 4.9. Open it and save it as **Classes List2.**

In this exercise a report of classes and the members enrolled on each of the classes will be created. This is done by adding a **Class Member List** subreport to the **Classes List2** main report.

❐ Save the form **Class Member List** as a report (see Activity 4 Session 5) with the same name. Open this new report in design mode.

❐ Reorder the fields so that **Class No** is last in the row. Set the **Visible** property for this field to **No** so that it does not print. Remove the label for **Class No.**

❐ Edit the header to read **List of members.**

❐ Use the palette to alter the colour of fill and borders. Preview the report to check your settings. Save the report and close it.

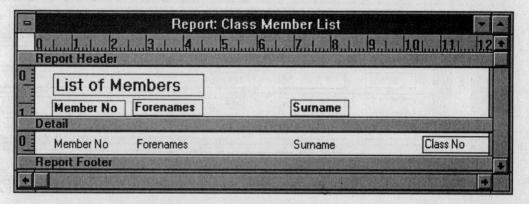

❐ Open the **Classes Lists2** report in design mode.

❐ Click on the **Sorting and Grouping** button and select **Class No** Ascending in the dialog box. Set the Group footer to Yes.

❐ Widen the group footer section to make room for the subreport.

❐ Open the *Window* menu and choose **Database:CHELMER** to display the Database Window.

❐ Click and drag the **Class Member List** report into the group footer section. You may need to re-arrange your windows so that you can readjust the position of the subreport.

❐ In the SubForm/SubReport properties window note that the link between the two reports is **Class No.**

❐ Set the **Can Shrink** and the **Can Grow** properties of the **Class No** Group footer section to Yes. (Click on the section header to select the section).

❐ Delete the **Class Member List** label. Preview the report.

❐ The report would look better if the field labels were in the **Class No** header. Use Sorting and Grouping and set class No group header to Yes. Cut and paste the headings from the Page header to the Class No header as illustrated.

❐ Preview, make final adjustments so that it looks similar to the following extract and save the report as **Classes List2** before printing it.

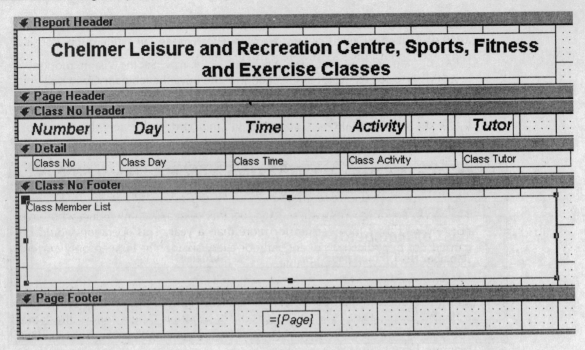

activity 4 designing action queries to modify data

Previously we have used queries to interrogate the database tables. Action queries can be used in a more powerful way to amend the tables. There are four types of action query, update queries, delete queries, append queries and make table queries.

An action query changes the data in your table or copies data from one table to another. Unlike the select queries we have already seen, an action query doesn't show the records it has retrieved for modification.

If you wish to see the result of the change made by an action query then will you need to either convert your action query to a select query or open the table (if you have created, appended to or deleted from it) to view the changes. The following activities explore the various action queries.

make table and delete query

These two action queries will be used together to deal with members who have not renewed their membership for more than a year. This operation would be carried out periodically, say annually or every six months to keep only current members in the **Membership** table.

Members who have not renewed their membership could simply be discarded or their information could be kept in a separate file for a further time period as historical information. Chelmer Leisure and Recreation Centre follow the latter course and make a table of old members before deleting them from the current membership table.

A make table query does just what it says and creates one table from another or others. Data is selected by means of a query to create the new table. A delete query deletes a group of records from one or more tables. The query you design will select the records that are to be deleted. When you run the query, Access retrieves the records you asked for and deletes them from the table.

In this activity we will create a table in which to store old member details before deleting all the members whose last renewal date was in 1992 or before. So that some records meet this criteria open the **Membership** table and add a couple of records where the **Date of Last Renewal** is before the end of 1992.

exercise 7 *archiving and removing out of date members*

❑ Start a new query. Add the **Membership** table to the query.

❑ Add all the fields from the table to the query by double-clicking on the table's title bar and dragging the highlighted area to the field cell.

❑ In the **Date of Last Renewal** column enter <1/1/93 into the criteria cell.

❑ You may wish to run the query to see which records are selected.

❑ To create the **Last renewed 92** table choose *Query-Make Table* or click on the *Make Table Query* button in the toolbar. Key in the name of the table **Last renewed 92**. This table will go into the current database so don't change the option setting. Leave the check boxes at their default values. Click on **OK.**

 ❑ Click on the **Run** button. A message box confirms the number of records that are being added to the new table. Click on the **OK** button to create the new table.

❐ Next change the query to a delete query using *Query-Delete* or click on the **Delete Query** button in the toolbar. In the **Date of Last Renewal** field the query is

Field:	Date of last renewal
Delete:	Where
Criteria:	<#01/01/93#

❐ Click on the **Run** button. A message box confirms the number of records that will be deleted. Click on **OK.**

❐ There is no need to save this query as it has performed its function.

❐ View the tables to see the effect of the make table and delete actions.

update query

An update query updates data in your tables. You choose the records and fields you want to update. When you run the query, Access retrieves the records you asked for (this is known as a dynaset) and makes the changes you specified. An example of an update query is increasing the credit limit of all customers that have credit limits of less than, say, £2000.

exercise 8

An example of an update query that Chelmer Leisure and Recreation Centre might use is when a member of staff changes. The update query can change the name of the **Class Tutor** in the **Classes** table.

❐ From the Database Window, click on the **Query** button and click on the **New** (and **New Query**) button.

❐ Add the table **Classes** to the query.

❐ Create a query with three fields, **Class No, Class Tutor** and **Class Activity.** In the criteria cell for **Class Tutor** put "Franks".

❐ Choose *Query-Update* and an **Update To:** row appears in the grid in the lower part of the query window.

❐ In the **Update To:** cell of the Class Tutor column type **"Knight".**

❐ An action query will change the data in your table. It is a good idea to check that your query will select the correct records before running the action query. You can do this by changing your action query into a selection query.

❐ First save the action query. Use *File-Save* and save it as **Update tutor.**

❐ To change to a select query use *Query-Select.* The lower grid changes to the select grid. Click on the **Datasheet** button on the toolbar to view the query's datasheet. The data that you see is the data that will be affected by your action query.

❏ To change back to the action query, first display the query design (click on Query Design button in the toolbar) and choose **Query-Update.**

❏ Click on the **Run** button on the toolbar. A message will appear telling you how many rows will be updated and giving you the opportunity to cancel. Click on **OK.**

❏ Close the query.

❏ Create a search query using the new tutors name as a criterion. Satisfy yourself that the action query has worked. Delete the action query. In the Database Window click on the query button highlight the action query and delete it by pressing the **Delete** key.

integrative exercises

exercise 9

Q. *What are the names and qualifications of the tutors taking class on 14/3/94?*

A. The tables needed are the **Bookings** table and the **Tutors** table. There is not a direct link between these tables so the **Classes** table must also be included in the query. Before creating this query review the data in the **Tutors** table and create records for the tutors employed by the centre.

Creating the query

❏ From the Database Window click on the **Query** button and click on **New** (and **New Query**).

❏ From the **Add Table** dialog box select the **Bookings, Tutors** and the **Classes** tables. These three tables should be shown in the query window with links between them.

❏ Add the fields **Date, Surname** and **Qualifications.**

❏ In the **Date** column set the criterion to #14/3/94# and hide this field. Run the query.

❏ Create a report based on this query.

exercise 10

Q. *How many members that attend Ladies' aerobics are non-smokers?*

A. The tables needed are the **Membership** table, **Class Lists** table and the **Classes** table.

Creating the query

☐ From the Database Window click on the **Query** button and click on **New** (and **New Query**).

☐ From the **Add Table** dialog box select the **Membership, Class Lists** and the **Classes** tables. These three tables should be shown in the query window with links between them.

☐ Add the fields **Surname, Smoker** and **Class Activity.**

☐ In the **Smoker** column set the criterion to No and hide this field.

☐ In the **Class Activity** column set the criterion to "Ladies' Aerobics" and hide this field.

☐ Click on the **Sigma** button, select Count for all the fields (only **Surname** will show). Run the query to discover the answer to the question

☐ Change the criterion for **Smoker** to find out the number of smokers attending Ladies' Aerobics.

exercise 11

Q. *What is the attendance profile of classes on Wednesdays?*

A. The **Classes** and **Class List** tables are required for this query. However, before constructing it use the **Class Lists** form to enter members into Wednesday's classes. A report containing a chart is a good method of presenting the answer to the query.

☐ Create a query as illustrated. Click on the **Sigma** button to display the Total row. Hide the **Class Day** field.

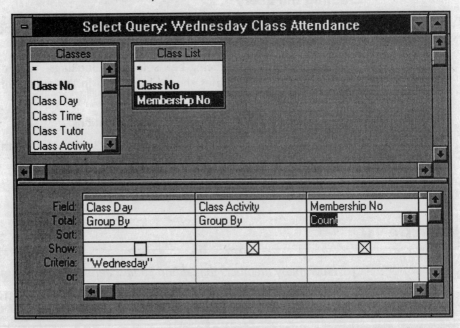

❑ Save the query as **Wednesday Class Attendance**.

❑ Create a Single column report based on this query using the ReportWizards. Add both fields, **Class Activity** and **CountofMembership** No to the report and sort on **Class Activity.**

❑ In the report footer create a chart, using the Chart tool. Base the chart on the **Wednesday Class Attendance** query. Select both fields for the chart. Reply No to 'Link the graph to the report?'.

❑ Save the report as **Wednesday Class Attendance,** and preview before printing.

Wednesday Class Attendance

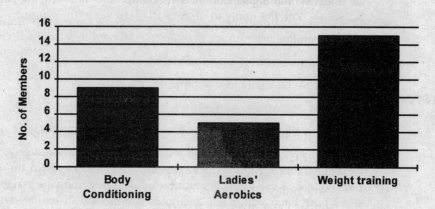

session eight
importing and exporting data

objectives

This session explores various issues associated with the importing and exporting of data from other sources. If you complete all of the activities in this session you will be able to:

❑ understand the distinction between importing data and attaching data

❑ import data from other standard database packages such as dBase III and IV and Paradox

❑ import spreadsheet data and text files

❑ export Access data into another Access database

❑ export Access data into a spreadsheet or a text file.

❑ use the clipboard to transfer data between applications.

Importing and exporting data is relatively straightforward with Access, especially between other standard packages and other packages in the Microsoft suite. Developers of the latest generation of database software have recognised that users now have significant databases established in earlier database packages and need to transfer data from these environments into any new database package that they acquire. Equally, users need to be able to integrate data in database, spreadsheet and word processing into appropriate documents. In general, no database or database product is stand alone; it must interface effectively with other related products. This session explores some of the more common types of importing and exporting that you may like to use. If you are an established user of databases you may wish to use your existing data within Access, or to convert your Access data into formats suitable for use in other database software. Importing and exporting allows you to develop databases and other applications relatively easily, and should be used wherever applicable.

However, this session can not hope to cover every different package that you might wish to use alongside Access. Instead a few more common applications are covered. This session then explains how to import and export dates to and from text files, spreadsheets and some common database formats. It also explains how you can attach tables from applications to your database and use them in the same way as Access tables.

This session is distinct from other sessions in that it is not integrated and the Activities do not develop one from another. You should select and attempt those activities for which you have the appropriate software and data. Nevertheless, it is important to explore some of the activities in this session and to start to understand the principles of importing and exporting of data.

activity 1 understanding importing, exporting and attaching files

Note: This activity explains the principles upon which some of the later activities in this session are based, but involves only thinking and not doing!

Access offers two different approaches to making use of existing data compiled with other database software:

Attached data behaves as if it is part of the Access database although it is not. The data can be edited in both Access and the other application and can be viewed as an Access table, although an Access table is not created. Attaching is useful when you wish to maintain the data in its original file format, whilst creating Access forms and reports.

Imported data has been converted from its original format into an Access table. A copy of the data is placed in a table in an Access database.

Access supports attaching and importing with dBase, Paradox, MS FoxPro, Btrieve and SQL.

Notes

1. If you want to add a table to an Access database this data can be imported into an existing Access database.

2. If you want to add data from an existing application to an Access table, you can append the data to an Access table, as long as its format matches that of the existing table entries i.e. it has the same fields with similar definitions.

3. Either attach or import - do not do both, because this will create more than one copy of the data. With more than one copy of the data it is difficult to be sure which is the most recent and to maintain file integrity.

Exporting data puts Access data into a format that other applications can use. Exporting data creates a separate file that contains the data stored in a table.

activity 2 importing data into an Access table

To import the data in a file into a table in the current Access database:

❒ switch to the Database window by pressing **F11** or clicking on it

❒ choose ***File-Import*** or click on the **Import** button

❒ choose the format of the data to be imported from the **Data Source** list box in the **Import** dialog box.

❒ select the directory from the **Directories** list box

❒ select the drive from the **Drives** list box

❒ Select the file you want to import and select the **Import** button.

When Access has imported the file that you have selected, it displays a message that it has successfully imported the file.

❒ click on **OK** and **CLOSE.**

If the **Database** window is displaying the database's tables, the newly imported table should appear in the list of tables.

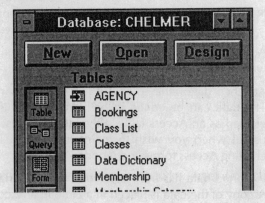

Figure 8.1 Database window showing an attached table

Activity 3 Attaching a table

To attach data stored in another file as a table in the current database:

❒ switch to the Database window by pressing F11 or clicking on it,

❒ choose *File-Attach Table* or click on the **Attach Table** button,

❒ choose the format of the data that you want to import from the **Data Source** list box in the **Import** dialogue box, and click on **OK.**

❒ select the filename of the file that you want to attach and choose **OK.** You can also change the drive and the directory as with Import.

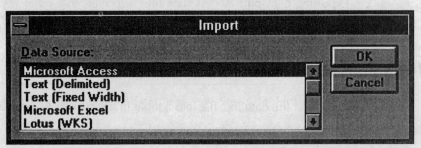

When Access has attached the file you have selected it displays a message saying the attachment is complete.

❒ click on **OK** and **Close**.

Attached tables are used in the same way as any other Access table. The table icon is displayed in the **Database** window, and provides a link to the attached table. Simply click on the table icon to use the table. Attached tables can be used with queries, forms and reports just like any other table.

To delete a link to an attached table, if you no longer require the link:

❒ select the icon for the attached table that is to be unattached

❏ select *Edit-Delete*

This deletes the link but the table remains intact, and could be re-attached at a later stage.

Access can use data from the following database formats and applications:

❏ Paradox

❏ Foxpro 2.0 and 2.5, dBase III and dBase IV

❏ Btrieve (with data definition files FILE.DDF and FIELD.DDF

❏ Access.

differences between attaching and importing

Imported and attached tables differ in the following respects:

1. They have different **icons** viz:

    Attached icon . Imported tables have the usual icon but are shown in upper case.

2. **Deleting a table.** When you delete an imported table, the tables contents are deleted. When you delete an attached table, the link is broken between the current database and the database that contains the table. The data is still available in the original database and any other databases that use the table as an attached table.

3. **Adding Data.** Imported data can be added to an existing table or placed in a new table. Attached tables are separate from existing tables in the database.

4. **Speed.** Attached tables are not an fast as tables stored in Access files because the data from the attached table must be constantly read form the original file. Access to data in attached tables can be speeded up by appropriate use of queries and indexes.

5. **Table design.** Attached tables can only be modified to a limited extent in Table design. Features such as filed names, data type, the order of fields, adding new fields or deleting fields can not be performed on attached tables.

6. **Importing or Attaching?** If you attach the data remains in another database format and can still be used just as Access tables are used, for example, to edit data, create queries, forms and reports that use data. If you intend to use your data only in Access you should import it. Access works faster with its own tables and Access tables can be customised more easily.

exercise 1 *importing, exporting and attaching files*

This exercise asks you to review some of the basic concepts associated with importing, exporting and attaching files. Answer the following questions:

❑ What are the advantages of importing a file compared with attaching it?

❑ How can you tell when viewing filenames with the Database window which files are imported and which files are attached?

❑ Why should you not both attach and import a file?

❑ What does exporting do?

activity 4 using dBase data with Access

dBase III and IV files can be imported or attached using the steps outlined in 8.2 and 8.3 above. There are only two special points to note:

1. In an imported table dBase field types are changed thus:

Character	➡	Text
Numeric	➡	Number
Float	➡	Number
Logical	➡	Yes/No
Date	➡	Date/Time
Memo	➡	Memo

In an attached table, the table continues with the original dBase field types.

2. In attaching a dBase table the speed with which Access operates with the data in the dBase file can be improved by selecting appropriate dBase index files.

exercise 2 *importing and attaching dBase data into Access*

In this exercise you first import, and then attach an existing dBase file into Access.

First you require a dBase file to import. Either create a file in dBase, or use an existing dBase file. You could create a file such as:

Field	Field Name	Type	Width	Dec	Index
1	AGENCYNO	Numeric	3		Y
2	SURNAME	Character	20		Y
3	INITIALS	Character	3		N
4	TITLE	Character	10		N
5	STREET	Character	30		N
6	TOWN	Character	20		Y
7	COUNTY	Character	20		N
8	POSTCODE	Character	10		N
9	DATEBIRTH	Date	8		Y
10	SEX	Logical	1		N
11	MARRIED	Logical	1		N
12	QUALIFICAT	Memo	10		N

This could be a dBase file held by an employment agency called **Agency.dbf.** Make a copy of this file so that you have two copies. You are going to use one of these copies to import and the other to attach.

Import the first copy thus:

☐ Switch to the **Database** window by pressing **F11** or clicking on the window.

☐ Choose *File-Import* or click on the **Import** button

☐ Choose the format of the data to be imported from the **Data Source** list box in the **Import** dialog box i.e. select dBase IV.

☐ Choose the directory from the **Directories** list box.

☐ Choose the drive from the **Drives** list box.

☐ Access displays the **Select File** dialog box.

☐ Select the .DBF file that you wish to import and select the **Import** button.

When Access has imported the file that you have selected, it displays a message that it has successfully imported the file.

☐ Click on **OK** and **Close** in the **Select File** dialog.

☐ You will now see **AGENCY** listed with the other tables in the database.

☐ Open this table, set **AGENCYNO** as the Primary Key.

☐ Set the index for **SURNAME** to Yes (Duplicates OK)

☐ Set the index for **TOWN** to Yes (Duplicates OK)

☐ Set the index for **DATEBIRTH** to Yes (Duplicates OK)

☐ Format **DATEBIRTH** to Short Date

☐ Yes/No fields result in −1 for true and 0 for false. Set format for **SEX** to ;"Male";"Female"

☐ Set format for **MARRIED** to ;"Married";"Single"

If the Database Window is displaying the database's tables, the newly imported table should appear in the list of tables (it will be shown in upper case). Click on the table name and in Design view examine the table and observe that the field types have been changed to be consistent with Access field types.

Use the second copy of the file to attach. Attach this table by following these steps:

☐ Switch to the **Database** window by pressing **F11** or clicking on it.

☐ Choose *File-Attach Table* or click on the **Attach Table** button.

☐ Choose the format of the data that you want to import from the **Data Source** List box in the **Attach** dialog box, i.e. select dBase IV and click on **OK.**

☐ Select the filename of the file that you want to attach and choose **Attach.**

☐ Select each dBase index file (.NDX or .MDX) one at a time and choose the **Select** button. Choose **Close.** In the **Select Unique Record Identifier** dialogue box choose the index which uniquely identifies each record in the table. Click on **OK.**

❑ When Access has attached the file it displays a message saying that the attachment is complete.

❑ Click on **OK** and **Close.**

If the Database Window is displaying the database' s tables, the newly attached table should appear in the list of tables. It will be indicated by an attached table icon.

Try to modify the attached and imported tables. Note that in Table Design an imported table can be modified in exactly the same way as any other Access table. The attached table can only be modified to a limited extent. You will find that you can not change the structure, but the following properties can be set: format, decimal places, caption, default value, validation rule and validation text. Try changing some of these.

Complete the exercise by deleting the link to the attached table thus;

❑ select the icon for the attached table that is to be unattached.

❑ select **Edit-Delete.**

activity 5 using Paradox data with Access

Paradox (versions 3.0 and 3.5) tables can be imported or attached using the steps outlined in 8.2 and 8.3 above. There are only two special points to note:

1. In an imported table Paradox field types are changed thus:

Alphanumeric	➡	Text
Number	➡	Number
Logical	➡	Yes/No
Date	➡	Date/Time
Memo	➡	Memo

    In an attached table, the table continues with the original Paradox field types.

2. If the Paradox table has an index file with a .PX extension, Access uses this file to keep track of the tables primary key. Keep this index file with the Paradox datafile, since you cannot open the attached table if Access can not find the file.

3. If you attach a Paradox table that does not have a primary key, the data can not be updated in Access. If you expect to want to update the table, define a primary key for the table in Paradox.

exercise 3 importing and attaching Access data into Paradox

In this exercise you first import, and then attach an existing Paradox file into Access. First you need a file to import and attach. If you do not have such a file you could create the agency table used in Exercise 2, or create the Classes table as a Paradox table, or alternatively refer to Activity 7 and export the Classes table to Paradox first and then try importing it and attaching it.

Repeat the same steps as in Exercise 2, except, on this occasion, Paradox needs to be selected in the **Data Source** list box. The other minor change is that it is not necessary to select index files.

activity 6 importing spreadsheet data and text files

It is possible to import spreadsheet data and text files into Access. Access can import files in the following spreadsheet and text formats:

Excel (versions 2.x, 3.0 and 4.0)

Lotus 1-2-3 or 1-2-3/W (.WKS, .WK1, and .WK3 files)

Delimited text (where text is separated into groups by commas, tabs or other characters)

Fixed width text (where values are arranged so that each field has a certain width).

When a spreadsheet or text file is imported, Access creates a new table to store the imported data, or, if you choose, adds it to an existing table.

There are a number of options to be selected in importing spreadsheet data and text files into Access, because it is necessary to define how the table should be created from the spreadsheet data or text file.

Importing spreadsheet data

Before attempting to import spreadsheet data into Access it is easiest if the data is in an appropriate format. The data must have the same type of data in each field and the same fields in every row. In addition, it is preferable if column headings of an appropriate type are inserted in the first row of the spreadsheet so that these can be used as field names. Access will look at the first row of data and assign a data type for each field on the basis of this first row. For example, if the first value for a field is a date, then Access assigns Date/Time data type to that field and assumes that all values for that field will be dates.

To import spreadsheet data into Access:

❐ Switch to the **Database** window by pressing **F11** or clicking on the window.

❐ Choose *File-Import* or click on the **Import** button.

❐ Select the appropriate format for the data that you want to import (e.g. Excel) from the **Data Source** list box in the **Import** dialog box. Click on **OK.**

❐ Access displays the **Select File** dialog box. Select the name of the spreadsheet that you want to import and click on the Import button.

Access will display an **Import Spreadsheet Options** dialog box.

❐ Select the **First Row Contains Field Names** check box if the spreadsheet range you are importing has labels in the first row that you want to use as the field names in the table.

Either:

❐ Select the **Create New Table** radio button if you want the data imported into a new table

or:

❐ Select the **Append to Existing Table** radio button and select one of the existing table names from the drop down list box. Note that to append to an existing table it is imperative that the data is in the same format as the existing table.

❐ Type the range name or range address that contains the data you want to import in the **Spreadsheet Range** text box. If you do not make an entry in the text box, Access imports the entire spreadsheet. Click on **OK.**

When the spreadsheet has been imported, a message is displayed that indicates whether Access found any errors whilst importing the spreadsheet. For example, if the first row in the spreadsheet contains entries that do not make valid field names when you have selected the **First Row Contains Field Names** check box, you cannot import data as it is. It is necessary to modify the spreadsheet data so that the first row contains valid field names or to select the **First Row Contains Field Names** check box and to clear it.

❐ After any modification to accommodate errors, click **OK** again. Click on **CLOSE.**

exercise 4 *importing spreadsheet data*

Note: To complete this exercise you need access to a copy of Excel or Lotus or other compatible spreadsheet package.

Create a spreadsheet in Excel or Lotus 1-2-3 into which you can enter data that matches the Classes table. Save this file as **Classes2.** As illustrated enter the field names in the first row, and then enter some records for specific classes, one record per row, as required.

	A	B	C	D	E	F	
					CLASSES2.XLS		
1	Class No	Class Day	Class Time	Class Tutor	Class Activity	Male/Female/Mixed	
2	26	Tuesday	14:00	Bates	Badminton	Female	
3	27	Tuesday	15:00	Bates	Badminton	Female	
4	28	Wednesday	09:00	Flowers	Multi-Gym	Mixed	
5	29	Thursday	21:00	Tonks	Multi-Gym	Male	
6							

Open Access and open the Database Window.

❐ Choose *File-Import*

❏ In the **Data Source** list box, in the **Import** dialog box choose the appropriate format for the data that you want to import (e.g. Excel)

❏ Select the name of the spreadsheet that you want to import. Choose the **Import** button.

❏ Access displays the **Import Spreadsheet Options** dialog box.

❏ Select the **First Row Contains Field Names** check box

❏ Select the **Create New Table** radio button. Access will create a table with the name of the spreadsheet selected e.g. **Classes2**

❏ A message is displayed stating the number of records successfully imported.

❏ Click on **Close.** Open the table in design view and edit the field properties, e.g. setting primary key.

Using the same spreadsheet also try to append the data to an existing table, in this case the table **Classes.** Note: highlight the file you wish to append to before using *File-Import.*

importing delimited text files into Access

A delimited text file is a text file in which fields are separated by a special character, such as a comma or a tab. Data in a text file intended for importing into a table must be in an appropriate format. As with spreadsheets, the text file must have the same type of data in each field and the same fields in every row. Again the first row may be used as field names, and Access uses the first row of data as a basis for assigning data types.

To import a delimited text file:

❏ Open a database

❏ Choose *File-Import*

❏ In the **Data Source** list box select Text(Delimited) and then choose **OK.**

❏ Select the text file to be imported and then choose the **Import** button. The **Import Text Options** dialog box will be displayed.

❏ Select appropriate import options. For example, choose to use the first row as field names by clicking on the **First Row Contains Field Names** box. Choose whether to **Create New Table,** or **Append to Existing Table,** and specify the **Text Delimiter** that has been used.

❏ When all options have been selected, choose **OK.** Access creates a new table with the same name as the original text file, unless you choose to append data to an existing file. Choose **Close.**

exercise 5 *importing delimited text files*

Note: To complete this exercise you need access to a copy of an appropriate word processing package, such as Word for Windows.

Create a delimited text file into which you can enter data that matches the Classes table. If you are working with Word for Windows you may choose to do this be creating a table, but text delimited by commas or tabs will work equally well. Save this file as **Classes3**. As in Figure 8.2, enter the field names in the first row, and then enter some records for specific classes, one record per row, as required.

Class No	Class Day	Class Time	Class Tutor	Class Activity	Male/Female/Mixed
26	Tuesday	14.00	Miss Bates	Badminton	Female
27	Tuesday	15.00	Miss Bates	Badminton	Female
28	Wednesday	09.00	Mr Flowers	Multi-gym	Mixed
29	Thursday	21.00	Mr Tonks	Multi-gym	Male

Figure 8.2 A delimited text file for importing into an Access table

Open Access and open the **Database** window.

❏ Choose *File-Import*

❏ In the **Data Source** list box, in the **Import** dialog box select Text(Delimited) and then choose OK.

❏ Select the name of the text file that you want to import. Choose the **Import** button.

❏ Access displays the **Import Text Options** dialog box.

❏ Select the **First Row Contains Field Names** check box

❏ Select the **Create New Table** radio button. Access will create a table with the name of the text file selected e.g. **Classes3**

View this table in Datasheet view, and then in Design view. Are you satisfied with the field names and data types that Access has assigned? Do they match the names and data types that we used when we defined Classes? Change any data types and field names to suit your taste

Using the same text file also try to append the data to an existing table, in this case the table Classes.

Notes

1. We have just explored a further way of creating text and entering it in a database. Normally it is more satisfactory to enter data directly into a database, but on occasions an existing word processed file, say, in this instance of the classes on offer, or the names and addresses of some members may usefully be incorporated into an Access database, either simply so that it is merged with other similar data, or because it is easier to sort, group and query the data in database format.

2. We do not describe importing fixed-width text fields here.

activity 7 exporting a table

Data can be exported from Access tables to text files, spreadsheets to any of the database formats from which importing can be executed. Data can also be exported to a Word for Windows mail merge data file, which can then be used to create form letter, mailing labels and other merged documents. Data may be exported to other database applications so that it can be merged with other data in other files.

Important Note: Access allows table and field names that can contain up to 64 characters and can include spaces. Most other database packages and other applications work with shorter maximum table and field names, and do not allow spaces in names. When you export a table with table or field names that are not acceptable to another application, Access adjusts the names. For example, if you export data to a dBase table, Access truncates any names longer than 10 characters. It is therefore important to check that after such truncation you will be left with a set of unique field and table names.

To export data in a table to a file in a format that other applications can use:

❏ switch to the **Database** window by pressing **F11** or clicking on it,

❏ choose *File-Export* or click on the **Export** button,

❏ select the format of the data you want to export from the **Data Destination** list box in the **Export** dialog box and click on **OK,**

❏ select the table to be exported and click on **OK,**

❏ select the name of the file where you want the data exported to and select **OK,**

❏ select any information Access needs to export the table. The information that you are asked for depends on the data format selected earlier.

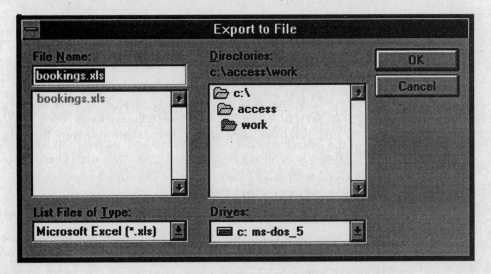

Exporting to a database or spreadsheet file

To export data to a database or spreadsheet file:

1. Switch to the database containing the table that you wish to export

2. Choose *File-Export.* Access displays the **Export** dialog box.

3. Select the spreadsheet or database format required from the Data Destination list box, and choose OK.

4. Access displays a list of tables in the database. Select the table or query to be exported from the Objects list box and choose **OK.**

5. Access displays the **Export To File** dialog box. Enter a filename for the data to be exported, and then choose OK.

exercise 6 exporting a table to dBase

Note: To complete this exercise you require either dBase III or IV on your system. dBase field names are only 10 characters long so you may need to revise your Access field names.

Export the table that was imported in Exercise 1, Classes.

❒ Switch to the **database containing the table Classes.**

❒ Choose *File-Export*

❒ Select the format of the data that is to be exported, say dBase III from the **Data Destination** list box in the **Export** dialog box and click on **OK.**

❒ Select the table to be exported and click on **OK.**

❒ Enter the name of the file to where you want the data exported, say **Classes4,** and select **OK.**

exercise 7 exporting a table to a spreadsheet

Note: To complete this exercise you require a spreadsheet package such as Excel or Lotus 1-2-3.

Export the table that was imported in Exercise 4, Classes, following the same steps as in Exercise 6 but this time selecting, say Excel, from the Data Destination list box. Enter the name of the file to where you want the data exported as **Classes 5.**

exporting a table to a text file

It may often be appropriate to select a set of records from a table and export them to a word processor for further formatting or for integration into a text based document.

To export an Access table to a text file:

1.   Switch to the database containing the table that you wish to export

2.   Choose *File-Export.* Access displays the **Export** dialog box.

3.   Select Text(Delimited) or Text(Fixed Width) from the **Data Destination** list box, and choose **OK.**

4.   Access displays a list of tables in the database. Select the table to be exported from the Tables list box and choose **OK.**

5.   Access displays the **Export To File** dialog box. Enter a filename for the data to be exported, and then choose **OK.**

6.   Access displays the **Export Text Options** dialog box. If necessary, specify text options, and then choose **OK.**

exercise 8 *exporting a table to a word processor*

Suppose we wish to create a brochure detailing the opportunities for Ladies leisure and recreational activities available at Chelmer Leisure and Recreation Centre. This leaflet will be essentially a word processed document containing text about the activities and the Centre. However, embedded in the document will be a list of Keep Fit and Multi-gym Classes for Ladies. In order to extract this information from our Access **Classes** table, and insert the data into the leaflet we need first to select the appropriate records by the use of a query, convert the result of the query to a table, and then export the data in the table to a word processor file.

To execute the query:

1.   Click on the **Query** button in the Database Window and click on the **New** button to create a new query.

2.   In the **Add Table** dialog box, choose **Classes.** Click on **Close.**

3.   Add the appropriate fields to the query.

4.   Use criteria to select the required records.

5.   Display the dynaset.

Note: The following steps 6 and 7 are only required for Access 1 as Access 2 allows exporting of queries.

6.   Choose *Query-Make Table.* Key in a suitable name for the table. Click on **OK.**

7.   Click on **Run** and a message box will display the number of records that are being added to the new table. Click on **OK** to create the new table.

To export the data to a word processor file:

1.   Switch to Chelmer.

2.   Choose *File-Export.* Access displays the **Export** dialog box.

3.   Select Text(Delimited) from the **Data Destination** list box, and choose **OK.**

4. Access displays a list of tables in the Chelmer database. Select the newly created query which is to be exported i.e. select from the **Objects** list box and choose **OK.**

5. Access displays the **Export To File** dialog box. Enter a filename for the data to be exported, and then choose **OK.**

6. Access displays the **Export Text Options** dialog box. If necessary, specify text options, and then choose **OK.**

exporting Access data to another Access database

Exporting and importing are two sides of the same process. Data can be transferred between Access databases, either by importing or exporting. You import when the current database is the database where you need a copy of the table or other object and you export when you are in the database that contains the object or data you want copied to another database.

To export a table or other database object:

❏ follow the steps for exporting a table.

❏ to select an object other than a table select the object type from the **Object Type** drop-down list box, and then select the object of that type that you wish to export.

❏ when Access prompts for the name of a file, select one of the existing databases.

❏ enter the name of the object in the current database or type in a new one.

After exporting, the object is in both databases and there is no link between the two copies of the object. So, for example, if the object is updated in one database it will not be updated in another.

activity 8 using the clipboard to transfer data

In addition to transferring data between Access and other applications by importing, attaching and exporting data, information can be transferred between applications using the clipboard. Transferring data using the clipboard is very straightforward, provided the data is in an acceptable format. It is especially easy is you are working with Excel and Word alongside Access.

The Clipboard is the Windows temporary area where it can store information from any applications designed to use it. The basic procedure is to:

❏ select the data to be moved

❏ select *Edit-Copy* or *Edit-Cut* depending upon whether you also wish to retain the data in its original location or not.

❏ switch to the application into which you wish to import data

❏ select *Edit-Paste.*

This procedure can be adopted, for example, for:

❑ moving Access data into an Excel (or other) spreadsheet

❑ moving Access data into a Word for Windows document in the form of a table.

❑ moving Access objects from one database to another.

exercise 9 *using the clipboard to move Access data into a Word document*

Chelmer Leisure and Recreation Centre may find it useful to have a list of those members who are children or, in other words, have a Membership Category of Junior or Junior Club. First we need to create a query to select appropriate records, and then we can select appropriate records on the screen and use *Edit-Copy* and *Edit-Paste* to insert those records in a word processed document.

To create a query:

❑ Click on the **Query** button in the Database Window and click on the **New** button to create a new query.

❑ In the **Add Table** dialog box, choose **Membership.** Click on **Close.**

❑ Add the following fields to the query

> **Membership Category**
> **Forenames**
> **Surname**
> **Date of Birth**
> **Date of Joining**
> **Sporting Interests**
> **Sex.**

❑ Use a criterion in the **Membership Category** field to select categories 3 *or* 4.

❑ Display the dynaset. Select the dynaset.

❑ Copy the selection to the clipboard, switch to the word processor and paste the table from the clipboard.

Another case where Chelmer Leisure and Recreation Centre would wish to move Access data into a document would be to create a list of classes intended for a publicity document such as a poster or leaflet.

To create a query:

❑ Click on the **Query** button in the Database Window and click on the **New** button to create a new query.

❑ In the **Add Table** dialog box, choose **Classes.** Click on **Close.**

❑ Add the following fields to the query:

> **Class Day**
> **Class Time**
> **Class Activity**
> **Male/Female/Mixed.**

❏ Display the dynaset. Select the dynaset.

❏ Copy the selection to the clipboard, switch to the word processor and paste the table from the clipboard.

How could you amend the query to produce a leaflet targeted at male members?

exercise 10 *using the clipboard to move Access data into an Excel spreadsheet*

This exercise investigates how bookings table data can be pasted into an Excel spreadsheet to perform additional analysis.

❏ Create a query based on the **Bookings** table. add the fields **Booking No** and **Date.**

❏ Click on the **Sigma** button to create totals. select Count for **Booking No** and Group by for **Date.**

❏ Use *Edit-Select all Records* and *Edit-Copy.*

❏ Switch to Excel

❏ Use *Edit-Paste* and the data is pasted in Excel.

The average number of bookings per day can be found, which could have been done using Access, however Excel could be used to calculate the median and mode of this data. Other more sophisticated statistical analysis could be used on Access data transferred to Excel such as forecasting using a linear regression technique.

session nine

macros

objectives

This session introduces macros. Macros are basically a list of instructions, rather like short programs. When using Access there may be occasions when the same series of actions is performed again and again. To save time these actions may be recorded as a macro so that one command, to run the macro, can replace the need to issue a series of commands.

By performing a series of actions macros can automate your database application. Forms can be designed with buttons to which macros can be assigned. When a button is clicked its associated macro could display a form or generate a report. An example of this would be a button labelled New Member which when clicked would display a blank membership form ready to take a new member's details. The button labelled New Member would be on a separate form and there could be other buttons on that form such as Make Booking, Renew Membership etc.

Another use for a macro is in complex validation. A macro can be attached to a control such that when data is entered this data may be checked by the macro to see if it is valid. The macro can display message boxes so that the person entering the data is informed of any mistakes and can be given help as to the correct entry that they should be making.

Macros in Access are powerful and perform many tasks that in other database management systems could only be achieved by writing a program, which involves learning the programming language. Creating macros, however, does require a clear understanding of your database application so that you can plan exactly what you want each macro to do. In this session, you will be introduced to some macros, which while not being comprehensive should cover some of the basics. At the end of this session you should be able to

❏ create simple macros

❏ assign macros to buttons or events

❏ use macros to validate data entry

❏ create a form that uses macros to enter report criteria

activity 1 the macro window

Macros are entered in Macro Windows, just as you enter a query using a Query Window or a form using a Form Window.

The Macro Window is usually shown with two columns, **Action** and **Comment,** as illustrated in Figure 9.1. In the action column the action for the macro is selected, the action being selected from a drop down list associated with that cell. In the Comments column you can add comments to add as a reminder of the function of the macro.

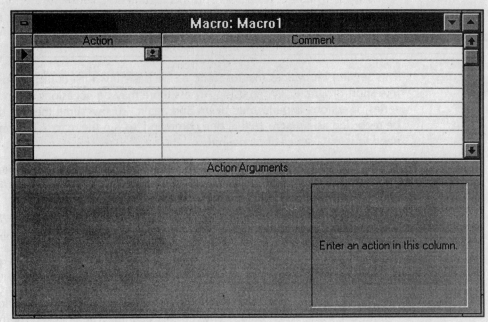

Figure 9.1 Macro Window

Exercise 1 A macro to open a form

This macro is easy to create and one which is frequently used. This exercise will consider construction of the macro stage by stage. At each stage relevant explanation is given.

❏ Click on the **Macro** button in the Database Window and click on the **New** button to display the Macro Window.

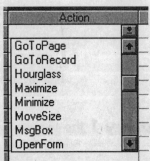

The first action of this macro is **OpenForm.** There are many actions to chose from as you will discover when you open the list box of the Action cell.

❏ Open the Action cell list box. Scroll through the actions and select the Open-Form action. When you do this you will see that an argument section appears in the lower left of the Macro Window.

Whatever action is selected there will nearly always be an argument section to complete. Some actions require more arguments than others, refer to the section on Understanding Actions and Arguments.

❐ Open the Form Name list in the Action Arguments section and select Membership. Leave the action arguments as their default values.

The View argument opens the form in form run mode. The Data mode argument of Edit allows the form to be edited. The Where condition specifies which record is displayed when the form opens. If this argument is left blank then the form is opened displaying the first record.

Form Name	Membership
View	Form
Filter Name	
Where Condition	
Data Mode	Edit
Window Mode	Normal

❐ Key into the **Comment** column the description **Open Membership form.**

❐ Save the Macro with the name **Chelmer.**

Note: A macro must be saved before it can be run or executed. Choose *File-Save* or press F12 to save the macro. In the **Save As** dialog box type a descriptive name for the macro. Click on **OK.**

❐ The macro can be tested by running it. Click on the **Run** button in the toolbar. The **Membership** form should be displayed with the first record showing.

Note: There are several different ways in which a macro can be run or executed. Refer to the section Executing Macros for details of the different methods.

❐ Close the form and close the macro. The macro name should be displayed in the Database Window.

activity 2 modifying a macro

A macro may need to be edited to change its actions or to correct an error. All or part of a macro may be copied from one macro window to another to save having to repeat work that has already been done. Macros may be copied from one database to another.

Normally a macro is edited to change its actions, usually to improve or refine them. Display the macro window that you wish to modify. Editing may be achieved using either the mouse or the keyboard.

exercise 2 editing a macro

In this exercise the macro created in the last exercise will be opened and edited so that when it opens the Membership form it displays the form ready to accept a new record. This is useful when a new member's details are to be entered.

☐ Open the macro **Chelmer** in design mode.

☐ For the second action of the macro select the **GoToRecord** action.

☐ To define which record to go to the **Record** argument is used. Open the list box associated with this argument and select **New.**

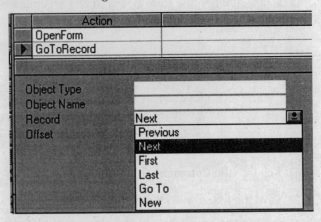

☐ Save the macro and run it. This time the **Membership** form should be displayed ready to accept a new record.

☐ Close the form and the macro.

exercise 3 *sizing and positioning the form*

To add a further refinement to the macro to open the form, the size of the form can be set. If the size is not set then the form will be displayed at the last size used when the form was displayed in design mode. By sizing and positioning a form from a macro gives consistency to your database application.

☐ Open the macro **Chelmer** in design mode.

☐ Insert a row in the macro sheet below the **OpenForm** action. Highlight the second row and use *Edit-Insert Row* to insert a blank row.

☐ In the new row select the action **MoveSize.** Set the arguments as shown in the following table:

Right	The new horizontal position of the window's upper left corner, measured from the left edge of its containing window	4 cm
Down	The new vertical position of the window's upper left corner, measured from the top edge of its containing window	1 cm
Width	The window's new width	15 cm
Height	The window's new height	12 cm

☐ Save the macro and run it.

❏ You may need to adjust the sizes in the **MoveSize** arguments to suit your form. To do this close the **Membership** form, edit and save the macro.

❏ Save the changes and run the macro. The Membership form should display nicely and be ready to accept a new record.

❏ Close the **Membership** form and the macro.

understanding action and arguments

The macro actions available in Access can duplicate commands that would be chosen from the menus as well as control many processes such as synchronising the records that forms display. There are many actions available so by means of illustration a few actions will be considered along with their associated arguments. If the action duplicates a command which would generate a dialog box then the arguments are the selections that would be made in that dialog box. Three of the many actions are illustrated below.

Action	Argument	Function
FindRecord	Find What Where Match Case Direction Search as Formatted Search In Find First	Finds the next record after the current record meeting the specified criteria. Searches through a table, form, or dynaset.
OpenForm	Form Name View Filter Name Where Condition Data Mode Window Mode	Opens or activates a form in one of its views.
OpenReport	Report Name View Filter Name Where Condition	Opens a report in the view specified and filters the records before printing.

By defining the arguments, for example, the name of a report in the Report Name argument, then the appropriate action is carried out.

executing macros

You can run a macro in many ways. If you are creating quick macros for immediate use, you may want to run them by choosing them from the Macro window or the Database window. To create a system that is more automated or one that is easier to use, you can run a macro in a variety of ways which are outlined briefly below and are discussed in more detail later in the session.

Running from the macro window

A macro can be run from its macro window. This capability is useful for testing a macro. To run the macro click on the run button on the toolbar or choose *Macro-Run.* If the active Macro window contains a group of macros, only the first macro in the macro window runs. to run a specific macro in the group see activity 9.8.

From any window

Choose *File-Run Macro* and in the **Run Macro** dialog box select or key in the name of the macro. Click on **OK.**

From the database window

This is a convenient way of running a macro. To run a macro from the database window, open any forms or reports that are expected by the macro. Click on the Macro button to display the list of macros. Double-click on the macro name or select the name and click on the Run button.

From another macro

A macro can be run from another macro using the RunMacro action. The argument for this action is the name of the macro to be called. When the called macro has run Access returns control to the next action in the calling macro. The macro may run repeatedly if either the Repeat Count or Repeat Expression are set.

From an event

The running of a macro can be 'triggered' by an event. An event can be the opening or closing of a form or report or it can be the selecting of a control. For example a macro which opens a form can run when a field is selected. A macro which validates an entry can run when a field is exited. These kind of macro events make your database application much more professional in operation.

From a button

This is another way to make your database application more professional. Command buttons are a very easy addition to a form. By clicking on the button the macro can be performed such as opening another form.

From a shortcut key

It is a good idea to assign frequently used macros to a short-cut key, for example Ctrl-p could be assigned to a macro that performs printing. By pressing the short-cut key combination the macro will run.

activity 3 creating macro groups

It is useful to keep related macros together and Access offers the facility to group macros. Therefore it is possible to have more than one macro in a macro window. This also has the added advantage that it reduces the number of macro windows. Many macros are small, only a few lines long and if each required a separate macro window then it would be difficult to keep track of them all. To distinguish macros in one window each has its own name. The macro name is entered in the Macro Name column of the window and this column is displayed by clicking on the **Macro Names** button (see Appendix 3 or 4) in the toolbar or by choosing *Display-Names.* This column is displayed to the left of the Action column.

Each macro in the window begins with the action to the right of its name. The macro ends when it reaches the beginning of the next macro or it runs out of actions. There is no need for a particular end action.

When a Macro window contains several macros then to refer to a specific macro within the group use the following syntax:

macrowindowname.macroname

where a full stop separates the macro window name from the macro name, for example Chelmer.NewBooking. To run a particular macro in a group choose *File-Run Macro* and type the name using the syntax described above. Note that if the macroname is omitted then the first macro in the group will run.

exercise 4 creating a macro group

In this exercise another macro will be added to the Chelmer macro. This will be another open form macro to open the booking form ready to take a new booking.

❏ Display the **Chelmer** macro window in design view.

❏ Click on the **Macro Names** button in the toolbar.

❏ Leave a couple of blank rows below the existing macro and in the Macro Name column put **NewBooking.**

❏ On the next row select the action **OpenForm.** Set the Form argument to **Bookings.**

❏ The second action is **GoToRecord,** with the argument of **Record** set to **New.**

Macro Name	Action
	OpenForm
	GoToRecord
NewBooking	OpenForm
	GoToRecord

❏ Save the macro.

❏ To run this part of the macro group select *File-Run Macro.*

❏ In the **Run Macro** dialog box add to the macro name, so that it reads **Chelmer.NewBooking** and click on **OK.**

❏ Close the form and close the macro.

activity 4 adding command buttons to a form

A macro can be assigned to a command button so that when the button is clicked the macro runs. Buttons may be added to existing forms which are based on tables or they can be added to blank forms. A blank form which does not have an associated table can be created, this type of form is known as an unbound from. By adding buttons to the form it can become a menu form.

A macro can be made convenient to run by assigning it to a button to a form, either existing or blank. The button can then be clicked to run the macro.

1. Open the form in design view and display it by the side of the Database Window.

2. Click the **Macro** button in the Database window.

3. Drag the name of the macro on to the form where the button is to appear and release.

4. The button will have the name of the macro. If wished this can be changed by editing the text on the button.

5. Save the form with the button.

6. Display the form in Run mode and click on the button to run the macro.

exercise 5 *creating a blank form and adding buttons to it*

In this exercise an unbound blank form will be created which will only contain two command buttons. The first command button to be added will be one which when clicked on will open the **Membership** form ready to accept a new member's details. The second button will open the **Bookings** form ready to accept a new booking. To create a blank unbound form:

❑ From the Database Window click on the **Form** button and click on **New.** Leave the Table/query box empty as this form is not bound to a table or query.

To add a command button:

❑ Click on the **Blank form** button. Display the new blank form and the Database Window side by side. Click on the **Macro** button of the Database Window and select **Chelmer.**

❑ Drag the macro onto the form. A button appears with the name Chelmer on it.

❑ The name on the button can be changed by either editing the **Caption** property or directly editing the text on the button. Edit the name of the button to read **New Member.** You should find that the **On Push** or **On Click** property is set to Chelmer, i.e. the first macro in the macrogroup Chelmer will run when the button is clicked (pushed).

❑ Set the properties of the form as follows (if the form is not selected use *Edit-Select Form* to select it):

Property	Setting
Caption	Form Menu (the name that will appear in the title bar of the form)
DefaultView	Single Form
ScrollBars	Neither

❑ Save the form as **Form Menu.** Run the form and click on the **New Member** button you have just created. Close the **Membership** form.

❑ Return to design view of the **Form Menu** form.

❑ Drag the Chelmer macro onto the form. A button appears with the name Chelmer on it.

❑ The name on the button can be changed by editing the **Caption** property. Edit the name of the button to read **Make Booking.**

❑ You should also edit the **On Push** (**On Click**) property which is set to Chelmer, to Chelmer.NewBooking so that the macro Chelmer.NewBooking will run when the button is clicked. In Access 2 **Chelmer.New Booking** may be chosen from the On Click drop down list.

❑ You may add a title and adjust fonts as illustrated below. Save the form and try the new button.

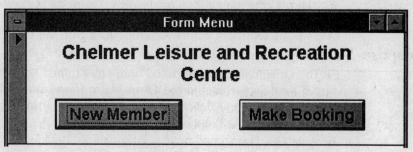

exercise 6 *adding a button to an existing form*

This will be a very simple macro to close the open object, which might be a form or report. In the preceeding exercise to close after adding a new member or taking a new booking would be simple if a button labelled **Close** was added to both the **Membership** and **Bookings** form.

The macro to close an object is simple and it can be added to the **Chelmer** macrogroup. To add this macro:

Access 1

❑ Display the **Chelmer** macro in design view.

❑ Leave a couple of blank rows after the NewBooking macro and in the Name column put Close.

❑ In the corresponding Action column select the action Close. By leaving the arguments blank this means that close will work with the active window.

❒ Save and close the macro.

To add a **Close** command button to the **Membership** form:

❒ Display the **Membership** form in design view.

❒ Use the **Command Button** tool from the Toolbox to draw a button at the bottom of the form. Set the properties for this button:

Property	Setting
Caption	Close (or you may prefer Cancel)
On Push	Chelmer.Close

Access 2

❒ Display Membership form in design view.

❒ Use Command Button tool from the Toolbox to draw a button at the bottom of the form. The Command Button Wizard starts.

❒ Select **Form Operations** from the **Categories** list and **Close Form** from the **When button is pressed** list. Click on Next>.

❒ Choose a picture or text from the button. Give the button the name **Close Membership Form** and click on Finish.

Access 1 & 2

❒ Save the form. Try out the macro, clicking on the **Close** button should close the form.

❒ The same macro can be called from other forms. Add a **Close** button to both the **Bookings** form and the **Form Menu** form using either the Access 1 or Access 2 method described above. Notice that in Access 2 the On Click property is set to Event Procedure.

❒ Save the forms and test your macros.

activity 5 assigning a macro to a key

It is useful to be able to assign a frequently used macro to a keystroke as this gives the operator more choice when using the database. The example we shall consider is that of Ctrl-n to display the Membership form ready to accept a new members record and Ctrl-b to display the Booking form. Examples of other short-cut keys that could be used are Crtl-x to close or Crtl-p to print.

A separate macro needs to be created in which the key assignments are set. All key assignments are kept in this macro as a group. So that Access knows this is a key assignment macro it is saved with the name **AutoKeys.** In the AutoKeys macro each key combination has a name and this name must follow the naming convention shown in the table below:

Key Combination	Macro Name
Ctrl-*letter*	^*letter*
Ctrl-number	^*number*
Function key	{F1} and so on
Ctrl-*Function key*	^{F1} and so on
Shift-*Function key*	+{F1} and so on
Insert	{Insert}
Ctrl-Insert	^{Insert}
Shift-Insert	+{Insert}
Delete	{Delete} or {Del}
Ctrl-Delete	^{Delete} or ^{Del}
Shift-Delete	+{Delete} or +{Del}

To assign a macro to a shortcut key:

1. Create and save the macros and/or macro groups to which you wish to assign shortcut keys.

2. Open a new macro window and display the **Macro Name** column. This macro will become a macro group in which all shortcut keys are defined.

3. In the macro name column put the macro name, for example, ^p.

4. The action for this macro will be a RunMacro action which will refer to one of the macros you have already created. See the following section for more detail on the RunMacro action.

5. State the macro name that you are calling in the **Macro Name** argument. Use the correct syntax, i.e. if the macro is in a group then use *macrogroup-name.macroname.*

6. Use the **Comment** column to note which macro is being called.

7. Choose *View-Options* to display the **Option** dialog box. Select Keyboard and you will see that the name for the Key Assignment Macro is **AutoKeys.** It is possible to set a different name for this macro using this dialog box. Close the dialog box.

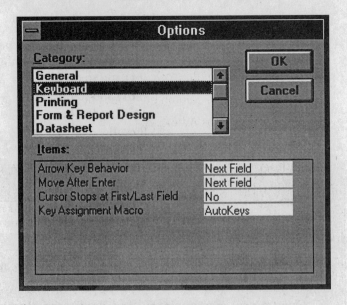

☐ Save the shortcut key macro as AutoKeys.

☐ Any shortcut keys you wish to set up later must be added to this macro.

the RunMacro action

A macro can be run from within another macro by using the RunMacro action. The arguments for the RunMacro action are the name of the macro to be run, and the number of times the macro is to repeat. The macro may be set to repeat a set number of times or an expression can be used to test whether the macro has been performed the required number of times.

When the main (or calling) macro is run it performs its list of actions. When the RunMacro action is encountered the specified macro runs the required number of times. When that has finished Access returns control to the next action in the calling macro.

exercise 7 *assigning shortcut keys*

In this exercise the shortcut key Ctrl-m (^m) is to be assigned to the macro that opens the **Membership** form ready to accept a new members record and Ctrl-b (^b) to opening the **Bookings** form. To create an AutoKeys macro

☐ Open a new macro sheet. Display the Macro Name column.

☐ Put ^m in the Macro Name column.

☐ In the Action column select the **RunMacro** action and set the Macro Name argument to Chelmer (this is the first macro of the Chelmer group of macros).

☐ In the Comments column put Opens Membership form for new record.

❑ In the next row of the Macro Name column put ^b.

❑ In the Action column select the **RunMacro** action and set the Macro Name argument to Chelmer.NewBooking (this is the NewBooking macro of the Chelmer group of macros).

❑ In the Comments column put Opens Bookings form for new record.

❑ Save the macro as **AutoKeys.**

❑ Open the Form Menu and try using the shortcut key.

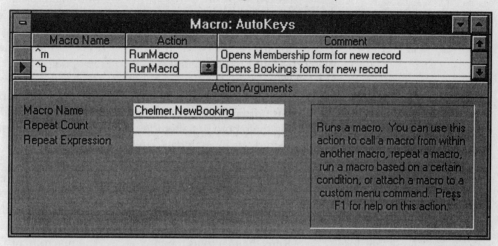

You may have noticed that in many Windows applications the shortcut letter in a menu or on a button is underlined. It is possible to do this, by displaying the form or report containing the button in design mode and editing the Caption so that an & precedes the letter to be underlined. For example, Make Booking would be typed as Make &Booking so that it appeared as Make <u>B</u>ooking on the button.

activity 6 understanding report and form events

Specific events in forms and reports can be used to 'trigger' the running of a macro. Examples of events are the opening of a form, the user selecting or exiting from a field control or the user double-clicking on a field.

By assigning macros to events the database system becomes more professional as set procedures within the system become automated. Event driven macros can be used to open multiple forms together, printing reports using specific queries, or creating error checks that are more extensive than those available through control properties. There are more form events than report events.

The events for a form or report can be found in the table of properties. Forms, controls and reports have different events associated with them. The following tables illustrate some of the events to which macros can be assigned.

Events in a form or record

Form Property	Event	Example of use
OnOpen	Runs the macro when the form opens but before displaying a record	The macro may open or close other forms when the form opens
OnInsert	Runs the macro when the user begins to enter data into a new record	The macro can display extra information or a warning message
BeforeUpdate	Runs the macro after the user has finished changing or entering the record but before the record is updated in the database	The macro can display a dialog box asking the user to confirm that the record be updated.
AfterUpdate	Runs the macro after the user has finished changing or entering the record but after the record has been updated in the database.	The macro can update other forms using the data in the new record.
OnDelete	Runs the macro when the user deletes a record but before the record is actually deleted.	The macro may ask for confirmation as to whether the record should be deleted.
OnClose	Runs the macro as the form is about to close but has not disappeared from the screen.	The macro may ask whether data may be transferred when the form is closed.

Events in a form control

Form Control Property	Event	Example of use
OnEnter	Runs the macro when a control is clicked i.e. just as it receives the focus	The macro may ask for a password before allowing data entry.
OnPush (On Click)	Runs the macro when a command button is clicked	The caption on the button usually indicates the function of the macro, for example Print.
BeforeUpdate	Runs the macro after the user leaves a control but before the control is changed	The macro can validate the data that has been entered and ask for it to be corrected.
OnDoubleClick	Runs the macro when the user double clicks on a control or its label	Can display a form with information regarding data entry.
OnExit	Runs the macro when the user attempts to move to another control but before the focus moves away	Can define the next control using the GoToControl action.

Events in a report

Report event	Event description	Example of use
OnOpen	Runs the macro when the report opens but before printing	Displays a form in which to enter criteria.

Assigning a macro to an event

To assign a macro to an event first create and save the macro. To assign it to the required form, report or control

1. Open the required form or report in design view.
2. Select the form, report or control to which the macro is to be assigned.

To	Do This
Select a form or report	Click on the background in a form. Click outside a report section. Choose either *Edit-Select Form* or *Edit-Select Report*
Select a report section	Click on the section header
Select a control	Click on the control

3. Display the properties window by clicking on the **Properties** button in the toolbar.
4. Select the required event in the properties table.
5. Open the combo box and select the macro name to be assigned to this event. In Access 1, if the macro is part of a group, select the group's name and edit it to add a dot and the name of the macro.
6. Save the changes made and test the macro.

Using conditions

Your macros can have the capability to make decisions about how they operate. Macros can test whether a condition is true and when that condition is true they can run actions you specify.

By adding the condition column to the macro window expressions can be added. Click on the **Conditions** button in the toolbar (see Appendix 3 or 4) to display the condition column. You enter in this Condition column expressions that can be evaluated as true or false. If the expression is true the macro action on its right runs. If the expression is False the macro action doesn't run.

Expressions test the values of control names, for example:

[Surname]="Smith"   True when Surname control contains the text *Smith*.

[Membership Fee]<20   True when the control *Membership Fee* is less than 20

exercise 8 using conditions to control the focus in a form

In this exercise a macro will be assigned to the **Member/Class** control in the **Bookings** form which will control whether the focus moves to the **Membership No** control or to the **Class No** control.

Macro: Booking			
Macro Name	Condition	Action	Comment
▶ Member/Class	[Member/Class]	GoToControl ⊟	
	Not [Member/Class]	GoToControl	
Date		GoToControl	

Action Arguments	
Control Name	[Membership No]

Moves the focus to a specified field or other

❏ Create the macro group Booking as illustrated. There are two macros in the group and they are named after the controls with which they are associated.

❏ The **Member/Class** macro has two conditions, one if the **Member/Class** control is true and the other if the **Member/Class** control is false. If the **Member/Class** control is true then the GoToControl action specifies **Membership No** (as illustrated). If the **Member/Class** control is false then the GoToControl action specifies **Class No.**

❏ To move the focus to **Date** after either a **Membership** or **Class** number has been entered, the macro Date is used. This macro uses a **GoToControl** action with the **Control Name** argument **Date.**

❏ Save the macro group as **Booking.**

❏ Display the Bookings form in design mode.

❏ Click on the **Member/Class** control and set the **On Exit** property to Booking. This means that the first macro in the macro group Bookings will run when this control is exited.

❏ Set the **On Exit** control of **Membership No** to Booking.Date. Repeat for the **Class No** control.

❏ Save the form and test the macro group by entering some data.

control reference syntax

To be able to refer to a control name from within a macro the correct syntax must be used. If the way in which the control is referred does not follow the rules of syntax then the macro will not work.

The syntax for referring to controls is as follows:

For a control on a form

Forms*!formname!controlname*

For a control on a report

Reports*!reportname!controlname*

For a control on a subform

Forms!*mainformname!subformname.Form!controlname*

If the name of the form, report or control contains spaces then it must be enclosed in square brackets for example

Forms![Membership Category]![Membership Fee]

If the macro is run from the form or report containing the control then the control can be referred to by the controlname alone, this is known as the short syntax, for example

[Membership Fee]

If you are in doubt always use the full syntax. If the short syntax is used in an inappropriate situation then the macro will not run.

exercise 9 *using a form to enter report criteria*

If a report is created that is based on a query then it is useful to be able to enter criteria for the report. The report that is to be used is the one based on the **When joined** query which listed members who have joined the centre during a defined time period. This query was created in Exercise 2.8. Use Report Wizards to create a single-column report from this query. Save the report with the name **When joined.**

A form will be created that will allow the start and end dates of the time period to be entered before the report is previewed.

The exercise involves creating an unbound form, a macro group, a module and also the underlying query and the report will be edited. Therefore this is a long exercise so follow the steps carefully.

Step 1

Step 1 is to create an unbound form

❏ From the Database Window click on the **Form** button and click on **New.** Leave the Table/Query box empty as this form is not bound to a table or query.

❏ Click on blank form.

❏ In design view set the properties for the form

Property	Setting
Caption	Period under investigation (the name that will appear in the title bar of the form)
DefaultView	Single Form
ScrollBars	Neither
ViewsAllowed	Form

❐ Add an unbound text box for each criterion you want to enter. There are two criteria to be entered so add two text boxes, use the completed form illustrated following as a guide.

❐ Set the properties for the text boxes as follows:

Property	Setting
ControlName (or Name)	Start Date (first text box)
	End Date (second text box)
	Use a ControlName that describes the type of criterion.
Format	Short Date (both text boxes)
	Use a Format that reflects the data type of the criterion.

❐ Edit the label of the first text box to read **Period beginning** and the second text box to read **Period ending** as illustrated.

❐ Add text to indicate the purpose of the form.

❐ Save the form, and giving it the name, **When joined.**

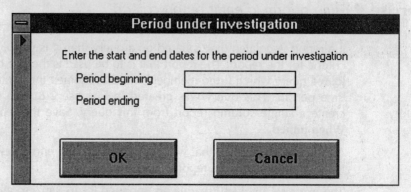

Your form will not look like this yet as you have only used design mode. The OK and Cancel command buttons will be added to the form after you create macros for them.

Step 2

Step 2 is to create a module that is used by one of the macros

Modules have not been introduced as they involve programming and it is not the intention of this book to discuss programming Access other than superficially as in this example. The module being created is a copy of one of the modules that is available with the North Wind Traders sample database that comes with Access. By recreating it you will see how to create a module.

❐ From the database window click on the **Module** button and click on **New.** Type the line

Function IsLoaded (MyFormName)

and press Enter. The menu bar will change to display IsLoaded in the Procedure box.

❐ Key in the rest of the module exactly as illustrated. The line End Function is pre-set and you add the lines inbetween. Those of you familiar with Basic will notice that a For...Next loop and an If statement are used. Note the apostrophe indicates that the text to the right of it is a comment.

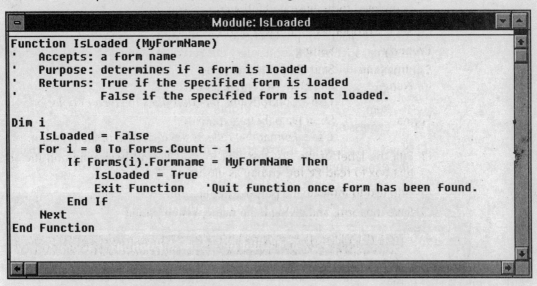

```
Module: IsLoaded

Function IsLoaded (MyFormName)
'    Accepts: a form name
'    Purpose: determines if a form is loaded
'    Returns: True if the specified form is loaded
'             False if the specified form is not loaded.

Dim i
    IsLoaded = False
    For i = 0 To Forms.Count - 1
        If Forms(i).Formname = MyFormName Then
            IsLoaded = True
            Exit Function    'Quit function once form has been found.
        End If
    Next
End Function
```

☐ Save the module with the name **IsLoaded** and close it.

Step 3

Step 3 is to create the macros for the form

The three macros used by the form will be kept in one macro group as illustrated at the end of this step.

☐ In the Database Window, click the **Macro** button, and then choose the **New** button.

☐ Create a macro that opens the unbound **When joined** form. Display the macro names column. Give the macro the name **Open Dialog,** and select the OpenForm action. Then set the action arguments for OpenForm as follows.

Argument	Setting
Form Name	When joined
View	Form
Data Mode	Edit
Window Mode	Dialog

☐ Add a second action that cancels previewing or printing the report. This action will only take place if the form doesn't load. Click the Conditions button, and type the following expression in the Condition column:

   Not IsLoaded("When joined")

Select CancelEvent as the action for this condition being true. The function IsLoaded checks whether the named form is loaded.

☐ Add a macro to the group that closes the form. Give the macro a name such as Close Dialog. Select the Close action. Set the action arguments as follows.

Argument	Setting
Object Type	Form
Object Name	When joined

❏ Create a macro for the **OK** button. This macro hides the form. Give the macro a name, such as OK, and select the SetValue action. Then set its action arguments as follows.

Argument	Setting
Item	Visible
Expression	No

❏ Save and close the macro group. Give the macro group a name that reflects the general purpose of the group; in this case, **When joined.**

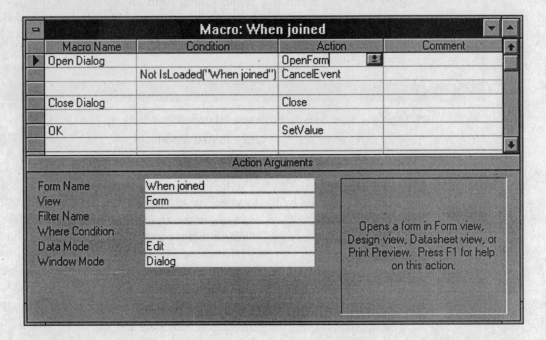

Step 4

To add OK and Cancel command buttons to the form

❏ Reopen the unbound form **When joined** in Design view.

❏ Using the Toolbox (first switch off the Wizards button in Access 2), add a command button for OK, and set its properties as follows.

Property	Setting
Caption	OK
OnPush	When joined.OK
(On Click)	(macrogroup.macroname)

❏ Add a command button for Cancel, and set its properties as follows.

Property	Setting
Caption	Cancel
OnPush	When joined. Close Dialog

❏ Save and close the form.

Step 5

To edit the criteria in the underlying query **When joined.**

❏ Open the **When joined** query in Design view.

❏ Replace the criteria for the **Date of Joining** field. In the new criteria expression, the controls in the **When joined** form are used. Enter the following replacement expression to refer to controls named **Start Date and End Date:**

Between [Forms]![When joined]![Start Date] And [Forms]![When joined]![End Date]

❏ Save the changes and close the query.

Step 6

To attach the macros to the **When joined** report

❏ In Design view of the main report, set the following properties:

Property	Setting
OnOpen	When joined.Open Dialog
	(Name of the macro that opens the unbound When joined form)
OnClose	When joined.Close Dialog
	(Name of the macro that closes the unbound When joined form)

❏ Try putting two unbound controls into the report header so that the title reads List of members that joined between *Start date* and *End date*. Save the report and run it.

activity 7 using macros for data validation

When a table is defined it is possible to set Validation Rules to validate data being entered. One rule used prevented a Category No of greater than 6 being entered as there are only six categories of membership. Validation rules are limited in the validation that they can perform and macros can take validation one stage further. The kind of validation that a macro can perform is to check whether a member signing for a class is the right sex for that class. This will be considered in the following exercise. Another validation that could be performed is that of checking that a room is available at a certain day and time before a booking is accepted.

exercise10 validating bookings for classes

This exercise uses a macro that will check whether a person booking a class is of the right sex. It will prevent a female member booking into a male class and vice versa. When a booking is made the **Class Lists** main/subform is used. The membership number is entered into the subform **(Class Member List).** To check whether the member is male or female the membership data needs to accessed. This can be done by opening the membership form at the record of the membership number just entered.

To prevent the membership form from displaying on the screen the form can be opened as hidden by a validation macro that is assigned to the Before Update property of the Membership No control. To create this validation macro:

❏ In the Database Window, click the **Macro** button, and then choose the **New** button.

❏ Select the OpenForm action. Then set the action arguments for OpenForm as follows.

Argument	Setting
Form Name	Membership
View	Form
Where	[Membership No]=Forms![Class Lists]![Class Member List].Form![Membership No]
Data Mode	Read Only
Window Mode	Hidden

❏ Add a second action that displays a message box. This action will only take place if the member is male and the class is female only. Click the Conditions button, and type the following expression (in one line) in the Condition column:

Forms![Membership]![Sex] And Forms![Class

Lists]![Male/Female/Mixed]="Female"

Select MsgBox as the action for this condition being true. Set the properties for the message box as follows.

Argument	Setting
Message	This is a female only class
Beep	Yes
Type	None
Title	Classes Validation

❏ Add a third action that cancels the event. This action is also dependant upon the condition in the row above and to indicate this an ellipsis, three dots in a row (...) are put in the condition column. Select the CancelEvent action.

❏ Add a fourth action that displays a message box. This action will only take place if the member is female and the class is male only. Click the Conditions button, and type the following expression in the Condition column:

Not Forms![Membership]![Sex] And Forms![Class

Lists]![Male/Female/Mixed]="Male"

Select **MsgBox** as the action for this condition being true. Set the properties for the message box as follows.

Argument	Setting
Message	This is a male only class
Beep	Yes
Type	None
Title	Classes Validation

❑ Add a sixth action that cancels the event. This action is also dependant upon the condition in the row above and to indicate this an ellipsis, three dots in a row (...) are put in the condition column. Select the CancelEvent action.

❑ The final action is Close. Set its arguments as follows.

Argument	Setting
Object Type	Form
Object Name	Membership

❑ Save the macro using the name **Male Female Validation.**

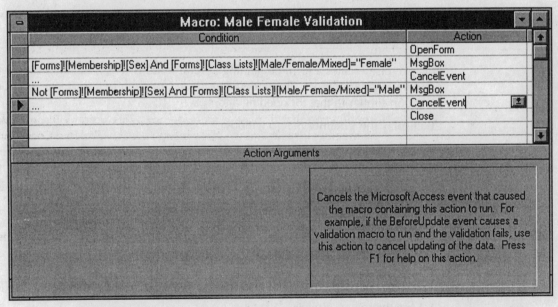

❑ Open the **Class Member List** form in design view. Display the form property sheet, open the Before update property of the form and select Male Female Validation. Save and close the form.

❑ Select the **Class Lists** Main/sub form and open it, try entering a female member into a male class and vice versa to test your macro. Use Edit-Undo Current Record to remove deliberate mistakes. If it doesn't work it is likely that a name has been mistyped. Open the macro in design view and check it carefully.

activity 8 running a macro at start-up time

To give a database application a professional look a macro can be written which will run when the database is opened. This macro can open required forms and set any defaults. Typically a start-up macro would open a form which displayed a main menu for the database. This might have various buttons which the user can click depending upon the action they wish to take.

The macro to perform the start-up tasks is written as usual but to tell Access that it is the start-up macro it is saved with the name Autoexec. When the database is opened if there is a macro called Autoexec then it will be run.

It is possible to stop the macro Autoexec running if you wish to do some development work on the database by holding down the Shift key when the OK button is clicked or Enter is pressed to open the database.

integrative exercises

exercise 11 a report menu

This exercise creates a form containing several buttons which when clicked will preview a certain report. The underlying macro for each button opens a report, an action similar to that for opening a form.

❒ Display the **Chelmer** macro window.

❒ In the next convenient row put Membership Report as the name of this macro.

❒ Open the Action cell list box. Scroll through the actions and select the Open-Report action. Set the arguments for this action as follows:

Argument	Setting
Report Name	Members2
View	Preview

❒ Key into the **Comment** column the description **Preview Membership Report.**

❒ Save the macro group.

❒ In a similar fashion create macros to open the **Mailing, Classes4,** and **Bookings** reports.

❒ Create a blank unbound form. Add to it a title, e.g. Reports Menu and add four buttons one for each macro just created.

❒ Label each button and assign the appropriate macro to it. Remember to use the right syntax, e.g. Chelmer.Mailing for the On Push (On Click) property. Save the form as **Reports Menu** and run it.

Exercise 12 A query menu

This exercise creates a form containing several buttons which when clicked will run a certain query. The underlying macro for each button opens a report, an action similar to that for opening a form.

❑ Display the **Chelmer** macro window.

❑ In the next convenient row put **Sporting Interests** as the name of this macro.

❑ Open the Action cell list box. Scroll through the actions and select the Open-Query action. Set the argument for this action as follows (leave the others at their default settings):

Argument	Setting
Query Name	Members sporting interests

❑ Key into the **Comment** column the description **Sporting Interests Query.**

❑ Save the macro group.

❑ In a similar fashion create macros to open the **Member Ages, Fitness Suite Bookings,** and **When joined** queries.

❑ Create a blank unbound form. Add to it a title, e.g. Queries Menu and add four buttons one for each macro just created.

❑ Label each button and assign the appropriate macro to it. Remember to use the right syntax, e.g. Chelmer.Sporting Interests for the On Push (On Click) property. Save the form as **Query Menu** and run it.

creating a database application

objectives

In the earlier sessions in this book we have explored the creation and use of tables, queries, reports, forms and macros. In order to create a fully operational database system, known as an application, it is necessary to link all of these components together. In this session we explore some of the issues associated with the creation of a working application. At the end of this session you should:

❏ understand the issues and stages in the design of an application

❏ be able to use forms and macros to create a series of linked menus

❏ be able to create a simple application for the use and maintenance of one table

❏ appreciate the complexity of relational database design.

A major underlying objective of this session is to attempt to begin to draw the various components of the Chelmer Database that you have created in this book into a partial application. In order to retain this integrative focus, this session, unlike most others in this book, will not seek to explore the wide range of features that can be used in the design of Applications, such as drop-down menus, menu bars and pop-up forms, but will instead use some of the basic features and focus on the integration of the database components into a basic application, which the reader is welcome to refine later.

activity 1 understanding applications

Why do we need applications? Earlier sessions have introduced you to the creation of the component parts of applications: tables, forms, reports, queries and macros. (Modules might also be included in an Application but we have not attempted these in this book.) You may think that you have already created an application! Indeed through the Database window you are able to select tables, call up a form, edit data in tables, perform queries on tables and produce reports. This might be adequate for a relatively small personal or in-house database, but real Applications are tailored for specific environments. A Leisure Management System would not access the database components through the Database window. Users expect to start the system up, and view a main menu which offers them one or a series of options, such as add a new member or make a booking. The user does not want to have to remember the name of the table which needs to be accessed in order to perform these actions. The user expects to be able to click on a button or choose a menu option and move straight into the form that allows them to perform the appropriate data entry. So for example, an opening or main menu screen might appear as in Figure 10.1.

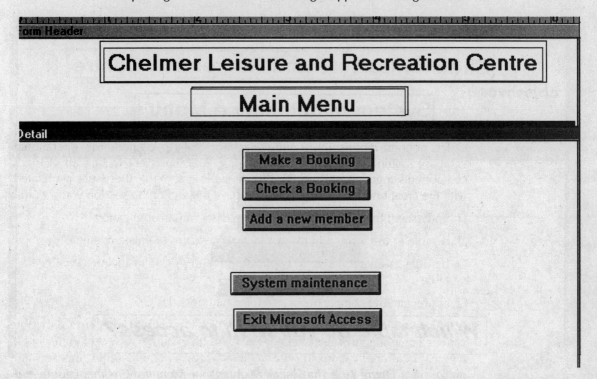

Figure 10.1 The Main Menu for Chelmer Leisure and Recreation Centre Database in Design View

When the user clicks on the first option a form, such as **Bookings** would be displayed.

When the user clicked on System Maintenance an additional menu would be displayed which would offer further options, perhaps as displayed in Figure 10.2

Clicking on one of these buttons would, for instance lead to a further menu for the actions that can be performed on

Membership table, as for example, in Figure 10.3.

What then is a database Application? The Access User's Guide offers a succinct definition:

'A Database Application is a set of related Microsoft Access database objects that you can use to accomplish a particular database task. For example, if you use a certain set of forms and reports frequently, you can create an application that gives you easy access to these forms and reports and displays them conveniently in the Microsoft Access window.'

In Session 9 you developed some simple macros that could be used with forms and reports. You can use macros to create an application, or custom workspace, and to add features to your application. For example, you can create custom menu bars for forms, assign common actions to menu commands or key combinations, and automate various tasks such as printing daily reports or backing up your database.

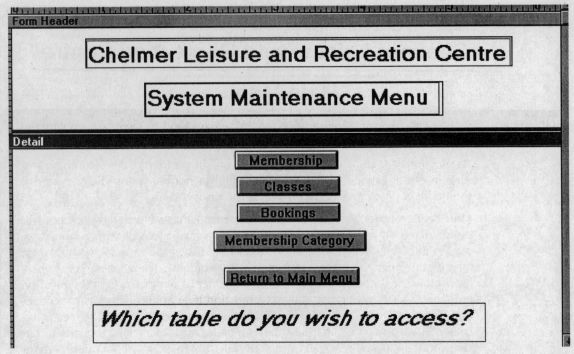

Figure 10.2 The System Maintenance Menu for Chelmer Leisure and Recreation Centre Database

Note: We have created the database components first and are now proceeding to integrate them into one application. This is not the way these things should be done! However, it is easier for the beginner to start to understand some of the components before attempting to integrate those components. If we were designing a database Application for real the same data analysis that led to the table design as shown in Figure 1.1 should consider the way in which that data is to be used. This would determine which forms, reports, queries, macros and modules were necessary and the function of each of these.

exercise 1 understanding applications

Figure 10.3 shows a menu for adding records to the **Membership** table. Draw on paper a similar menu for adding data to the **Classes** table. Indicate which of the forms and reports that you have already created might be accessed via this menu.

activity 2 creating a simple application

The sample Application illustrated in the earlier Figures in this session is extremely simplistic. For example, only forms are used for the display of menus, and windows, pull-down menus, menu bars and pop-up forms are not used. Yet even these simple menus start to illustrate some important features of good application design:

Screen design in an application is a type of Form design, and there all of the same design considerations must be taken into account. For example, it is important to choose easily legible fonts and font sizes, and to create an uncluttered screen.

Design must depend upon the application. In particular the sequencing of screens should make it easy to run through a normal task sequence, and it should be easy to move between related but distinct tasks.

Most systems have three types of users: systems managers (who have responsibility for maintain the system, managers (seeking management reports and summary data), and operators (who, for example, are on the desk taking bookings, meeting members and answering members enquiries). These users seek to perform different operations using the system. Menus and menu options must be grouped in such a way that different users find their applications easily accessible. Hence, for example, in Figure 10.1, the Main Menu for the Chelmer Database it is easy to go straight into desk functions such as making a booking, but other functions that might be more useful to managers are ' hidden' under system Maintenance. An additional refinement would be that workstations on the bookings desk did not display the System Maintenance options at all. This would lend greater security on workstations that were in a public access area.

A real system based on multiple tables is very complex to create and would involve much more input than you would probably wish to pursue. Instead, in Exercise 10.2 we create a small application based solely on the Membership table, and using some of the forms and reports that we have already created, as well as some special forms which will display the menus.

exercise 2 *creating the main or opening menu for the membership table*

We wish to create the Main Menu for the Chelmer Leisure and Recreation Centre as in Figure 10.1. The process has two stages: the creation of the form, and the creation of and linking of macros to the form. Where possible we use macros that were created in Session 9.

First to create a form:

❐ Open a new form and stretch it.

❐ Add a form header and footer

❐ Open the form header and insert the title text in Figure 10.1

❐ Open the Detail Band and insert the buttons as in Figure 10.1

❐ Save the form as **Main Menu**.

Next review and create appropriate macros. Macros similar to those required have already been created in Session 9.

We need:

Button	Macro
Make a booking	Opens a booking form (e.g. **Booking**), such as NewBooking
Check a Booking	Opens a booking form at the first record, ready for the user to search using ***Edit-Find***.
Add a New Member	Opens a form, such as **Membership**.
System Maintenance	Opens a form, e.g. **System Maintenance Menu**.
Exit Microsoft Access	Closes the active window.

When you have checked that you have all of the above macros:

❑ Open the form again in Design View.

❑ Add the macros to the buttons in turn, by Clicking on the button and inserting the macro name as the OnPush property, on the Properties Sheet.

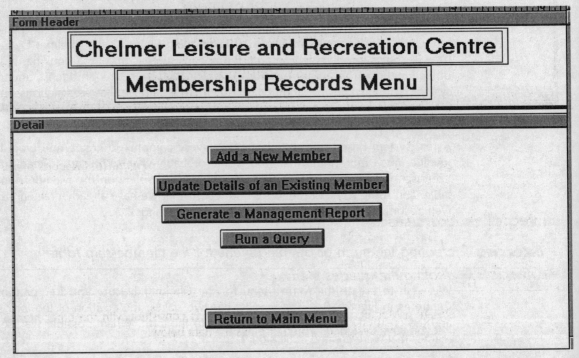

Figure 10.3 Membership Table Menu

exercise 3 creating the system maintenance menu

Using a similar approach to that used in Exercise 2, create the System Maintenance Menu shown in Figure 10.2

exercise 4 creating the management reports menu

The Report Menu can be created using similar principles to those outlined in Exercise 11 Session 9. Try modifying the menu that you created in that exercise to look like Figure 10.4

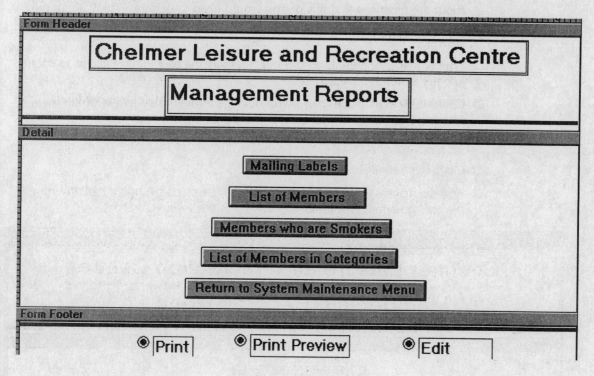

Figure 10.4 Reports Menu

integrative exercises

exercise 6 creating the queries menu

Design a Membership Queries Menu which is consistent with the other menus that you have designed, which displays the data below.

> Chelmer Leisure and Recreation Centre
> Membership Queries Menu
>
> New Query
> Existing Query

exercise 7 designing a bookings table main menu.

❑ Design a Bookings Main Menu for the **Bookings** table which is similar to that for the Membership table.

❑ What' s wrong with this menu for the person on the bookings desk? Think about the functions that this person would need to perform. Think about the questions that customers might ask, for which they would need to provide an answer.

❑ Which, if any, of these functions might require the user to have access to data in other tables in the database?

❑ Could customers make their own bookings through a system with the main menu in Figure 10.1? What additional security might be advisable?

appendix 1
basic Windows operations

Some readers will not be familiar with Windows and Access may well be one of the first Windows products encountered by many users. Any reader who has not previously used Windows is strongly recommended to run through the Windows tutorial which introduces users to mouse techniques and the basic operation of Windows. This appendix briefly summarises some of the key operations and should act as a ready reference to some of the terminology that is used elsewhere in the book.

mouse techniques

The basic mouse techniques are listed in the table below, with a simple description of each technique.

To	Do this
Point	Position the mouse pointer on or next to something
Click	Position the pointer and then quickly press and release the left mouse button
Double click	Position the pointer and then quickly press and release the left mouse button twice
Drag	Position the pointer. Press and hold down the left mouse button as you move the mouse to the desired position. The release the button.

mouse pointer shapes

When the mouse is pointed to different parts of the screen, the pointer shape changes allowing you to perform different tasks. Some commands also change the pointer shape.

The table below lists some common pointer shapes as encountered in Access:

Pointer shape	Meaning
I	The pointer over the text area. Click to position an insertion point where text may be typed.
⤡	The pointer appears over menus, non-text areas of windows, inactive windows, scroll bars, or toolbar. You can choose a menu and command, click a button. You can use the pointer to drag to make a selection.

Pointer shape	Meaning
	The pointer is over the selection bar, for example, at the edge of a table, or at the left edge of a cell. You can select a cell, a row, or several rows.
	Access is performing a task that will take a few seconds
	Appears along the borders between window sections or columns. Drag to resize the section or column.
	The pointer appears after you press Shift-F1. You can point to any item on the screen and click to view specific Help.
	The pointer is on a window border. Depending on which border the pointer will assume one of the shapes opposite. Drag to resize the window.
	This pointer appears when you have selected the Move or Size command from the Control menu. You can move the window to a new position or drag the window border.
	This pointer appears over the grey bar at the top of a column in a table, query, or filter. Click to select the column.
	This pointer appears in the record selection bar. Click to select record.
	This is the drag and drop pointer appears when you make a selection and drag the selection to its new location, releasing the mouse button to drop or insert the selection.
	This is the zoom pointer which appears in print preview.
	The pointer is on a control sizing handle. Depending on which handle the pointer will assume one of the shapes opposite. Drag to resize the control.
	In form or report design this pointer is used to move an individual label or control.
	In form or report design this pointer is used to move a label and control or a selected set of controls.
	This pointer appears with a Toolbox icon and indicates the position of the control on the form or report design. Click to position the control.

basics of windows: a quick review

The Windows screen has the following features:

Menu bar

The menu bar shows the titles of the various pull down menus that are available with a given application. To select a menu option, first select the menu by placing the mouse pointer over the name of the menu on the menu bar and click the left mouse button. The menu will appear. Move the mouse pointer to the menu option you require and click the left mouse button again. Note that any menu options displayed in light grey are not currently available. Menus can also be accessed via the keyboard. For example, to select the file menu press **ALT+F** i.e. press **ALT** together with the initial letter of the menu option.

Control menu

The **control** menu is found on all windows whether they be application windows or document windows. To access the **Control** menu click on the control menu box in the upper left corner of the window, or press **ALT+SPACEBAR.** The exact contents are different for different windows, but typically basic windows operations such as restore, move, size, minimise, maximise, close and switch to are represented.

Title bar

The title bar tells you which window is displayed. By pointing the mouse at the window's title bar, and then dragging the title bar to a new location the window can be moved.

Maximise, minimise and restore buttons

Clicking on the **MAXIMISE** button enlarges a window to its maximum size, so that is fills the whole desktop.

Clicking on the **RESTORE** button will restore a maximised window to its previous size.

Clicking on the **MINIMISE** button reduces the window to a small icon at the bottom of the screen. When you shrink an application window to an icon, the application is still running in memory, but its window is not taking up space on your desktop.

Dialog boxes

Windows uses dialog boxes to request information from you and to provide information to you. Most dialog boxes include options, with each option asking for a different kind of information.

After all of the requested information has been supplied you choose a command button to carry out the command. Two command buttons that feature on every dialog box are **OK** and **CANCEL. OK** causes the command to be executed.

CANCEL cancels the operation and removes the dialog box from the screen. These buttons represent the two means of quitting from a dialog box. To choose a command button, click on it, or if the button is currently active, press **ENTER.**

There are a number of different kinds of dialog boxes. These are:

Text boxes are boxes where you are allowed to type in text, such as a filename. The presence of a flashing vertical bar, or the insertion point, indicates that the text box is active and that you may enter text. If the text box is not active, place the mouse pointer on the box and click. The insertion point will then appear in the box.

List boxes show a column of available choices. Items can be selected from a list box by double clicking on the item, or clicking once on the item and then clicking on the OK button.

Check boxes offer a list of options that you can switch on and off. You can select as many or as few check box options as are applicable. When an option in a check box is selected it contains an X; otherwise the box is empty. To select a check box, click on the empty box.

Option buttons appear as a list of mutually exclusive items. You can select only one option from the list at a time. You can change a selection by selecting a different button. The selected button contains a black dot. To select an option button, click on it.

Scroll bars appear at the side of windows and list boxes. They appear when the information contained in a window can not be displayed wholly within that window. Both vertical and horizontal scroll bars may be present depending on whether the document is too long or too wide to fit on the screen. The small box in the middle of the bar represents the position of the currently displayed text within the whole document. You can move to a different position in the text by moving this box. You can move this box either by clicking on the scroll bar arrow boxes, clicking on the scroll bar itself, or dragging the box.

appendix 2
data, data dictionary and list of forms, queries and reports

Data

Membership table data

Membership No	Category	Surname	Forenames	Title	Street
1	2	Walker	Andrew J	Mr	16 Dovecot Close
2	1	Cartwright	Denise	Mrs	27 Bowling Green Rd
3	6	Perry	Jason R	Mr	59 Church Street
4	2	Forsythe	Ann M	Miss	2 Ferndale Close
5	1	Jameson	Donna	Mrs	25 Alder Drive
6	3	Robinson	Petra	Miss	16 Lowton Lane
7	5	Harris	David J	Mr	55 Coven Road
8	2	Shangali	Imran	Mr	47 High Street
9	1	Barrett	Martha A	Mrs	7 Oldcott Way
10	1	Weiner	George W F	Mr	6 Church Street
11	6	Ali	David	Mr	33 Meirton Road
12	2	Young	Aileen	Ms	78 Highgate Street
13	5	Gray	Ivor P	Mr	4 The Parade
14	5	Swift	Freda	Miss	23 Ferndale Close
15	1	Davies	Sandra M	Mrs	61 Hallfield Road
16	1	Robinson	Rebecca	Mrs	9 Moss Street
17	2	Everett	Alan	Mr	12 Stanley Street
18	4	Locker	Liam	Mr	2 Beech Close
19	4	Locker	Alison	Miss	2 Beech Close
20	1	Jones	Edward R	Mr	17 Mayfield Avenue

	Town	County	Post Code	Telephone No	Occupation	Date of Birth
1	Chelmer	Cheshire	CH2 6TR	0777 569236	Builder	12/3/52
2	Meirton	Cheshire	CH9 2EV	0777 552099	Housewife	29/11/60
3	Chelmer	Cheshire	CH1 8YU			3/6/81
4	Chelmer	Cheshire		0777 569945	Receptionist	5/8/73
5	Chelmer	Cheshire	CH2 7FN		Housewife	4/12/70
6	Branford	Staffs	ST10 2DZ	0778 890523		7/7/84
7	Chelmer	Cheshire	CH3 8PS	0777 569311	Retired	22/5/28
8	Chelmer	Cheshire	CH1 7JH	0777 561553	Accountant	15/3/55
9	Meirton	Cheshire	CH9 3DR	0777 557822	Teacher	25/11/60
10	Chelmer	Cheshire	CH1 8YV		Electrician	10/2/58
11	Chelmer	Cheshire	CH4 5KD	0777 569066		14/7/80
12	Branford	Staffs	ST10 4RT	0778 894471	Civil Servant	25/10/51
13	Chelmer	Cheshire	CH1 7ER	0777 565715	Unemployed	12/4/47
14	Chelmer	Cheshire	CH2 8PN	0777 567351	Retired	14/9/27
15	Meirton	Cheshire	CH9 1YJ	0778 891441	Clerk	1/2/65
16	Chelmer	Cheshire	CH2 8SE	0777 568812	Housewife	18/5/68
17	Chelmer	Cheshire	CH3 3CJ		Draughtsperson	30/7/57
18	Chelmer	Cheshire	CH3 8UH			30/12/83
19	Chelmer	Cheshire	CH3 8UH			30/12/83
20	Chelmer	Cheshire	CH2 9OL	0777 567333	Bus Driver	22/12/58

	Date of Joining	Date of Last Renewal	Sporting Interests	Smoker	Sex
1	3/2/92	3/2/93	Tennis, squash	Yes	Yes
2	16/7/91	16/7/93	Aerobics, swimming, running, squash	No	No
3	12/12/93	12/12/93	Judo, Karate	No	Yes
4	16/9/91	16/9/93		No	No
5	15/6/92	15/6/93	Aerobics, squash	Yes	No
6	3/1/94	3/1/94	Swimming, Judo	No	No
7	1/2/94	1/2/94	Badminton, cricket	Yes	Yes
8	6/4/92	6/4/93	Weight training, squash	No	Yes
9	4/10/93	4/10/93	Keep fit, swimming	No	No
10	15/7/92	15/7/93	Weight training, squash	No	Yes
11	2/10/93	2/10/93	Judo, swimming, football	No	Yes
12	9/8/92	9/8/93	Keep fit, Aerobics, squash	Yes	No
13	5/1/94	5/1/94		Yes	Yes
14	16/9/93	16/9/93		No	No
15	5/4/92	5/4/93	Aerobics, squash, swimming	Yes	No
16	6/12/91	6/12/93	Tennis, Aerobics	No	No
17	5/11/93	5/11/93	Squash, Fitness training, football	No	Yes
18	13/6/92	13/6/93		No	Yes
19	13/6/92	13/6/93		No	No
20	17/5/91	17/5/93	Weight training	Yes	Yes

Membership category table data

Category No	Category Type	Membership fee
1	Senior	£25.00
2	Senior Club	£30.00
3	Junior	£10.00
4	Junior Club	£15.00
5	Concessionary	£18.00
6	Youth Club	£20.00

Classes table data

Class No	Class Day	Class Time	Class Tutor	Class Activity	Male/Female /Mixed
1	Monday	10:00	Evans	Ladies' Aerobics	Female
2	Monday	11:00	Franks	Weight Training	Male
3	Monday	15:00	Latham	Body Conditioning	Mixed
4	Monday	19:00	Wheildon	Step Aerobics	Mixed
5	Tuesday	10:00	Jackson	Men's Multi-gym	Male
6	Tuesday	14:00	Adams	Ladies' Multi-gym	Female
7	Tuesday	19:00	Jackson	Family Multi-gym	Mixed
8	Wednesday	10:00	Evans	Ladies' Aerobics	Female
9	Wednesday	14:00	Latham	Body Conditioning	Mixed
10	Wednesday	15:00	Franks	Weight training	Female
11	Wednesday	19:00	Franks	Weight Training	Mixed
12	Thursday	11:00	Latham	Weight Training	Male
13	Thursday	14:00	Wheildon	Step Aerobics	Mixed
14	Thursday	15:00	Adams	Multi-gym	Mixed
15	Thursday	19:00	Latham	Body Conditioning	Mixed
16	Friday	10:00	Latham	Body Conditioning	Female
17	Friday	11:00	Wheildon	Step Aerobics	Mixed
18	Friday	14:00	Jackson	Men's Multi-gym	Male

Bookings table data

Booking No	Room/hall/ court No	Membership No	Class No	Date	Time	Member/Class
1	Fitness Suite		1	14/3/94	10:00	Class
2	Fitness Suite		2	14/3/94	11:00	Class
3	Sports hall 2		3	14/3/94	15:00	Class
4	Sports hall 1		4	14/3/94	19:00	Class
5	Fitness Suite		5	15/3/94	10:00	Class
6	Fitness Suite		6	15/3/94	14:00	Class
7	Fitness Suite		7	15/3/94	19:00	Class
8	Fitness Suite		8	16/3/94	10:00	Class
9	Sports hall 2		9	16/3/94	14:00	Class
10	Sports hall 2		10	16/3/94	15:00	Class
11	Sports hall 2		11	16/3/94	19:00	Class
12	Sports hall 2		12	17/3/94	11:00	Class
13	Sports hall 2		13	17/4/94	14:00	Class
14	Fitness Suite		14	17/3/94	15:00	Class
15	Sports hall 2		15	17/3/94	19:00	Class
16	Sports hall 2		16	18/3/94	10:00	Class
17	Sports hall 2		17	18/3/94	11:00	Class
18	Fitness Suite		18	18/3/94	14:00	Class
19	Court 1	2		14/3/94	18:00	Member
20	Court 2	17		17/3/94	14:00	Member
21	Court 3	15		15/3/94	11:00	Member
22	Court 1	12		16/3/94	19:00	Member

Class List table data

Class No	Membership No
1	2
1	5
1	16
4	4
4	6
5	7
5	10
5	1

Data dictionary

Data dictionary table

Field Name	Data Type	Description	Length		Index Name
Table Name	Text		50		Primary Key
Field Name	Text		50		Primary Key
Data Type	Text		50		
Description	Text		50		
Length	Text		50		
Format	Text		50		
Default Value	Text		50		
Validation Rule	Text		50		
Validation Text	Text		50		
Required	Text		50		
Index Name	Text		50		

Bookings table (**Bookings** is the first field for each record)

Field Name	Data Type	Description	Length	Format	Default value
Booking No	Counter		4		
Class No	Long		4		
Date	Date/Time		8	d/m/yy	
Member/Class	Yes/No		1		
Membership No	Long		4		
Room/Hall/Court	Text		20		
Time	Date/Time		8	hh:mm Short time	

Field Name	Validation Rule	Validation Text	Required	Index Name
Booking No				Primary Key
Class No				Reference
Date			Yes	Multi
Member/Class			*Yes*	
Membership No				Reference
Room/Hall/Court			Yes	Single
Time			Yes	Multi

Classes table (**Classes** is the first field for each record)

Field Name	Data Type	Description	Length	Format	Default value
Class Activity	Text		20		
Class Day	Text		10		
Class No	Counter		4		
Class Time	Date/Time		8	hh:mm Short time	
Class Tutor	Text		30		
Male/Female/Mixed	Text		10		

Field Name	Validation Rule	Validation Text	Required	Index Name
Class Activity			Yes	
Class Day			Yes	
Class No				Primary Key
Class Time			Yes	
Class Tutor				Single, Reference
Male/Female/Mixed	"Male" or "Female" or "Mixed"	Please enter Male Female or Mixed		

Membership table (**Membership** is the first field for each record)

Field Name	Data Type	Description	Length	Format	Default value
County	Text		20		Cheshire
Date of Birth	Date/Time		8	d/m/yy	
Date of Joining	Date/Time		8	d/m/yy	
Date of Last Renewal	Date/Time		8	d/m/yy	
Forenames	Text		30		
Membership Category	Byte	Categories are 1-Senior, 2-	1		
Membership No	Counter		4		
Occupation	Text		50		
Post Code	Text		10	>	
Sex	Yes/No		1	"Male";"Female"	
Smoker	Yes/No		1	"Smoker";"Non-Smoker"	
Sporting Interests	Memo		0		
Street	Text		30		
Surname	Text		25		
Telephone No	Text		12		
Title	Text		10		
Town	Text		25		Cheshire

Field Name	Validation Rule	Validation Text	Required	Index Name
County			Yes	
Date of Birth				Single
Date of Joining			Yes	Single
Date of Last Renewal			Yes	
Forenames				Multi
Membership Category	<=6	Please enter a category between 1 and 6		
Membership No				Primary Key
Occupation				
Post Code				
Sex				
Smoker				
Sporting Interests				
Street			Yes	
Surname			Yes	Multi
Telephone No				
Title				
Town			Yes	

Membership Category table (Membership Category is the first field for each record)

Field Name	Data Type	Description	Length	Format	Default value
Category No	Byte		1		
Category Type	Text		15		
Membership Fee	Currency		8		

Field Name	Validation Rule	Validation Text	Required	Index Name
Category No			Yes	Primary Key
Category Type			Yes	
Membership Fee			Yes	

Tutors table (Tutor is the first field for each record)

Field Name	Data Type	Description	Length	Format	Default value
County	Text		20		Cheshire
Date of Birth	Date/Time		8	d/m/yy	
Initials	Text		3		
National Insurance No	Text		10		
Post Code	Text		10		
Qualifications	Memo		0		
Street	Text		30		
Surname	Text		25		
Telephone No	Text		12		
Title	Text		10		
Town	Text		25		Chelmer

Field Name	Validation Rule	Validation Text	Required	Index Name
County			Yes	
Date of Birth				Single
Initials				Multi
National Insurance No				
Post Code				
Qualifications				
Street			Yes	
Surname			Yes	Primary key, Multi
Telephone No				
Title				
Town			Yes	

Class List table (Class List is the first field for each record)

Field Name	Data Type	Description	Length	Format	Default value
Class No	Long		4		
Membership No	Long		4		

Field Name	Validation Rule	Validation Text	Required	Index Name
Class No				Primary Key
Membership No				Primary Key

Tables

Membership
Membership Category
Classes
Bookings
Dictionary (1.7)
Tutors
Class List (7.4)
Last Renewed 92 (7.7)

Reports

Name	Exercises
Members	4.1,4.2,4.7
Categories	4.3,6.14
Mailing	4.4,9.11
Classes	4.6,4.8,5.12
Members2	4.7,5.10,5.11,5.12
Classes2	4.9,7.6
Smokers	4.10
Classes List	4.11
Classes3	5.15
Classes4	6.3, 9.11
Classes List2	7.6
Bookings	5.9,9.11
Class Member List(Sub-report)	7.6
Wednesday Class Attendance	7.11

Forms

Name	Exercises
Membership	3.1,3.5,3.6,3.7,3.9,5.1,5.3,5.4,5.5,5.6, 5.7,6.13,9.1,9.2,9.3,9.5,9.6,9.7
Membership Category	3.2,3.4,3.8
Membership2	3.10
Tutor	3.12
Bookings2	5.2
Classes	3.11,5.13
Bookings	3.11,9.5,9.6,9.7,9.8
Classes2	3.12,5.12
Classes3	6.1,6.2,6.7
Class Member List (Sub-form)	7.4,9.10
Class Lists	7.5
Main Menu	10.2
Membership Menu	10.3
System Maintenance Menu	10.4
Queries Menu	10.5
Bookings Menu	10.6
Form Menu	9.5,9.6
When Joined	9.9

Queries

Name	Exercises
Members sporting interests	2.2,2.3,2.4
Addresses of male smokers	2.7
Occupations of female members	2.7
Sporting Interest	2.8
Sports Hall 1 Bookings	5.14
Member ages	2.9,9.12
Average ages	2.12
When joined	2.8,9.9,9.12
New members	4.4
Fitness suite bookings	5.8,9.12
Recent fees paid	7.2
Activities in fitness suite	7.3
Wednesday Class Attendance	7.11

Macros

Name	Exercises
Chelmer	9.1,9.2,9.3,9.6,9.11
Chelmer.NewBooking	9.4
Autokeys	9.7
Booking	9.8
Male Female Validation	9.10

Database window

Button	Button name	Description
	Print preview	Shows how the datasheet, form or report will appear when printed
	New query	Creates a new query based on the query or table selected in the database window, if one is selected.
	New form	Creates a new form based on the query or table selected in the database window, if one is selected
	Undo	Undoes your most recent action
	Help	Opens help

Design view (tables)

	Design view	Switches you to the design view of a table, query, or form.
	Datasheet view	Switches you to the datasheet view of a table, query, or form
	Properties	Displays or conceals the property sheet for the selected control, section or database object.
	Primary key	Makes the selected field or fields the primary key for the table.

Design view (queries)

	Totals	Displays or conceals the Totals row in the QBE grid
	Run	Runs a query, or, in a macro window, a macro.

Datasheet view (tables and queries)

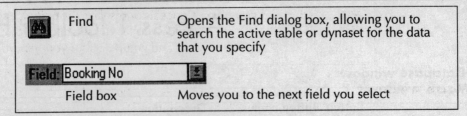

	Find	Opens the Find dialog box, allowing you to search the active table or dynaset for the data that you specify
Field: Booking No	Field box	Moves you to the next field you select

Design view (forms window)

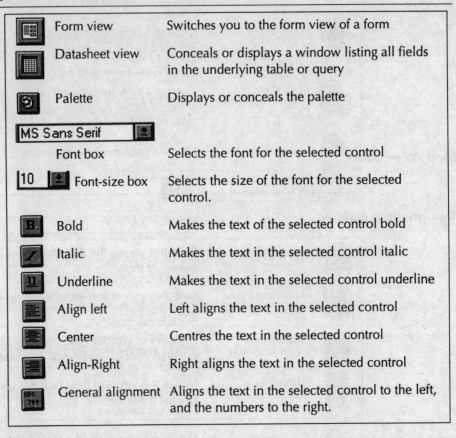

	Form view	Switches you to the form view of a form
	Datasheet view	Conceals or displays a window listing all fields in the underlying table or query
	Palette	Displays or conceals the palette
MS Sans Serif	Font box	Selects the font for the selected control
10	Font-size box	Selects the size of the font for the selected control.
B	Bold	Makes the text of the selected control bold
I	Italic	Makes the text in the selected control italic
U	Underline	Makes the text in the selected control underline
	Align left	Left aligns the text in the selected control
	Center	Centres the text in the selected control
	Align-Right	Right aligns the text in the selected control
	General alignment	Aligns the text in the selected control to the left, and the numbers to the right.

Datasheet and form view (forms window)

	Edit filter/sort	Opens the Filter window to create or edit a filter
	Apply/Sort Filter	Applies the current filter
	Show all records	Displays all records in underlying table by removing any applied filters.

Report window

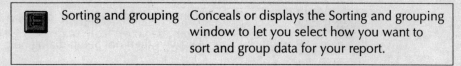

| | Sorting and grouping | Conceals or displays the Sorting and grouping window to let you select how you want to sort and group data for your report. |

Macro window

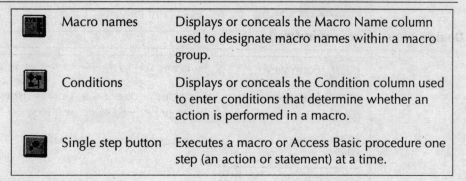

	Macro names	Displays or conceals the Macro Name column used to designate macro names within a macro group.
	Conditions	Displays or conceals the Condition column used to enter conditions that determine whether an action is performed in a macro.
	Single step button	Executes a macro or Access Basic procedure one step (an action or statement) at a time.

Module window

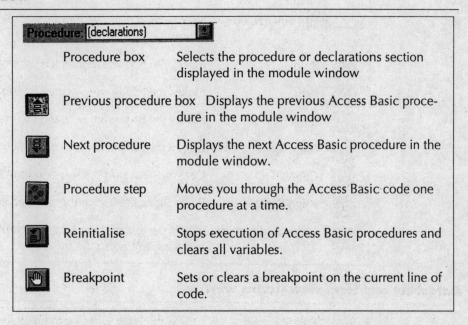

Procedure: [declarations]

	Procedure box	Selects the procedure or declarations section displayed in the module window
	Previous procedure box	Displays the previous Access Basic procedure in the module window
	Next procedure	Displays the next Access Basic procedure in the module window.
	Procedure step	Moves you through the Access Basic code one procedure at a time.
	Reinitialise	Stops execution of Access Basic procedures and clears all variables.
	Breakpoint	Sets or clears a breakpoint on the current line of code.

Print preview and sample preview window

Print...	Print	Prints the datasheet, form, or report.
Setup...	Setup	Displays the Print Setup dialog box.
Zoom	Zoom	Switches between showing a magnified portion of the page or the entire page.
Cancel	Cancel	Exits Print Preview

Database window

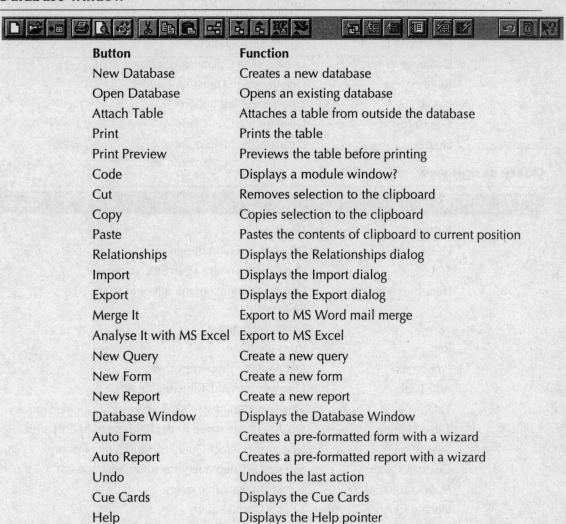

Button	Function
New Database	Creates a new database
Open Database	Opens an existing database
Attach Table	Attaches a table from outside the database
Print	Prints the table
Print Preview	Previews the table before printing
Code	Displays a module window?
Cut	Removes selection to the clipboard
Copy	Copies selection to the clipboard
Paste	Pastes the contents of clipboard to current position
Relationships	Displays the Relationships dialog
Import	Displays the Import dialog
Export	Displays the Export dialog
Merge It	Export to MS Word mail merge
Analyse It with MS Excel	Export to MS Excel
New Query	Create a new query
New Form	Create a new form
New Report	Create a new report
Database Window	Displays the Database Window
Auto Form	Creates a pre-formatted form with a wizard
Auto Report	Creates a pre-formatted report with a wizard
Undo	Undoes the last action
Cue Cards	Displays the Cue Cards
Help	Displays the Help pointer

Table design view

Button	Function
Design View	Displays table design
Datasheet View	Displays the data in the table in the form of a datasheet
Save	Saves the table

Properties	Displays the properties sheet
Indexes	Displays the Indexes dialog box
Set Primary Key	Sets primary key for selected field(s)
Insert Row	Insert a row
Delete Row	Delete a row
New Query	Create a new query
New Form	Create a new form
New Report	Create a new report
Database Window	Displays the Database Window
Build	Displays the Expression builder
Undo	Undoes the last action
Cue Cards	Displays the Cue Cards
Help	Displays the Help pointer

Query design view

Button	Function
Design View	Displays query in design view
SQL	Displays the query as an SQL statement
Datasheet View	Displays the data in the query in the form of a datasheet
Save	Saves the query
Run	Runs the query
Properties	Displays the properties sheet
Add Table	Displays the Add Table dialog box
Total	Displays total row in QBE grid for statistical summary
Table Names	Displays table name under field name in QBE grid
Select Query	Selects the Select Query (default type of query)
Crosstab Query	Selects Crosstab query for summarising data
Make-Table Query	Selects Make Table query
Update Query	Selects Update query
Append Query	Selects Append query
Delete Query	Selects Delete query
New Query	Create a new query
New Form	Create a new form
New Report	Create a new report
Database Window	Displays the Database Window
Build	Displays the Expression builder
Undo	Undoes the last action

| Cue Cards | Displays the Cue Cards |
| Help | Displays the Help pointer |

Datasheet view (tables)

Button	Function
Design View	Displays table design
Datasheet View	Displays the data in the table in the form of a datasheet
Print	Prints the datasheet
Print Preview	Displays the print preview
New	Goto new record
Cut	Remove selection to clipboard
Copy	Copy selection to clipboard
Paste	Paste from clipboard to current position
Find	Search for selected data
Sort Ascending	Displays records in ascending order of current field
Sort Descending	Displays records in descending order of current field
Edit Filter/Sort	Displays filter design window
Apply Filter/Sort	Applies filter to records
Show All Records	Remove filter and show natural order
New Query	Create a new query
New Form	Create a new form
New Report	Create a new report
Database Window	Displays the Database Window
Auto Form	Creates a pre-formatted form with a wizard
Auto Report	Creates a pre-formatted report with a wizard
Undo Current Field/Record	Undoes the current field or record
Undo	Undoes the last action
Cue Cards	Displays the Cue Cards
Help	Displays the Help pointer

Datasheet view (queries)

Button	Function
Design View	Displays table design
SQL	Displays the query as an SQL statement
Datasheet View	Displays the data in the table in the form of a datasheet

Print	Prints the dynaset
Print Preview	Displays the print preview
New	Goto new record
Cut	Remove selection to clipboard
Copy	Copy selection to clipboard
Paste	Paste from clipboard to current position
Find	Search for selected data
New Query	Create a new query
New Form	Create a new form
New Report	Create a new report
Database Window	Displays the Database Window
Auto Form	Creates a pre-formatted form with a wizard
Auto Report	Creates a pre-formatted report with a wizard
Undo Current Field/Record	Undoes the current field or record
Undo	Undoes the last action
Cue Cards	Displays the Cue Cards
Help	Displays the Help pointer

Form run view

Button	Function
Design View	Displays form design
Form View	Runs the form
Datasheet View	Displays the datasheet
Print	Prints the dynaset
Print Preview	Displays the print preview
New	Goto new record
Cut	Remove selection to clipboard
Copy	Copy selection to clipboard
Paste	Paste from clipboard to current position
Find	Search for selected data
Sort Ascending	Displays records in ascending order of current field
Sort Descending	Displays records in descending order of current field
Edit Filter/Sort	Displays filter design window
Apply Filter/Sort	Applies filter to records
Show All Records	Remove filter and show natural order
Database Window	Displays the Database Window
Undo Current Field/Record	Undoes the current field or record

Undo	Undoes the last action
Cue Cards	Displays the Cue Cards
Help	Displays the Help pointer

Form Design View

Button	Function
Design View	Displays form design
Form View	Runs the form
Datasheet View	Displays the datasheet
Save	Saves the form
Print Preview	Displays the print preview
Properties	Displays the properties sheet
Field List	Displays the field list window
Code	Displays an Access Basic form module in the Module window.
Toolbox	Displays the Toolbox window
Palette	Displays the Palette window
Font Name	Displays list of font names
Font Size	Displays list of font sizes
Bold	Applies bold typeface
Italic	Applies italic typeface
Left align	Left aligns contents of label or control
Centre align	Centre aligns contents of label or control
Right align	Right aligns contents of label or control
Database Window	Displays Database Window
Undo	Undoes the last action
Cue Cards	Displays the Cue Cards
Help	Displays the Help pointer

Report Design View

Button	Function
Design View	Displays report in design view
Print Preview	Displays a print preview
Sample Preview	Displays a sample print preview
Save	Saves the report
Sorting and Grouping	Displays the Sorting and Grouping dialog box
Properties	Displays the properties sheet

Field List	Displays the field list window
Code	Displays an Access Basic report module in the Module window.
Toolbox	Displays the Toolbox window
Palette	Displays the Palette window
Font Name	Displays list of font names
Font Size	Displays list of font sizes
Bold	Applies bold typeface
Italic	Applies italic typeface
Left align	Left aligns contents of label or control
Centre align	Centre aligns contents of label or control
Right align	Right aligns contents of label or control
Database Window	Displays Database Window
Undo	Undoes the last action
Cue Cards	Displays the Cue Cards
Help	Displays the Help pointer

Report and Form Print Preview

Button	Function
Close Window	Closes preview and returns to design
Print	Prints
Print Setup	Displays print setup dialog box
Zoom	Toggle to zoom in or out
Publish it with MS Word	Saves the output of a table, query, form, report, or module to a file in one of the following file formats: Microsoft Excel (.XLS), Rich Text Format (.RTF), or MS-DOS Text (.TXT).
Analyse it with MS Excel	Saves the output of a table, query, form, report, or module to a file in one of the following file formats: Microsoft Excel (.XLS), Rich Text Format (.RTF), or MS-DOS Text (.TXT).
Mail it	Saves the output of a table, query, form, report, or module to a file, and then attaches the file to a message in your electronic mail program
Database Window	Displays the Database Window
Cue Cards	Displays the Cue Cards
Help	Displays the Help pointer

Macro Design

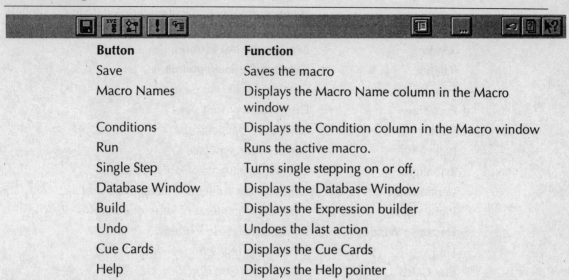

Button	Function
Save	Saves the macro
Macro Names	Displays the Macro Name column in the Macro window
Conditions	Displays the Condition column in the Macro window
Run	Runs the active macro.
Single Step	Turns single stepping on or off.
Database Window	Displays the Database Window
Build	Displays the Expression builder
Undo	Undoes the last action
Cue Cards	Displays the Cue Cards
Help	Displays the Help pointer

Module Design

Button	Function
Save	Saves the module
Object	List box for selecting an object
Procedure	List box for selecting a procedure
Previous procedure	Displays the previous procedure in the current module
Next procedure	Displays the next procedure in the current module
New procedure	Creates a Sub or Function procedure in the Module window
Run	Continues Access Basic code execution after an interruption
Compile loaded modules	Compiles all procedures in all modules in the current database.
Step Into	Executes one statement at a time
Step Over	Executes one statement at a time, treating a call to a Sub or Function procedure as one step.
Reset	Terminates execution of Access Basic procedures and clears all variables.
Breakpoint	Sets or removes a breakpoint.
Build	Displays Expression builder
Immediate Window	Displays the Immediate window to test and debug the procedures created in the Module window

Calls	Displays the Calls dialog box, in which you can trace all the currently active procedures that your code has called.
Undo	Undoes the last action
Help	Displays the Help pointer

index

Excel for Business Students

Using Excel for Windows versions 3 & 4

J Muir

This book is aimed at students who need to learn Excel 3 or 4 to acquire spreadsheet skills. Both Excel and its business applications are explained in simple terms, and the author has deliberately avoided biasing the examples towards areas where specialised knowledge of accountancy is required.

It is known to be used on the following courses: BA Business, Accounting Foundation courses, DMS, HND Computing, BTEC National Travel and Tourism, MSc Business IT, BTEC Business Studies, GNVQ Intermediate and Advanced Business.

Review comments

'Excellent – the only authoritative text on the market.'

'Well explained and illustrated, with good examples.'

'Excellent course book that will be used extensively.'

Lecturers

1st edition • 192 pp • 245 x 190 mm • 1993 • ISBN 1 85805 029 4

Programming in Visual Basic

P K MacBride

This book assumes a basic knowledge of programming (for instance, using Pascal or BASIC). It uses simple examples to introduce the different programming approach required by Visual Basic, a screen-based object-oriented program. The book is suitable for use with versions 2.0 and 3.0. It is expected to be used on the following courses: BTEC National and Higher National Computing, Computing degree courses.

1st edition • 200 pp (approx) • 245 x 190 mm • June 1994 • ISBN 1 85805 092 8

Word for Windows 2.0

An Active-Learning Approach

Sue Coles & Jenny Rowley

This book is intended for students on a wide range of business and other courses who need to know how to use MS Word for Windows, one of the industry standard word processing packages.

It is known to be used on the following courses: BTEC National Computer Studies, Computer Applications, A Level Computing, HND Computing, HND Business and Finance, BTEC First IT.

Review comments

'Excellent value – precise, to the point and easy to follow.'

'Exactly what's required.'

'An excellent book at a student-affordable price.'   Lecturers

1st edition • 160 pp • 245 x 190 mm • 1993 • ISBN 1 85805 047 2

WordPerfect 6.0 for Windows

An Active-Learning Approach

E Leonard

This book not only provides a self-teaching text for any student needing to know how to use WordPerfect 6.0 for Windows, it also meets the wordprocessing requirements of all four levels of C & G 7261. As a result it is ideal for anyone for whom the basics of wordprocessing are a requirement.

1st edition • 208 pp (approx) 245 x 190 mm • July 1994 • ISBN 1 85805 065 0

Works for Windows

An Active-Learning Approach

D Weale

This book provides an easy-to-follow, self-teaching text for students who need a good working knowledge of Works for Windows.

1st edition • 208 pp • 245 x 190 mm • April 1994 • ISBN 1 85805 073 1